BRITISH MUSICAL TI
SINCE 1950

Robert Gordon is Professor of Theatre and Performance at Goldsmiths, University of London, UK, and Director of the Pinter Research Centre in Performance and Creative Writing. He has published books on Tom Stoppard and Harold Pinter, on modern acting theories, and edited *The Oxford Handbook of Sondheim Studies;* he is co-editor of *The Oxford Handbook of the British Musical.*

Olaf Jubin is Reader in Media Studies and Musical Theatre at Regent's University London, UK, and a Visiting Lecturer on the M.A. in Musical Theatre at Goldsmiths, University of London, UK. He has written and co-edited several books on musical theatre and the mass media and is co-editor of *The Oxford Handbook of the British Musical.*

Millie Taylor is Professor of Musical Theatre at the University of Winchester, UK. She worked as a freelance musical director and, for almost 20 years, toured Britain and Europe with a variety of musicals including *West Side Story, The Rocky Horror Show, Little Shop of Horrors* and *Sweeney Todd.* Her publications include: *Singing for Musicals: A Practical Guide* (2008); *Musical Theatre, Realism and Entertainment* (2012); and, with Dominic Symonds, the textbook *Studying Musical Theatre: Theory and Practice* (2014).

THE THEATRE OF HAROLD PINTER
by Mark Taylor-Batty

THE THEATRE OF TIMBERLAKE WERTENBAKER
by Sophie Bush

THE THEATRE OF TENNESSEE WILLIAMS
by Brenda Murphy

MODERN ASIAN THEATRE AND PERFORMANCE 1900–2000
by Kevin J. Wetmore, Siyuan Liu and Erin B. Mee

BRITISH MUSICAL THEATRE SINCE 1950

Robert Gordon, Olaf Jubin and Millie Taylor

Series Editors: Patrick Lonergan and Kevin J. Wetmore, Jr.

Bloomsbury Methuen Drama
An imprint of Bloomsbury Publishing Plc

B L O O M S B U R Y
LONDON · OXFORD · NEW YORK · NEW DELHI · SYDNEY

Bloomsbury Methuen Drama

An imprint of Bloomsbury Publishing Plc

Imprint previously known as Methuen Drama

50 Bedford Square	1385 Broadway
London	New York
WC1B 3DP	NY 10018
UK	USA

www.bloomsbury.com

BLOOMSBURY, METHUEN DRAMA and the Diana logo are trademarks of Bloomsbury Publishing Plc

First published 2016

British Library Cataloguing-in-Publication Data
A catalogue record for this book is available from the British Library.

ISBN:	HB:	978-1-4725-8437-3
	PB:	978-1-4725-8436-6
	ePDF:	978-1-4725-8439-7
	ePub:	978-1-4725-8438-0

Library of Congress Cataloging-in-Publication Data
A catalog record for this book is available from the Library of Congress.

Series: Critical Companions

Cover image: Luis Enrique Ascui/Stringer/Getty Images

Typeset by RefineCatch Limited, Bungay, Suffolk

CONTENTS

Contents

LIST OF ILLUSTRATIONS

*These two photographs are included in this form to illustrate how performance photography
has changed in the intervening years. A photographer was employed to take production shots,
often at a dress rehearsal, on black-and-white film. The photographer provided a contact sheet
of images from the negatives from which photographs were chosen; 10″ by 8″ photographs
were then printed. This image is from the original contact sheet and contains two consecutive
photographs from the performance/photo-shoot.

INTRODUCTION

The overwhelming success of *Jesus Christ Superstar* as a concept album in 1970 made British musical theatre a global phenomenon for the first time since the First World War. More than half of the musicals that young British and American theatregoers – and many others around the world – are familiar with today were created in Britain after 1970. These are most likely to include *Joseph and His Technicolor Dreamcoat* (1973 West End), *Jesus Christ Superstar* (1973 West End), *The Rocky Horror Show* (1973 West End), *Evita* (1978 West End), *Cats* (1981), *Blood Brothers* (1983 West End), *Les Misérables* (1985 West End), *The Phantom of the Opera* (1986), *Miss Saigon* (1989), *Mamma Mia!* (1999), *Billy Elliot* (2005) and *Matilda* (2011 West End).

These shows did not emerge out of the ether fully formed. In fact the first English musical comedy can be said to be John Gay's *The Beggar's Opera*, a sensational success in London in 1728 that established the genre known as ballad opera, which became dominant in Britain and subsequently in its North American colonies during the eighteenth century. British musical theatre has made an international impact in four distinct historical epochs: (a) eighteenth-century ballad opera; (b) Gilbert and Sullivan's comic opera between 1871 and 1896; (c) English musical comedy between 1892 and 1918; and (d) the explosion of British musicals globally since *Jesus Christ Superstar*. Yet there is surprisingly little critical literature that situates the enormous recent success of British musicals within an historical perspective. By examining developments in the British musical since the Second World War, this book aims to provide a context within which to comprehend the contemporary phenomenon.

Until now, most scholarly research in the field of musical theatre has focused almost exclusively on the Broadway musical. At times this has unfortunately led some American authors and artists to judge British musicals according to *Broadway* categories and *Broadway* ideas of craftsmanship, an inadvertent essentializing of those aesthetics. In this context, the works of British songwriters and librettists tend to be viewed merely as footnotes to the development of the American musical, revealing a cultural blind spot that has typically resulted in regarding the art form as inherently American. For instance, in his coffee-table book *More Broadway Musicals*, Martin Gottfried discusses *Cats* (1981) and *The Phantom of the Opera* (1986) at length as *Broadway* shows. How inappropriate this is becomes clear if the same parameters are applied to other musicals: both *Annie Get Your Gun* (1946) and *The Producers* (2001) have played successfully in Berlin, but nobody would have the idea of categorizing either of them as a *German* musical.

When film scholar Gerald Mast claimed that for '[Tim] Rice and [Andrew Lloyd] Webber, London's West End has become New Haven, where shows try out before coming to New York,'[1] he seemed oblivious to the notion that as British citizens, the aim of the composer and lyricist might actually be to see their musicals premiered in London, their hometown. While some British artists may well have harboured dreams of a New York production, their first and most pressing aim was (and remains) always to find appreciation in their own (artistic) community, a word that is significant in this context, as one of the striking characteristics of the British musical is that it focuses on the community and is far less preoccupied with the individual (and individual success) than its American counterpart.

Although the modern British musical has undoubtedly been inspired by Broadway, it has a very specific relationship with and relevance within British society, its theatrical traditions, social mores and history. It is the intention of the authors to highlight how those factors have shaped British musical theatre since 1950 and to show how every musical gains meaning from the artistic, political and cultural climate that has bred, nurtured and embraced it.

As such this book deals with issues such as interculturalism and multiculturalism, social class, gender and sexuality that provide the background against which discussions of individual musicals can be contextualized. Clearly one of the most important developments in the UK since the Second World War, the end of the Empire (1945–67) and the formation of a Commonwealth of Nations (1949), has been the migration of citizens from former colonies to the British mainland, a migration that has brought an intensely rich variety of cultures to British musical theatre. The British policy of multiculturalism has been instrumental, though, in encouraging a positive recognition of cultural difference that – in theory at least – celebrates diverse cultures and social contexts rather than promoting assimilation into a supposedly 'British' way of life.

What it means to be British continues to be in flux, as the notion of British identity develops progressively to include a greater diversity of cultural backgrounds with their varied performance traditions. Significantly, the particular mix of cultures derives from a colonial history that is unique to Britain. As diasporic communities have become increasingly confident with regard to their hybrid cultural identities, intercultural forms of performance have emerged that speak of multiple cultural roots. The performance of a pre-1960s British identity that can be perceived, for example, in either *Me and My Girl* (1937) or *Salad Days* (1954) has been transformed in musicals such as *Bend It Like Beckham* (2015) or the hip-hop dance musical *Into the Hoods* (2006).

In parallel with this increase in cultural diversity, a liberalization of laws began that determined the rights of women and homosexuals. Once they had achieved the vote and were represented in parliament, feminists focused on the fight for equal pay for equal work – a battle that was documented in the film *Made in Dagenham* (2010) and its subsequent musical of the same name (2014). Although the battle has still not been won, recent legislation makes inequality harder to defend. However, in many respects the representation of women has been transformed, as is most obvious in the production of *Mamma Mia!* (1999). The book of this show, which focuses on female relationships and points of view, was written by a woman, and the director and producer were also female, a very unusual combination even in today's West End.

Increasing cultural diversity and the progress towards the equality of women together with the democratization of higher education have been instrumental in partially eroding class and gender boundaries. Britain is still a class-based society, however, and current political measures appear to be designed to destroy the opportunities for social mobility that were increasing from the 1960s to early 2000s. In inner cities in particular there remain pockets of poverty and deprivation and an underclass that has little access to the social mobility, equality of opportunity or gender equality that should be available to all; this situation is parallel to that of the early 1980s depicted in *Blood Brothers* (West End 1983). Since many immigrant communities are housed in poorer areas on first arrival, and may not have the linguistic skills or legal knowledge to access opportunities that might promote social mobility, new class structures have emerged to replace the old.

Although *Bombay Dreams* (2002) contrasts the worlds of Mumbai's slums and film-making community, highlighting the gulf between the two, its performance on a British stage by British Asian performers emphasizes its pertinence to a contemporary British context as issues of class, race, migration and gender are bound together in a story of oppression and deprivation. At different historical times *Oliver!* (1960), *Oh What a Lovely War!* (1963) and *Blood Brothers* (1983) exemplify how varied types of musico-dramaturgical structures can represent issues of class and social inequality in different ways.

Substantial changes have recently and only gradually been made to the legislative framework for lesbian, gay, bisexual and transgender equality: homosexual activity between consenting adults was legalized in England and Wales in 1967, but as late as 1980 in Scotland and 1982 in Northern Ireland, while legal protection against discrimination for LGBT individuals followed in 2010. Same-sex civil partnerships were legalized in 2005 and same-sex marriage in 2014. Since 1967 there has been a slow development towards an equal representation of sexual difference in musical theatre. When homosexuality was illegal, hidden codes were used to speak across the footlights, as in *Salad Days*. The next stage was the public acceptance of alternative sexualities seen in *The Rocky Horror Show* (1973 West End) where sexual difference is overt, but only for the alien characters. *Privates on Parade* (1977) presents gay characters as witty and sympathetic, but in accordance with its 1950s setting they are still constructed as stereotypes – closeted, extremely camp or in drag. It is not until the late 1990s and 2000s that gay characters appear who live 'normal' lives, have relationships, jobs and families. *Billy Elliot* (2005) and *Soho Cinders* (2008) engage with this mainstreaming or normalizing of gay characters and relationships.

British politics is not necessarily overt in all the musicals discussed here, but a British sensibility does inform even the most globally successful musicals such as *Mamma Mia!* (1999) and *The Phantom of the Opera* (1986), and consequently one of the functions of this book is to question what a British sensibility or aesthetic might be. Twelve of the most successful musicals that appeared in the West End during the period between 1950 and the present have been chosen; these also demonstrate something of the diversity of practice over 65 years. Naturally there are many important musicals that have been omitted, and this selection should not be perceived as establishing any sort of canon. Significantly, this book provides a specifically British context within which these musicals can be viewed so that the individual case studies and the strategies for looking at them, along with the other musicals we might have mentioned, provide a catalyst for further research.

A book on British musical theatre therefore raises questions about what might constitute a British musical, which in a global commercial market becomes increasingly hard to define. *Jesus Christ Superstar* (1970, concept album) might be regarded as British because of its authorship by Tim Rice and Andrew Lloyd Webber, but does an author or composer's nationality mean that *Matilda* (2010) is Australian, *Les Misérables* (1985, West End) French or *Bombay Dreams* (2002) Indian? Perhaps the source of the finance or the geographical base of the producers should be considered, but increasingly musicals are financed by multinational conglomerates or by groups of producers from the West End and Broadway. *Bend It Like Beckham* (2015), for example, has eight producer names above the title that include film, media and theatre producers with experience in India, Africa, the West End and on Broadway, so the finance is international; this was much less the case in 1950. Perhaps, and this is what is proposed here, British musicals are those that contain stories pertinent to British audiences, that are developed in British theatres, whether subsidized or commercial. *Matilda* (2008) and *Les Misérables*, for example, were both developed in the British subsidized sector at the Royal Shakespeare Company before transferring to West End theatres. *Oh What a Lovely War!* (1963) was the product of a devising process at the Theatre Royal Stratford East; *Blood Brothers* was written for a school performance and first performed at the Liverpool Playhouse in 1982; *The Rocky Horror Show* opened in 1973 at the Royal Court's Theatre Upstairs. By contrast *Billy Elliot* (2005) and *Oliver!* (1960), *The Phantom of the Opera* (1986) and *Mamma Mia!* (1999) were all first performed in the West End.

The book is structured in three parts, reflecting the expertise and expressing the individual viewpoints of three authors. Each part consists of an essay on a particular topic illustrated by four case studies that offer close readings of specific musicals in order to outline the relationship between the aesthetic form of the work and its social or cultural context. In Part One Robert Gordon presents a reflection of the ways in which musicals have responded to the major events of social and political history since 1950; Millie Taylor provides an assessment of the ways in which musical theatre is derived from and interacts with popular culture in Part Two; while Olaf Jubin identifies and analyses innovations in the approach to narrative in British musicals since 1970 in Part Three.

These three key themes locate the musicals under discussion within a British sociocultural milieu and thus the work as a whole articulates a British aesthetic that is distinct from its American counterpart. Although all three parts identify a set of specifically 'British' cultural attitudes that determine the aesthetics of the musical, the authors have made no attempt to 'harmonize' their views or integrate their perspectives to produce a single approach to a multidisciplinary field of study. Robert Gordon writes as a theatre director, scholar and playwright; Millie Taylor from the standpoint of a professional musician, musical director and academic musicologist; while Olaf Jubin is a specialist musical theatre and film historian and media critic. We hope that the differences between our approaches will play against one another dialectically in order to draw students and scholars into critical discussion and debate rather than passive acceptance of a univocal critical attitude.

All forms of popular entertainment need to respond to and to some degree reflect the taste, the preoccupations as well as the living circumstances of the people that make up its audience, otherwise it ceases to be engaging as well as relevant, which in turn may spell doom for its commercial prospects. How exactly this played out for the British musical since 1950 is the subject of this volume. By focusing on what makes British musicals uniquely *British* – as opposed to American – the authors intend to challenge the historically inaccurate and culturally biased view of the British musical as a second-rate imitation of a superior Broadway model. The British musical is simply different – so as the French would say: 'Vive la différence!'

PART I
MUSICALS AND SOCIAL CHANGE
Robert Gordon

1.1 BRITISH THEATRE AND SOCIETY
AFTER THE SECOND WORLD WAR

In 1950 Britain was an exhausted nation. Having stood alone in 1940 against
the might of German military forces, Britain had, seemingly against all the
odds, survived the nightly terrors of the Blitz to achieve, with the help of the
Allies, a remarkable victory over the Nazis in the Second World War.[1]
Military triumph, however, was accompanied by what appeared to be
economic defeat: the enormous cost of a six-year war had utterly depleted
Britain's financial reserves and the country was by 1950 not only bankrupt
but being forced to dismantle the largest Empire since that of the Romans.[2]
British people were psychologically confronting the loss of their reputation
as the twentieth century's most powerful and influential nation,[3] a loss that
on a personal level would undermine the confident mentality that had
promoted the innate sense of superiority manifest in the imperial project
from the mid-eighteenth century onwards.[4]

The rationing of food and 'luxury' goods introduced during the war
continued until 1954. Britain had in 1939 entered an age of austerity for
possibly the first time in its history.[5] Obviously popular culture was
profoundly affected by the great transformation in the nation's fortunes, and
this can clearly be seen in the changes in the form and style of British
musicals that occurred between 1945 and 1954. The stunning impact of both
Oklahoma! (Theatre Royal, Drury Lane) and *Annie Get Your Gun* (Coliseum)
in 1947 led to the transfer of a succession of Broadway hits in the 1950s and
1960s. Obviously London's war-weary West End could not compete with the
ebullience of Broadway theatre in originating and popularizing a certain
type of musical.

In their fulsome laudation of these two colourful and rumbustious
American musicals, reviewers unfortunately promoted a corresponding view
that British musicals were genteel and old-fashioned, clinging to pre-war

manners and ideals and attempting to compensate in charm for their lack of energy. American male dancers appeared virile and strong; their British counterparts seemed by comparison effete and effeminate.[6] Although the most popular British musicals in fact ran longer in the West End than most of the Broadway shows,[7] British producers and writers lacked the imagination and drive to create English equivalents to the American blockbusters and continued instead to exploit pre-war conventions of operetta and musical comedy.

Paradoxically, the form of the Broadway musical was eventually challenged by a very different type of English musical, but this form only served to enhance the myth that British musicals were second-rate entertainments born of an inspired amateurism and dedicated to nostalgic recreations of Edwardian grandeur or naive celebrations of community spirit, while Broadway shows were, by contrast, well crafted, inventively choreographed and vividly designed affirmations of the American dream. It is a truism that popular culture involves a spontaneous response to and projection of the common-sense expectations, tensions and contradictions that constitute the individual's social experience. In challenging the notion that British musicals were inferior, one must ask why they held greater appeal than their more critically valued American counterparts in order to comprehend how they reflected the society and expressed the culture that produced them.

While the United States had replaced Britain as the world's leading superpower after the war, Britain was a nation in retreat from Empire, struggling to forge new social images and identities in the crippling aftermath of that conflict.[8] Both countries were heavily invested in the notion of a Cold War between the communist Soviet Empire and the capitalist West, but while the United States had the will and resources to wage a series of wars against the rise of communist regimes in Asia and South America, Britain carefully calculated the cost of the break-up of Empire, granting independence to each of its former colonies in turn, and gradually transforming the British Empire into the Commonwealth – a loose federation of nations that attempted to sustain British influence in the former colonies without maintaining colonial power and responsibility. At the deepest and most personal level, the disintegration of the Empire between 1945 and 1967 was a profound shock to the British psyche, reinforcing the sense that having won the war, the country had lost the peace.[9] Having built the most extensive Empire in history, Britain was now a small, relatively poor nation without any serious influence in the world.[10]

Yet the war did bring its victories. Working-class men had closely observed and interacted with upper-middle-class and upper-class officers; women had assumed traditionally 'masculine' jobs on farms, in factories and in the armed forces.[11] The general election at the end of the war swept the Labour party to a landslide victory, which was to have a profound effect on British society and politics until the 1980s.[12] The new Labour Government set out to create a Welfare State, establishing both the principle and foundations of the National Health Service, free secondary and higher education and social welfare for the infirm, the disabled and the elderly.[13] This represented a huge advance towards a genuine social democracy in the UK in line with developments in other Western European countries, and initiated an era of consensus politics that remained in place until it was challenged by the Conservative government of Margaret Thatcher in the early 1980s.

As part of the culture produced by society, all forms of theatre reflect, both directly and indirectly, the historical conditions and social circumstances of any given era. The relationship between popular entertainment and the society that produces it can be quite complex to comprehend because forms of entertainment usually disguise their economic aim (i.e. to make profit) through obscuring the ideological bias that constitutes their true meaning. By pretending to be 'only entertainment'[14] musicals disguise their underlying meanings by offering all kinds of pleasures to their audiences that may on the surface appear to have a very different import to their real significance. Most often the 'common-sense' meaning of a popular musical does not coincide with its true function as a commercial product. Creators of popular entertainment will seek to 'give the public what they want' in order to maximize profit. Marketing and audience research or simply a producer's hunch may have created the awareness that certain subjects and styles of performance will be popular, so musicals are created according to 'recipes' for the production of what it is believed the theatregoing public will enjoy. But theatre production is not an exact science and producers fail to capture the imagination or satisfy the taste of the public more often than they succeed.[15]

As with Hollywood films, producers of popular musicals therefore tend to be conservative in following trends that have proved commercially successful: Broadway producers invariably try to imitate a formula that has proved popular with minor variations that create an illusion of offering something new. Changing social conditions eventually result in changes in what Raymond Williams called 'structures of feeling',[16] accounting for major shifts in taste from one period to another. One of the most obvious recent examples is the way in which the trauma of the destruction of the World Trade Center in Manhattan on 9/11 brought to an end the epoch of bombastic musicals that deployed melodrama and spectacle to thrill and divert audiences with a rollercoaster of emotions and moods. *Thoroughly Modern Millie* (2002) may have been the first Broadway show to reflect the new *zeitgeist*, together with *The Producers* (2001), ushering in a period of retro musical comedy that continues to dominate Broadway musical theatre today.[17] Some musicals establish new trends largely because they are genuinely original – Lionel Bart's *Oliver!* is a show that in 1960 transformed the model of what a British musical could be. At its best, theatre can both reflect and challenge the predominant values of its time, so that although the industry does not necessarily provide an incentive for writers to do so, some musicals have done both.

The development of British musical theatre after the Second World War has clearly reflected changes in the sociocultural landscape. Before the war, Noel Coward and Ivor Novello were famous as directors for the extravagance and good taste of their staging; cast sizes were, by contemporary standards, enormous, and spectacle was if anything much grander than audiences are accustomed to at a large-scale West End show today.[18] Immediately after the war C. B. Cochran and other major West End producers continued with business as usual, presenting the same kind of shows that had succeeded immediately before the war. Ivor Novello's *Perchance to Dream* (1945) was a direct continuation of the series of spectacular operettas he had written and starred in before the war, and ran for 1,022 performances before embarking on a successful tour. In 1947, Cochran produced Vivian Ellis and A. P. Herbert's *Bless the Bride*, a huge hit starring newcomer Lizbeth Webb and the French singer Georges Guetary. It might have run far longer than it did, had not the producer for no good reason decided to replace it after a run of 886 performances with *Tough at the Top* in 1949. Novello continued to reign supreme as king of 'Ruritanian' operetta in *King's Rhapsody* (1949) at the Palace Theatre (841 performances). Both *Bless the Bride* and *King's Rhapsody* were operettas, a form that reinforced their sense of nostalgia for pre-war modes and styles.

Although John Snelson has argued persuasively that *Bless the Bride* (and *Tough at the Top*) paralleled *Oklahoma!* and *Annie Get Your Gun* in their excavation of the twentieth-century past as the source of the core values of the Allied nations in wartime,[19] the English musicals are on the surface more sophisticated and urbane, lacking the vitality of the pioneer milieu in which the American shows are often set, and referring to a class-ridden, aristocratic past rather than the populist democracy of the American west. What changed the scale and scope of the post-war British musical was not merely austerity (although that was a factor); the deaths of C. B. Cochran and Novello in January and March of 1951 represented the end of the pre-war theatre culture. The rejection by the critics and public alike of Noel Coward's ill-fated attempt in 1946 to bring back lavish operetta to Drury Lane (*Pacific 1860*)[20] or write a more contemporary style of cynical musical comedy (*Ace of Clubs* in 1950), signalled the changing values of a society that was at first traumatized and later invigorated by the loss of its Empire. *Pacific 1860* (1946) showed how out of touch Coward was with the new style of American musicals: it was an ill-considered vehicle for American star Mary Martin, set in the make-believe colony of Samolo that might well have been written in 1930.

Coward, Vivian Ellis and Noel Gay were masters of a gentle type of big band swing allied to a nostalgic style of light operetta music; and they continued to write in this 1930s style after the war. Sandy Wilson and Julian Slade employed the musical comedy format of Vivian Ellis and Noel Gay to compose nostalgic songs in the 1950s that harked back to those of the 1920s and 1930s. That is why British musicals appeared both dated and tame in comparison with the Broadway shows that transferred to London in the 1950s, such as *Guys and Dolls* (1950), *Wonderful Town* (1953), *The Pajama Game* (1954), *Damn Yankees* (1955), even though *Ace of Clubs* and *Gay's the Word* (1951) deliberately aimed to compete with such American musicals on their own terms – the former an imitation of the dark comic style and seedy nightclub setting of *Pal Joey* (1940), the latter Novello's typically English riposte to Broadway, self-reflexively burlesquing the Ruritanian fantasies of his own spectacular pre-war operettas and including an English equivalent to Berlin's 'There's No Business Like Show Business' in 'Vitality', the punchy retrospective tribute to British show business performers that became a signature number for its legendary leading lady, Cicely Courtneidge. It is significant that 'Vitality', in spite of its homage to Irving Berlin, is a nostalgic tribute to the 'old' British performers of music hall and variety. Surprisingly, Novello's musical was an enormous success, while *Ace of Clubs* was a damp squib. Coward returned to period musicals with *After the Ball* (1954), his adaptation of Oscar Wilde's *Lady Windermere's Fan*, but was not to succeed with a musical until *Sail Away* opened on Broadway in 1961.

1.2 INNOVATION AND NOSTALGIA: CAMP IN THE POST-WAR BRITISH MUSICAL

The first genuinely innovative West End musicals after the war were Sandy Wilson's *The Boy Friend* (1953) and *Salad Days* (1954) by Julian Slade and Dorothy Reynolds. Neither had originated in the West End: *The Boy Friend* had started life as a one-act musical at a theatre club called the Players' Theatre in Charing Cross, while *Salad Days* began as a summer holiday entertainment at the Bristol Old Vic theatre. When the shows transferred to the West End, however, both ran for over 2,000 performances, becoming the two longest-running West End musicals of the 1950s. *The Boy Friend* had a small band of piano, percussion and bass, while *Salad Days* was scored for two pianos; as small-scale musicals – the equivalent of the 'Little' revues during the war – they were peculiarly British in their seeming nonchalance, responding to the conformism of the Cold War ethos emphasized by the change from a Labour to a Conservative government in 1951 by inventing an anarchically comic style of carnivalesque entertainment that exploited elements of both revue and pre-war musical comedy. When food rationing ended in 1954, artists perceived an overt contradiction between the gradually improving material conditions and the continuation of a repressive social regime that enshrined conservative attitudes to gender, sexuality and class. This perception provides a strong motivation for *Salad Days*, which satirized such retrogressive beliefs in a zany allegory that provided different meanings for different groups of its audience.

Both *The Boy Friend* and *Salad Days* treat their audiences as privileged members of a clandestine club, gathering together in private to escape the privations of war, austerity and bureaucratically enforced conformism. Their responses to the Cold War culture of the early 1950s was as typically English as *Guys and Dolls* or *The Pajama Game* are typically American responses to that cultural crisis. These small-scale shows were not by any means the only British musicals to succeed in the West End after the war, and their popularity was not solely a response to the American imports but equally to the lavish period spectacle of *Bless the Bride*, to Novello's nostalgic fantasia of imperial culture, *King's Rhapsody*, the American-influenced *Zip Goes a Million* (1951, 544 performances), a star vehicle for George Formby, and *Wedding in Paris* (Hans May, Vera Caspary and Sonny Miller, 1954, 411 performances) – all much bigger shows in much bigger theatres.[21] The sociocultural study of popular entertainment focuses on the ways that it has connected with the audience; one indicator (if not always the most telling) is therefore the number of performances a production achieved. Many shows that are totally ignored by American scholars because they failed to repeat their success on Broadway demand close reading, sociological or otherwise, as manifestations of British popular taste.

Wilson and Slade were homosexual writers who expressed their sensibility in the face of rigid censorship and the Cold War hysteria that in the wake of the unmasking of Guy Burgess and Donald Maclean in 1951 as Soviet agents, invariably connected homosexuality with treachery.[22] Although the concept of sexual 'normality' was seriously challenged by the Kinsey report in America, which in 1948 suggested as a result of extensive research that men could be grouped on a seven-point scale, between totally heterosexual and totally homosexual with most men somewhere in between, homosexual men were subject to regular victimization in the early 1950s by the police force, who employed young policemen as *agent provocateurs* to entrap men in public lavatories.[23]

Most of those arrested in the police purge during the autumn and winter of 1953–4 were ordinary men whose personal tragedies did not make headlines,[24] but the arrest of Sir John Gielgud for 'importuning' in 1953 caused a huge stir in theatrical and social circles; young men also took the opportunity to rob or blackmail homosexuals with the threat of 'outing' them, leading to cases such as that of the distinguished scientist Alan Turing, whose eventual suicide was unquestionably a result of police persecution.[25] With public life preserving a hypocritical façade of respectable conformity, it is no wonder that the apparently impromptu nature of the fun promoted by such shows as *Salad Days* exploited a camp aesthetic, which deployed nostalgia together with the disorientating effects of pastiche and parody to project a coded 'gay' identity.[26] The uninhibited cultivation of joy and pleasure in such shows was 'gay' in the innocent sense of the word, but to those in the know it was also 'gay' in a way that insiders recognized as potentially subversive.

Camp has virtually no equivalent in American popular culture until the 1960s when it began to be used to indicate certain aspects of a gay sensibility. From at least the early nineteenth century, however, a strain of drollery can be identified in popular English culture that we might today recognize as camp. Its po-faced mockery of ridiculous (because outdated) conventions is evident in pantomime from the earliest harlequinades to the Christmas pantomimes of today, while Victorian entertainments such as extravaganza, burlesque[27] (which were later exploited in the Savoy operas) and music hall contain elements that one might retrospectively view as camp in their mockery of outmoded forms and clichés. This tradition of facetious mockery only becomes visible as part of a homosexual subculture in the 1890s when the flamboyant dandyism of the Wildean decadent begins to be imitated through its louchely parodic performance ('se camper') by working-class homosexuals, both in drag and out of it.

While the 'retro' conceit of *The Boy Friend* might be regarded as camp, the show does not mock its original models, but pays affectionate tribute to them at the same time as it recognizes that the lived experience they once represented is dead and gone. An affectionate pastiche of the 1920s Broadway musical comedy – its actual models were Vincent Youmans' *No, No, Nanette* (1924) and Rodgers and Hart's *The Girl Friend* (1926) – *The Boy Friend*'s transfer to Broadway marked the debut of Julie Andrews in a starring role.[28] The show is a celebration of nostalgia, brittle and self-reflexive, but in the form of homage rather than critique. The musical pastiche was more convincingly accomplished in London than New York because British popular music had not changed as much as its American counterpart; at the same time a British parody of the 1920s Broadway musical would in 1953 have sounded more exotic than a spoof of Noel Gay or Vivian Ellis. Although British culture had embraced American ragtime, jazz and swing as the new twentieth-century pop sound, inter-war British musical theatre composers such as Vivian Ellis, Ivor Novello, Noel Coward and Noel Gay preferred a nostalgic Edwardian style, spiced with ragtime and swing.

Jazz was not a mode with which British composers felt comfortable until the late 1950s, so the kind of modernity expressed by George Gershwin and Harold Arlen, much as it may have been enjoyed by West End audiences of Broadway musical comedies in the 1920s and 1930s, was never part of the British musical theatre vocabulary. Novello and Coward's musical tastes were formed before the end of the First World War by listening to Franz Lehár, Lionel Monckton, Paul Rubens, Ivan Caryll, Leslie Stuart, Edward

Figure 1 An affectionate pastiche of 1920s Broadway musical comedy – the revival of *The Boy Friend* at the Open Air Theatre Regent's Park 2006. Photograph by Marilyn Kingwill. Courtesy of ArenaPAL.

German, Oscar Straus – in fact the repertoire of operetta and musical comedy that was dominant before the 1920s. So Sandy Wilson was in fact returning to the ragtime style of pre-Gershwin musical comedy that can be observed in the work of Jerome Kern, Vincent Youmans and DeSylva/Brown/Henderson rather than the more seriously jazz-inflected music of Gershwin, Arlen or Cole Porter or the big-band swing sound of Richard Rodgers in his shows with Hammerstein or his 1930s shows with Hart.

While the American musicals of the 'golden age' – for example, *On the Town*, (1944) *Annie Get Your Gun* (1946), *Kiss Me Kate* (1948), *South Pacific* (1949) and *Guys and Dolls* (1950) – showcased the glories of mid-century American swing music, with their sophisticated orchestrations and exciting rhythmic inventiveness, Julian Slade and Sandy Wilson orchestrated their tuneful scores for a minimum of instruments. Slade and his writing partner Dorothy Reynolds were both actors, so their work was bound to emphasize theatrical wit and innuendo rather than complicated musical arrangements. Lushly melodic without being musically sophisticated, the Slade/Reynolds shows recapitulated from the vantage point of the 1950s the nostalgic music of the vanished pastoral that motivates much earlier twentieth-century English music, its hopeless yearning to find an image of modernity paradoxically constituting a perverse nostalgia for lost Edwardian glory (as ironically manifest in the number 'We Said We Wouldn't Look Back').[29]

What Slade and Reynolds invented in place of genuine modernity was a peculiar form of theatrical and musical camp – creating a hothouse environment of charming eccentricity and whimsical celebration that seemed to have only a tenuous link with contemporary reality but in retrospect can be seen as a coherent and absurdist satire on the repressive regime of Cold War conformity. In some respects, Slade and Wilson became victims of their own camp creations: when they were immortalized as Julian and Sandy by Kenneth Williams and Hugh Paddick in the famous radio comedy *Round the Horne* (1956–8), the association between musical theatre and gay men became an inevitable if initially covert aspect of popular British cultural mythology. A tradition dominated by homosexual writers was over three decades transformed from high camp (Sandy Wilson's *Valmouth*, 1958) to 'queer' (*The Rocky Horror Show*, 1973, and Neil Bartlett's *Night after Night*, 1993), running alongside the persistence of burlesque and camp in more mainstream theatre (e.g. Peter Nichols' *Privates on Parade*, 1977, and *Poppy*, 1982, Alan Bennett's *Forty Years On*, 1968, and *The History Boys*, 2005, Victoria Wood's *Acorn Antiques*, 2005, Stiles and Drewe's *Betty Blue Eyes*, 2011).

15

Case Study 1: *Salad Days*

Utopian versus nostalgic impulses

Julian Slade and Dorothy Reynolds' *Salad Days* (1954) must surely rate as the most eccentric musical ever to achieve mainstream commercial success in the West End. The longest-running British musical until *Oliver!* (1960), it has been constantly revived by amateur societies, received a few professional productions and even been filmed for television. Whereas some professional productions made the show seem like a relic from a bygone age, whose refined, middle-class manners – a throwback to a pre-Beatles Britain – could make no sense in an era that had witnessed heavy metal, glam rock, punk aggression and Northern soul, its durability was recently proved by a highly successful revival presented at the Riverside Studios in 2009 and again in 2010–11.[30] Yet even in its own rather more genteel epoch of 1950s repression, *Salad Days* was unique: a musical without a strong plot, about a couple of young university graduates, Timothy and Jane, who get married for convenience, are paid to look after a magic piano that forces people to dance, and end up encountering a flying saucer (in the shape of a large saucer) piloted by the hero's uncle.

From a present-day vantage point it may be worthwhile to compare *Salad Days* with the contemporaneous European avant-garde theatre of Ionesco, Adamov, and even Beckett[31] rather than view it in its immediate context of Terence Rattigan's critically acclaimed well-made plays. For while its bizarre allegorical form verges on the surreal, its camp humour, like that of the absurdist N. F. Simpson, draws on the uniquely English popular tradition of the naughty seaside postcard and was entirely pertinent to British society circa 1954.

Many theorists of the musical as a genre[32] view its psychological function as the creation of pleasure/jouissance of a utopian nature, offering a glimpse of the possibility of pure freedom; indeed Siân Adiseshiah reads *Salad Days* in exactly this way. In the only academic article entirely devoted to the 1954 show, she aims to

> [reposition] the show as an articulation of utopian desire for the 'not-yet' of a more liberated future [. . .] *Salad Days* uses both utopian and nostalgic sensibilities, and this article explores ways in which the utopian modes challenge ideological boundaries, and the backward glance signifies mourning for lost opportunities.[33]

While this is a percipient response to the ambivalence of a text that, like much of 1950s literature, art and theatre, looks forward to a yet-to-be-imagined future while it romanticizes a pre-war past, the essay fails to recognize the satirical drive of a show whose music expresses a degree of nostalgia for the simple pleasures of a – wholly imagined – prelapsarian past, while its libretto strains to demystify the ideology of a lifeless present. Dance, because it is capable of directly producing an ecstatic affect, is the art that comes closest to expressing the impulse towards Utopia. As do many musicals, *Salad Days* bases its thematic patterns directly on its own self-reflexive nature as an entertainment. Because it is the function of a musical to provide singing and dancing as entertainment, a show like *Salad Days* achieves maximum value by making singing and dancing the key to its own meaning as a drama.

The muted melancholy of 'We Said We Wouldn't Look Back', the most iconic number in the show, echoed perfectly the mood of a middle-class London audience in the mid-1950s. The period of austerity initiated by the Second World War was only beginning to end, and Britain's post-imperial identity had not been formed in any positive way. The initial euphoria of victory had given way to a profound sense of loss and deprivation after a realization of the extent of the country's economic debt.

A Conservative government under Churchill harked back to the pre-1939 idyll of the 'green and pleasant land' without being able to offer a correspondingly optimistic vision of the future. Middle-class citizens of 40 or over would have had nostalgic memories of life before the war; even during the war life had been exciting, individuals believing in the noble cause to which their personal sacrifices were dedicated. Post-war existence must have appeared a dreary anti-climax, so that the ambivalence of 'We Said We Wouldn't Look Back' with its contrast between nostalgia for an ideal past and fear of an ill-defined future struck a chord with its first audiences:

> It's hard to forget the plays, the dances,
> The walks by the river in Spring,
> [...]
> So if I let nostalgia blind me
> And my resolution is slack,
> I'll remind you to remind me
> We said we wouldn't look back. (5)

After the young couple has said farewell to the university in Act One, Scene 1, Timothy is particularly depressed by the thought of starting life in the 'real' world, so Jane arranges to meet him the following week in the London park where they had had a picnic 'the day we cut the Shakespeare exam to go to the first night of *Hamlet*' (4). Even at university, it appears as if the experience of genuine pleasure demands the rejection of authority's rules.

The pleasures of carnival versus social authority

Most of the scenes in *Salad Days* dramatize the operation of different social institutions – the university, the family, the Civil Service, marriage, political life, the police force, and so on. The 'naughtiness' that flies in the face of each form of social authority represents a genteel kind of comic rebellion, a subversion of authority from the inside rather than a radical revolution against the social order from without. All authority figures, including the university dons, Timothy's uncles and the police, appear in this topsy-turvy world of trivial pursuits to undermine their own value system by means of a peculiar need for fun or pleasure. Stage censorship in Britain was still extremely strict in 1954, so that the only way any serious political attitude could be articulated was in the guise of comedy or symbolism. Reynolds and Slade employed an unique mixture of comedy and allegory to mask their true intentions, but the rather fey gentility of *Salad Days* suggests that the social satire is itself rather disguised: as middle-class people, they themselves were partly invested in the culture they are mocking, while as members of the theatrical profession (one of whom – Slade – was homosexual) they stood outside the system as bohemians, highly sensitive to the grotesque contradictions that in their view rendered its repressiveness absurd.

The structure of *Salad Days* follows the pattern of a revue rather than the conventional model of a musical comedy plotted to reveal the cause-and-effect relationship of character and narrative. While the events that occur do form a vaguely coherent story, the connections between one incident and another are so tenuous as to seem entirely fanciful. Like its great comic antecedent *The Importance of Being Earnest* (1895), the world represented by *Salad Days* seems hermetically sealed off from the untidy complications of reality, while at the same time its rarefied alternative universe offers an illuminatingly distorted symbol of the 'real' world. Every scene appears to exist for itself as a kind of comic sketch but, taken together, they build up a picture of a cosy middle-class milieu that was itself hermetically sealed against intrusion by the concerns of working-class life or the wider world beyond. Undergirding the polite if faintly camp surface of every scene is the recurrent trope of middle-class conformity subverted by the demand of the unconscious for pleasure – mostly represented in the show by odd types of anti-authoritarian revelry.

The show is surely the only musical that starts with a gang of singing academics – as four male and four female dons in cap and gown process on stage, followed by Timothy and Jane, who are celebrating their graduation as BAs. This scene takes the form of a pseudo-Gilbert and Sullivan number, which begins portentously but soon degenerates into silly comedy:[34]

> You clearly think there's nothing drearier
> Than a poor old don,
> Don't judge us by our grim exterior
> That is all put on.
> For if you stray by chance one day
> And come on a gaggle of dons at play
> You would then say that an old M.A.
> Is quite the gayest of the gay. (2)

This is the first instance in which the audience witnesses authority subverted from within by the authority figure's own desire for fun or penchant for the ridiculous. The formality of the picture is in total contradiction to the dons' open admission of their own desire for childish diversion:

> Oh the things that are done by a don!
> We may look dry and dusty
> But under the gown
> You will find a clown
> Who is game for anything lusty! (2)

By the time they have enumerated the many 'mad things' they have done in somewhat immature defiance of academic authority, their dignified demeanour has given way to uncontrolled carnival celebration: '[T]hey are all dancing with Bacchic abandon round Timothy and Jane ...' (3).

The Establishment as a family

The ritualistic portentousness of Timothy's mother, father and Aunt Prue at their breakfast routine in Scene 2 echoes the dons' number but, surprisingly, his parents have none of the dons' sense of fun so that there is no hint of

Dionysiac frenzy at all. It is left to Aunt Prue to subvert the authority of his parents as best she can:

> **Mother and Father** Timothy's late. Timothy's late.
>   [. . .]
> **Mother** He's later each day, can you guess what the cause is?
> **Father** Timothy's lazy. Timothy's days
>   Are spent in reclining.
> **Aunt** It's only a phase.
>   [. . .]
> **Mother** Well, speak to him darling, no time like the present.
> **Aunt** No need to be pompous, just pointed and pleasant. (5, 6)

When Timothy does enter, the three of them sing a hackneyed refrain of banal admonition:

> Find yourself something to do, dear,
> Find yourself something to do.
> Choose a niche, a niche in which
> You can nestle and know that it's you.

The lyrics make it obvious that Tim's family is a paradigm for the Establishment: he has uncles in the diplomatic service (Clam), in Parliament (Augustine), the Army (General Sir Hector), and Uncle Zed, whose profession is not named but who later turns out to be a space scientist.

Aunt Prue's insistence that there are five uncles is confirmed by Timothy's parents as '[f]our [. . .] and the one we don't mention', who has obviously done something scandalous, putting him beyond the pale of polite society. The parents' circumlocution emblematizes the hypocritical tendency to cover up any socially embarrassing reality. The Establishment is here represented in the form of a middle-class family that comprises a cabal euphemistically defending a nepotistic system of self-promotion that preserves the values of the *status quo*.

Significantly, Jane begins Scene 3 in the park with an echo of the previous song's admonition: 'Timothy's late! Timothy's late!' (8). But instead of reprimanding him, she immediately acknowledges her contentment: 'Never mind! I'm happy to wait. / I've nothing to do' (8). Here she explicitly rejects the utilitarian philosophy of her mother and of Timothy's family in favour of her own simple hedonism: 'But now I'm happy, now I'm free, / And the

Summer sun's enough for me' (8), permitting herself to daydream about falling in love to avoid the conventional society marriage her mother is determined to arrange for her:

> One happy day
> The Summer may
> Provide an Adonis of my own choosing.
> [...]
> I might be in love by the end of the season. (9)

When Timothy arrives, mechanically spouting his parents' truisms about work, Jane comes up with an extraordinarily subversive solution to their dilemma: 'I can imagine marrying someone I was fond of, and – used to; someone I'd known for – one – or two years, and who thought the same way as I about things' (10). Timothy proposes such a marriage of convenience to Jane, who pretends it is his clever idea after they agree that it would satisfy their parents if they married and he took 'the first job that came along' (10), after which the tramp who appeared during the very first moment of the show arrives with his portable piano and persuades them to look after it for four weeks at the rate of £7 per week – so the very first job has indeed come along![35] The number 'Oh, Look at Me, I'm Dancing' (13) demonstrates the piano's magic, which is the power to make people dance to its tunes.

Dancing in the park is a complete disruption of middle-class decorum, but Timothy and Jane have lost control of their legs, which Jane claims 'misbehave on every beat' (13). As the dance takes over, they experience something parallel to the 'Bacchic abandon' (3) of the dons in Scene 1. This instinctive response of the body to the piano's power is the musical's key emblem for the overcoming of the repressive conditioning of a middle-class upbringing. As already evidenced in the dons' performance, breaking out into spontaneous dance constitutes a Dionysiac rejection of outmoded forms of decorum.

The introduction of a stereotypical comic policeman, P. C. Lancelot Boot, in Scene 5 is redolent of a music hall turn. Described as 'high-spirited and jaunty' (18), he blows his whistle into a tree to provoke a bird to 'reply accordingly' (18) – ironically, an example of how an authority figure is perversely dedicated to the kind of eccentric jollity that authority exists to suppress. Immediately afterwards he conducts a flirtation with Rowena, the sales assistant from Gusset Creations; on the assumption that she has agreed

Figure 2 'The first job to come along': looking after a magic piano – Eleanor Drew (Jane), John Warner (Timothy) and Newton Blick (the Tramp) in *Salad Days*, Vaudeville Theatre 1954. Courtesy of ArenaPAL.

to a date after work, he 'twirls' and then 'twirls into Jane's arms' on her entrance (19), after which he exits. The constable's uncontrolled balletic propensity exposes the instinctive desire for larking about beneath the decorous uniform of his institutional role.

When Timothy enters pushing the piano surreptitiously, a scene of mutual confession ensues in which he and Jane admit that they have been too afraid to break the news to their parents of their marriage and their 'job' looking after Minnie, the piano. Jane is therefore obligated to go through with the ball her mother has organized for her 'Eligibles', while Timothy is obliged to meet his various uncles about getting a job. On the entrance of a bishop, Timothy begins to play the piano, magically forcing the bishop to dance before putting a half-crown into the hat held out by a stranger named Troppo. This mute character insists on giving Jane and Timothy the tip, and in pantomime gestures agrees to stay with the piano in a garage at night. When several passers-by enter, Timothy plays and they reprise 'Oh Look at Me, I'm Dancing', all dancing 'in a variety of styles' (21); 'Boot enters R, and makes a brief attempt to create order, then joins the dancing in a prominent position' (21).

In Scene 4, Jane's mother, Lady Raeburn is first seen under the hairdryer in a beauty parlour. Just as Scenes 1 and 2, this hilarious comic set piece is closely modelled on the type of revue sketch that might mock the way a respectable married woman would spend her time in the mid-1950s. Bored and listless, Lady Raeburn possesses an innate sense of her own superiority, so she patronizes and scolds the women doing her nails and hair in between her rambling telephone conversations with friends:

Hullo? . . . Margo, my dear, it's you. How lovely! However did you guess I was here? . . . Oh, *no*, my dear. I'm not made of money. I only come twice a week . . . (15, 16)

Superficially, the scene appears to hold up the action, having a tenuous link to the developing plot, but it serves the function of satirizing the frivolous existence of a middle-class wife. Lady Raeburn's is the life Jane is expected by society to lead after she is married, and the scene offers a grotesque depiction of its vacuity. The irony is that Lady Raeburn is seriously committed to the empty social rituals of her class, dutifully giving balls, attending parties, having her hair and face 'done' and meeting friends for lunch as though the fate of the nation depended on it.

'It's Hush-Hush': Cold War repression and communist spies

Sir Clamsby Williams' room in the Foreign Office establishes a further emblematic environment for what is essentially a satirical sketch on the civil service. Once again, the assumption of decorum is undermined by the somewhat surreal stage business of Sir Clamsby turning to the audience with a conspiratorial finger on his lips before hanging his umbrella and hat on a hat-stand that mysteriously appears and vanishes from the wings. He tiptoes to a safe, 'glances surreptitiously around then brings out a tea tray with teapot, cups etc.' (23). The final piece of this elaborate pantomime involves him taking a flower out of a vase and speaking into it as if it were a microphone to summon Fosdyke, his attaché. This bizarre pantomime is reminiscent of sketches in wartime and post-war intimate revues presented in small theatres in the West End between the early 1940s and mid-1950s.

In keeping with the air of conspiracy in the scene, Fosdyke can only whisper the breathless confession that he has recently been dancing in the park. This scene and subsequent song 'It's Hush-Hush' (24–26), constitutes a hilarious parody of the Cold War attitude of secrecy and repression that motivates much of *Salad Days*. Incisively targeting the paranoid culture of conformity engineered by the Conservative government since its return to power in 1951, it alludes to the absurdly complacent trust in the Oxbridge Establishment, which blinded the government and the secret service to the fact that the greatest danger of Soviet agents betraying state secrets lay within that very Establishment, with its cosy network of friends and family in high places. The infamous spies Guy Burgess, Kim Philby, Donald Maclean and Anthony Blunt were scions of the Establishment, Blunt remaining Surveyor of the Queen's Pictures until 1972, while Burgess and Maclean defected to the Soviet Union in 1951, and Philby in 1963. The scene mocks the self-defeating absurdity of trying to police oneself to avoid betraying official 'secrets'. To Timothy's simple question, 'How are you?' Uncle Clam answers, 'Don't ask dangerous questions', and later informs him, 'You must learn to conceal *everything* – even the things you don't know' (24).

Timothy is initially impressed by his uncle's apparently exalted status but he is quickly disabused of his mistake when Uncle Clam reveals his own supposed knowledge to be no more than a sham:

Timothy   It must be very exciting to know everything and to reveal nothing [...] Surely you know the secrets of all the nations? [...]

Uncle Clam   No, no! We only *pretend* to. That is what is meant by diplomacy. (24)

The song-and-dance number that ensues is a comic highlight of *Salad Days*, an inspired bit of topsy-turveydom that recalls both the ubiquitous patter-songs of Gilbert and Sullivan and the comic surrealism of Lewis Carroll's nonsense verses in *Alice's Adventures in Wonderland* and *Through the Looking Glass*.

> But all my jobs appeared to consist of,
> Much to my chagrin and dismay,
> Was a painfully comprehensive list of
> Things I must never do or say.
>
> Don't ever ask what job you're on
> It's Hush-Hush.

Don't ever ask where the Empire's gone
It's Hush-Hush. (25)

'Hush-Hush' was a colloquial term employed in the 1950s to indicate something that was 'top-secret' – often concerning the government's development of nuclear weapons or an international political manoeuvre involving spying.

The lyrics parade all the topical buzz-words of the Cold War as well as the ludicrous ways in which the public had occasionally been warned during the war not to divulge information carelessly that might be used by the enemy:

At Russian teas lest you forget
And make a remark you might regret
Write on a Soviet serviette
Necrasniette. (25)

The fantastical quality of the comic nonsense verse satirizes the earnest attempts of authority at the obsessive policing of social behaviour in a virtuoso theatrical *reductio ad absurdum*.

Pleasure and pastime: the subversive gay subtext

The following scene in a police inspector's office extends the satire on the lunatic earnestness of authority in the form of a comic duo between Boot and the Inspector, whose manic recycling of old music hall routines with dated *double-entendres* and outrageous *non-sequiturs* anticipates the sublime silliness of a Monty Python sketch. The genuine comic surprise in the scene occurs when Boot confesses that he not only failed to arrest anyone for dancing in the park, but he himself also joined in, at which point the inspector declares, 'Dancing's a bit of a hobby of mine. (*Decisively*) You were dancing. In what style?' (27), before taking out a gramophone record, playing tango music and asking Boot to dance: 'You be the lady – I'm taller' (27). In 1954 this would be a somewhat outrageous music hall joke about two 'butch' men dancing together as though one were in drag, while among the gay men and women in the original audience, this would have been a camp in-joke, destabilizing heteronormative gender assumptions and implying the faint possibility of a gay relationship between the policemen – the overt representation of which would have been forbidden on a public stage.

> **Inspector**   I'll lead, you follow. (*They dance a quick-step*)
> (*During the dance*) Lovely floor, isn't it? Do you come here often? (*After an elaborate turn which lands them close together*) Getting familiar?
>
> **Boot**   I think we're on the wrong track, sir. (28)

The Inspector's implication that Boot may be making sexual advances on him is as direct a reference to homosexuality as the censor would allow. This scene comes closest to exposing the hidden gay subtext that reinforces and makes political sense of the theme of repression in *Salad Days*, as Boot continues his demonstration of the various steps that he claims to have been dancing in the park, which the Inspector identifies as a Morris dance, Caucasian Fertility Rite, English folk dance, and ballet. The scene ends with a wonderful comic reversal:

> **Boot**   I wish to resign from the Force, sir.
>
> **Inspector**   Now relax, Boot.
>
> **Boot** (*removing his helmet; almost in tears*)   I'm a failure, sir.
>
> **Inspector** (*moving to the gramophone*)   I shall come along with you myself.
>
> **Boot**   To make an arrest, sir?
>
> **Inspector**   Certainly not, Boot. (*He takes a pair of ballet shoes from the gramophone cupboard*) To join in. (28, 29)

The police force whose task it is to protect society from disruptive pleasures is shown to be itself susceptible to such antisocial desires, a camp joke about the capitulation of authority to the power of Dionysiac impulses – the enemy within.

Act One concludes with what is symbolically the disintegration of social order into carnival riot as bystanders in the park, including Boot and the Inspector, frenziedly sing and dance 'out of breath' – 'Dancing, dancing, dancing, / Till we all fall down.' During that scene Nigel Danvers, one of Jane's eligible suitors, reads her an item in the newspaper about the impact of the magic piano:

> **Nigel**   The Minister of Pleasure and Pastime, Mr Augustine Williams, announced today that the peaceful seclusion of London's parks has lately been disrupted by an alarming outbreak of dancing. [...] In spite of frequent police intervention many Londoners have already danced to the piano, including one of the sentries at Buckingham Palace. (29)

Doubly ironic is the fact that Timothy's Uncle Augustine, the Minister of Pleasure and Pastime, is the government agent of censorship and repression, who secretly frequents a nightclub called 'The Cleopatra'. A scene in the Gusset Creations dress shop (Act Two, Scene 5) seems to have no other function in the show but to introduce a self-standing comic sketch about a fashion parade organized by the flamboyantly effeminate fashion designer Ambrose that goes horribly wrong, eventually being interrupted by Troppo with the news that the piano has been lost again and ending with Ambrose's melodramatic final line, 'I'm drained of all emotions. I'm a husk. Leave me' (53).

Reading 'against the grain'[36] the fact that this extremely camp scene has only a tangential connection with the central narrative betrays the absence in the text of any realistic representation of homosexuality, which the demands of stage censorship strictly prohibit. Like the dancing dictated by the magic piano, homoerotic desire is one of the subversive pleasures that those in authority such as Uncle Augustine have banned, at the same time pursuing other illicit pastimes on their own account. In this context the word 'gay' used with apparent innocence in many scenes and songs would in 1954 have a double meaning for those in the know.

The deep psychological need to escape the demands of the Freudian superego is not confined in the show to homoerotic pleasure but is manifest in any young person's simple joy of life as opposed to utilitarian pursuits. Jane's melodic song 'The Time of My Life' is a lyrical paean to the utopian pleasures the tramp's 'amazing dance' has permitted her and Timothy to enjoy: 'We're young and we're green as the leaf on the tree / For these are our salad days' (54). The celebration of simple pleasures prepares Jane for the strangest event in the whole whimsical narrative: a flying saucer arrives, carrying Electrode, a man from Planet Zed, with long blond hair, and dressed in science fiction fashion. The scientist who has navigated the saucer to earth turns out to be Uncle Zed, Timothy's fourth uncle, who has seen that they were in trouble on his 'panuro-scopo-telecinerama refracto vistavision set' (58) and now hurries them all on board the saucer to fly off in search of the piano. The show's final revelation is that the tramp is Timothy's fifth uncle – the black sheep of the family – the 'one we don't mention'.

In deliberate contradiction to the heteronormative love stories that shape the narratives of post-war American stage and screen musicals, a central heterosexual romance is not the key motif in shaping the plot of *Salad Days*. In fact its representation of marriage is perversely if sweetly Platonic. *Salad Days* follows the pattern of a *bildungsroman* which culminates in the discovery of the magic of 'being gay': the liberation is brought about by play, and the revelation engineered by a social drop-out who spends his life subverting the earnest values of a society that has become obsessed with respectable conformity to such an extent that its repression of the libido has extinguished any pleasure in living. The musical celebrates the triumph of utopian fantasy over psychological repression, advocating the freeing of the body (symbolized by dancing with Dionysiac abandon) over the excessive censoriousness demanded by bourgeois conformity. Rather than appearing to be an ancient relic, the doubleness of the show's allegorical defence of both everyday hedonism and more subversive gay pleasure allows *Salad Days* to reveal itself in intelligent revivals such as that by Tête à Tête as both hilarious and curiously modern. Future revivals may well explore the surreal stylization of the musical as a surprising echo of absurdist theatre.

1.3 ROCK AND ROLL AND THE THEATRE REVOLUTION

The values of the new post-war culture did not remain locked in the closet of 1950s conformism but instead began to be manifest in popular entertainment through the development of British jazz and blues music, and the first obvious visual display of youth culture in the new sartorial style of Teddy Boys and their rock 'n' roll counterparts.[37] The arrival in the UK of rock and roll (with the release of the film *Rock Around the Clock* in 1956) coincided with the beginning of the theatre revolution – as symbolized in the opening of Osborne's *Look Back in Anger* at the Royal Court, which gave the name to the literary movement of 'angry young men' (there were some women!) that represented a rebellious youthful counter-culture contemptuous of the stiff upper lip reticence of wartime society. Although America was an increasingly irresistible influence and a powerful image of modernity in mass culture[38] (including pop music, film, comic books and consumer goods), literature and theatre reflected explicitly *British* social and cultural values in an explosion of artistic creativity in the fields of poetry, the novel and particularly in the revolutionary British drama of John Osborne, Arnold Wesker, Harold Pinter, Brendan Behan, John Arden and Shelagh Delaney.

In spite of its repressive censorship, British drama had actually been in a process of transformation since the late 1940s: nonetheless the middlebrow form of the middle-class well-made West End play of Enid Bagnold, N. C. Hunter and Terence Rattigan remained dominant until the late 1950s. By 1955 the impact of radical Continental European writers was just beginning to make itself apparent in the experimental work of Joan Littlewood (e.g. her production of Bertolt Brecht's *Mother Courage*) at Stratford East in 1954 and Peter Hall (Ionesco's *The Lesson*, Beckett's *Waiting for Godot*) at the Arts Theatre Club in 1955, while the visit in 1956 of Brecht and Helene Weigel's Berliner Ensemble to the Palace Theatre in London proved a revelation to young directors, writers and designers.

For the first time in the history of British theatre, actors were permitted to project their own working-class identities on stage without masking them through the use of 'RP' (Received Pronunciation). Many of the new actors and writers were working class and came from a variety of regional backgrounds, promising that the full range of British social and cultural experience would manifest itself on British stages. After 1956, a new generation of proletarian actors such as Albert Finney, Tom Courtenay, Rita Tushingham, Barbara Windsor, Sean Connery and Michael Caine became famous on stage, while many soon became international film stars.

The Suez Crisis of 1956 was the last nail in the coffin of British colonialism. American intervention forced a humiliating climb-down by the British government who were exposed as having lied to Parliament, thereby revealing Conservative Party leaders as hypocritical adventurers, interfering in world politics without moral authority. Scepticism and mistrust of authority was equally discernible in the striking development of new types of musical with daring subject matter that differed substantially from that of 'golden age' American musicals. After the constrictions affecting middle-class gay writers like Wilson and Slade, the new wave of musicals appeared to pay no respect to old formalities: they were gritty, realistic and cynical, expressing a wholly different sociocultural attitude. Always excepting *West Side Story* (1957), they make Broadway musicals of the period seem rather tame.

Not a musical, but a play whose meaning and impact depends on its songs, *The Entertainer* was John Osborne's response to the Suez Crisis – a savage Brechtian exposure of the death of English music hall (a symbol for the disintegration of the Empire) by means of a pitiless portrayal of a 'dying' comedian; it was a major success for Laurence Olivier that transferred from the Royal Court to the West End in 1957. Quite possibly influenced by Osborne's play with music, *Expresso Bongo* (1958) starred the major Shakespearean star of the 1950s, Paul Scofield, as a seedy West End show business agent in a bitter exposé of the ruthless cupidity of the contemporary pop music industry. Also featuring the versatile Millicent Martin, Britain's first post-war musical theatre star, the show included pastiche rock and roll numbers as well as some very haunting jazz and blues songs by David Heneker, Julian More and Monty

Norman and ran for two years in the West End. Written by the affably Marxist playwright Wolf Mankowitz, the musical was loosely based on the meteoric rise of pop star Tommy Steele and exposed the Soho business of show for the greedy sham that it was. ('Nothing Is for Nothing' is one of the show's more memorable lyrics.) Another of the show's cynical numbers was Scofield's 'I've Never Had It So Good', whose deliberate echo of Prime Minister Harold Macmillan's often-quoted line that most British people 'had never had it so good' highlighted the selfish individualism of Tory Britain.[39] Macmillan's assertion signalled the rise of an age of affluence, in which many consumer goods were for the first time available to working-class people.[40] Such prosperity was clearly reflected in the new-found confidence of writers and producers to create distinctively British musicals but also in their ability to rival Broadway by producing flashier and slicker musicals such as *Grab Me a Gondola!* (1956), which challenged the Americans at their own game.[41]

An obvious 'cross-over' musical, *Lock Up Your Daughters* (1959) was Laurie Johnson and Lionel Bart's adaptation of Henry Fielding's lascivious eighteenth-century farce *Rape upon Rape*, a minor example of the unbridled sex comedy of the period. It was updated by some cosmetic slimming down of Fielding's book and the addition of 'period' songs, which are in fact pop songs orchestrated to suggest the period of the play. Like the gritty design style of Joan Littlewood's productions, the newly built Mermaid's open stage with its set by the revolutionary Sean Kenny again revealed the pervasive impact of Brecht and his designer Caspar Neher on the British theatre of the late 1950s. Yet again testing the boundaries between serious and popular theatre, Joan Littlewood's famous production of Lionel Bart's *Fings Ain't Wot They Used T'Be* was virtually unclassifiable. A verismo depiction of the Soho underworld it is set in a basement *spieler*,[42] whose denizens are tarts and gamblers. A seamier, English equivalent of *Guys and Dolls*, its characters are not, like the Broadway show, cartoon-like exaggerations, but flesh-and-blood inhabitants of the West End streets. An urban folk play, the show's pop score celebrates the irrepressible criminality of Soho life in a manner as brimming over with vitality as its plot is disorganized. Having cemented the reputation of pop songwriter Lionel Bart for wit and melody, the show transferred to the West End where it ran for two years.

In 1959 Wolf Mankowitz, David Heneker and Monty Norman followed *Expresso Bongo* with *Make Me an Offer*, which opened in Stratford East but soon transferred to the West End. Reflecting the Marxist orientation of its book writer, the show satirizes the East End business milieu of street market dealers while focusing realistically on a dysfunctional marriage; it also introduced the actor Daniel Massey to musical theatre. Gritty musicals like *Expresso Bongo, Fings* and *Make Me an Offer* may well have prompted John Osborne to assay a full-scale musical as a further elaboration of the dramaturgy he had explored in *The Entertainer*. *The World of Paul Slickey* opened at the Palace Theatre in 1959 to the most devastatingly bad reviews in living memory – and legend has it that Osborne was chased home down the Kings Road by irate theatregoers. In 1962, the percipient critic of modern drama George Wellwarth recognized the play itself as an expression of Osborne's stubbornly insistent honesty as a writer:

> If there is a prototype of the angry-young-man play, *The World of Paul Slickey* is it [...] There is so much direct criticism of society (castigation would perhaps be a better word) in it that just about everyone must have been made uncomfortable [...] *The World of Paul Slickey* is pure spit and vomit thrown directly into the teeth of the audience. Commercially it has been Osborne's least successful play; artistically it is his best. Inability to compromise may be disastrous from a diplomatic viewpoint, but art is not diplomacy: it is truth.[43]

Its pastiche Coward-esque satire on the upper classes with its grotesque portrayal of the aristocracy as hypocritical deceivers, specializing in transvestite fetishism, is allied to a parallel but connected plot of sleazy journalism; it constitutes Osborne's most rancid portrait of Little England – a dying civilization that refuses to lie down and do the honourable thing. Given his determination to offend complacent audiences by rubbing their noses in the corruption of British society concomitant upon the endemic system of class privilege, one might conclude that Osborne had succeeded triumphantly, but he was never to write another musical.

1.4 THE PLAY WITH MUSIC: POLITICAL THEATRE AND WORKING-CLASS CULTURE

A phenomenon that came to prominence at the time – and one that is possibly unique to British theatre – is the serious play with music.[44] Partly influenced by Brecht's drama, and partly by earlier forms of agitprop performance, this tradition of socially realist yet non-naturalistic drama was discernible, first at Joan Littlewood's Theatre Royal, Stratford East, which in 1946 originated *Uranium 235* and in 1956 premiered Brendan Behan's *The Quare Fellow*, a 'serious' play to which Littlewood added songs, and *The Hostage* in 1958 and then at the Royal Court in Osborne's *The Entertainer*, John Arden's *Sergeant Musgrave's Dance* (1959), and in the musical *The Lily White Boys* (1960). This tradition has led British critics and audiences to regard more adventurous musicals (*The World of Paul Slickey*, *Oh What a Lovely War!*) and plays with music as a form of drama deriving from such plays as Brecht's *The Good Person of Szechwan* (1943).

The success of the darkly satirical exposé of the pop music business *Expresso Bongo* in 1958 inspired a series of musicals revealing the criminal underbelly of society: Peter Wildeblood and Peter Greenwell's *The Crooked Mile* (1959) was a typical example of what was becoming a recognizable sub-genre, and its superb cast included the brilliant Irish actor Jack McGowran as the gangster Jug Ears, the great jazz singer Elizabeth Welch and the young Millicent Martin. Although a box-office failure, *Johnny the Priest* (1960) adapted by Peter Powell from a play by R. C. Sherriff with music by Anthony Hopkins, was a musically ambitious show featuring the rising star Jeremy Brett as an idealistic young priest: its score challenged *West Side Story* in the sophisticated use it made of symphonically elaborated jazz and a theme of juvenile delinquency and social reform that was serious and progressive. The range of social and political themes tackled by these ambitious English musicals can be further evidenced in the Royal Court production of Harry Cooke's *The Lily White Boys* (1960), a musical with lyrics by the poet Christopher Logue and music by Tony Kinsey and Bill Le Sage; its examination of the disillusionment of a generation of council estate youths who rise from juvenile delinquency to become scions of the middle-class professions featured future stars such as Albert Finney, Georgia Brown, Shirley Ann Field and Philip Locke, and again demonstrated the fine line between musical theatre and serious drama with music.

The kind of working-class aesthetic sponsored by Littlewood was promulgated in Scotland and the North of England in the productions of the 7:84 companies (Scotland and England), which among other types of theatre, specialized in giving audiences 'a good night out': the epic musical plays conceived by working-class intellectual John McGrath and his wife Elizabeth MacLennan explored the inequalities of British society in Marxist terms, developing an original form of folk theatre that combined pantomime, music hall, ceilidh,[45] film documentary and agitprop scenes in a highly original way.[46] More limited in scope, but nevertheless aimed directly at representing working-class experiences in accessible entertainment forms, Willy Russell's *Blood Brothers* (1983) and *Our Day Out* (1983) and Melvyn

Bragg/Howard Goodall's *The Hired Man* (1984) continued the tradition of committed left-wing musical theatre. This tradition can still be seen to animate *Billy Elliot: the Musical* (2005) and *Made in Dagenham* (2015).

Case Study 2: *Blood Brothers*

Thatcher's theatre: melodrama and political protest

The early years of Margaret Thatcher's government, which witnessed the abandonment of the left-wing and Marxist alternative theatres of the 1970s – often through savage cuts in their Arts Council funding – saw not only a concomitant aestheticization of theatre in the growth of visual and physical experimentation in alternative and in commercial theatre (*Cats*, 1981, *Starlight Express*, 1984, *Time*, 1986) but also a corresponding increase in the popularity of melodramas with a progressive liberal or vaguely left-wing agenda, for example, *Nicholas Nickleby* (1979), *The Hired Man* (1984), *Les Misérables* (1985).[47] *Blood Brothers* exploits the form of melodrama while at the same time subverting and deconstructing its traditionally deterministic acceptance of human destiny by contrasting the superstitious and reactionary belief in fate against a progressive interpretation of individual life as the interaction of genetic predisposition with social forces and structures that can be changed to produce different outcomes.

Central to the emotional impact of nineteenth-century melodrama was the regular use of music and occasional use of songs to heighten and underscore the fluctuating emotional dynamic of the drama.[48] As a musical, *Blood Brothers* utilizes both songs and musical underscore of action and dialogue for the same purposes but also to interrupt the unfolding narrative and reflect or comment upon it. Willy Russell's effective deployment of a popular vocabulary of British rhythm and blues, 'retro' rock and roll and Northern soul, all of which were extremely popular in Britain during the late 1970s/early 1980s, ensures that the drama captures the *Zeitgeist* and communicates with audiences on an immediate and visceral level.

Brechtian techniques: story-telling and scenography

From the opening lyric, *Blood Brothers* makes its audience aware that a story is being told. One might say that this was a style derived from Brecht's notion of epic theatre, which emphasizes overt story-telling over the 'Aristotelian' approach to plotting as pure enactment, yet the narrator acts as a kind of Greek chorus figure, heightening the spectator's awareness of significant points in the action in a manner that is reminiscent of Sophoclean tragedy: 'Tell me it's not true / Say it's just a story'.

The sung lines of the central character that open the show begin the interrogation of the relationship between reality and fiction that is to run throughout the narrative, establishing a self-reflexiveness that provokes an awareness of the connection between individual story and history itself, thereby questioning the status of any particular narrative as a representation of more general truths. Even though a theatre audience may when the action has unfolded feel that 'it's just a story', the method of telling the tale will have alerted them to its wider frame of historical reference, enabling them to subject their own understanding of that history to more sophisticated examination.

Certainly the self-reflexiveness of the sung and spoken narration is a convention of the type of folk tale referenced in the unfolding of the fable by a narrator:

> So did y'hear the story
> Of the Johnstone twins?
> As like each other as two new pins.
> Of one womb born, on the self same day
> How one was kept and one given away?

By portraying as urban myth the story of the two 'blood brothers', separated in their infancy by circumstance, the narrator encourages the audience to reflect on the moral and social significance of the tale even before they have encountered the two characters. The next stanza is a deliberate 'spoiler', placing an audience in a position of superior knowledge to the characters by revealing the final outcome of the tragic narrative at the beginning of the performance:

> An' did you never hear how the Johnstone's died
> Never knowing that they shared one name,
> Till the day they died, when a mother cried
> 'My own dear sons lie slain.'

The heightened diction of 'My own dear sons lie slain' draws attention to the archetypal meaning encoded in the archaic form of the legend. The Brechtian notion that actors and spectators should *judge* each character being represented is implied in the narrator's exhortation to the audience in the final stanza of the song, 'Then bring her [the mother] on and come judge for yourselves / How she came to play this part.' The notion that the boys' mother was 'playing a part' alludes to the idea that the form of society is a human construction; it implies that the British class system is not inevitable but arbitrary – so that any 'actor' in the drama might find herself in any role, depending on what class s/he was born into. If the class structure were abolished, the working-class mother might have attained privileges that would allow her to evade the 'destiny' of losing both her sons: this revelation exposes the injustice of the social hierarchy.

The original scenic staging of *Blood Brothers* made use of Brecht's aesthetic of complex simplicity, utilizing a highly effective but conventional method of back flats that could be 'flown' in and out very swiftly to indicate changes in location emblematically. The 'wings' of the stage were masked by brick walls with arches for exits on stage left that suggest Victorian public buildings and doors downstage right that represent the two council houses of the Johnstone family. The staging exemplifies Peter Brook's category of 'rough theatre' – its non-illusionistic realism deriving from the scenic minimalism of designer Jocelyn Herbert and others at the Royal Court as much as the Brechtian simplicity of Joan Littlewood's work. With no attempt at naturalistic scenic illusion, the episodic nature of the dramatization could be enhanced by effecting split-second shifts of location with characters wheeling furniture on and off in full view of the audience, while the narrator or Mrs Johnstone establishes the situation in spoken or sung narration. The songs, which explore or reveal characters' attitudes to events, are usually accompanied by stylized movement or dance that visually illustrates them or provides an ironically contrasting action or image.

'Easy Terms': the price of being poor

Running through the show is a thematic trope of escape from the harshness and banality of daily existence through romance and fun. The pretty, young Mrs Johnstone has a fantasy identification with the screen goddess Marilyn Monroe – ironically so, because everyone knows that Monroe's short life was tragic. But initially the man she marries compares her favourably with Monroe when he takes her dancing, another repeated motif that signals the desperate need of young working-class people for relief from their debilitating daily toil. Predictably Mrs Johnstone soon finds she is pregnant and is obliged to get married. Although she 'still fancied dancing' after the birth of her first child, Mrs Johnstone's song reveals, 'My husband wouldn't go / With a wife he said was twice the size of Marilyn Monroe / No more dancing'. The song she sings outlines the failure of her marriage as child rearing and work begin to age her prematurely, and her husband walks out on her when she falls pregnant once again, '[f]or a girl they say who looks a bit like Marilyn Monroe / And they go dancing'.

The narrator and a chorus of four actors play all the minor roles in the show, enhancing the sense of conscious role-play that pervades the performance. The off-stage wailing of four hungry children and the Milkman/Narrator's repeated interruptions of the song with demands for payment vividly elucidate Mrs Johnstone's problems as a single mother. She continues the song with one further interruption as she talks to her children: action and song merge seamlessly into the next scene in Mrs Lyons' house where Mrs Johnstone works as a cleaner. The idea of superstition, which comes to dominate both Mrs Johnstone's and Mrs Lyons' lives, is introduced when Mrs Lyons is about to place a pair of new shoes on the table and Mrs Johnstone warns her that it could bring bad luck, a notion immediately reinforced by the entrance of the Narrator:

> **Mrs Johnstone**   I'm not superstitious.
>
> **Narrator**   The Mother said.
>
> **Mrs Johnstone**   I'm not superstitious.
>
> **Narrator**   The Mother said.

Immediately after this the Narrator re-enters as a gynaecologist who examines Mrs Johnstone and informs her she will be giving birth to twins. The meta-theatricality of the performance is emphasized by the fact that both the narrator and Mrs Johnstone joke about the fact that he has played both milkman and gynaecologist, before she returns to the scene in Mrs Lyons' house, which in physical terms she has not actually left. Without consciously intending it, she lets slip to Mrs Lyons that she is expecting twins; this immediately causes Mrs Lyons to hatch a plan to tell her husband, who is out of the country on business, that she herself is pregnant, so that she can adopt one of the twins, pretending it is hers. Mrs Lyons' desperation is powerfully depicted in her spontaneous enactment of her fake 'pregnancy':

> Look, look, you're what, four months pregnant, but you're only just beginning to show[...] so, so I'm four months pregnant and I'm only

just beginning to show.(*She grabs a cushion and arranges it beneath her dress.*) Look, look, I could have got pregnant just before he went away. (86)

The snatches of song sung by each woman in explanation of their feelings help the audience accept the extraordinary plan as a rational solution to the desperate situation of each. What clinches the arrangement is both women's realization of the economic advantages of a child being socially privileged:

Mrs Johnstone And when he grew up
        He could never be told
        To stand and queue up
        For hours on end at the dole
        He'd grow up to be

Mrs Lyons and **Mrs Johnstone** A credit to me. (88)

The choice of words has a double significance: 'credit' can be understood straightforwardly to mean 'reflecting approbation', but the word is drawn from the language of economics and also implies the profit-and-loss ledger of a business deal. This second meaning is brought into play in the following scene as the audience understands how both women have made a bargain that requires each in her different way to 'live on credit' with a 'debt to be paid'.

As Mrs Johnstone's furniture is repossessed because she fails to make timely repayments she sings 'Easy Terms', which comments on the price paid for the escapist pleasure of youthful romance. Getting pregnant has led Mrs Johnstone into a bad marriage that ends in an unhappy divorce and leaves her with eight mouths to feed. The song expresses the lived experience of poverty in a metaphor drawn from the world of finance, employing the jargon of the salesman to designate the fate of those who must live on credit:

Living on the never never
Constant as the changing weather
Never sure
Who's at the door
Or the price I'll have to pay. (91)

The true price of being a working-class mother is the sadness of giving up a child in order to be allowed to continue living on credit.

Mrs Lyons becomes irrationally jealous and afraid whenever Mrs Johnstone seeks to touch the adopted baby and eventually dismisses her. In order to prevent Mrs Johnstone from ever revealing the true identity of the adopted boy, Mrs Lyons tells her about the superstition that if either one of twins who have been secretly parted ever learns the truth, they shall both die. The Narrator evokes Mrs Johnstone's guilt and superstitious fear in song:

> **Narrator**   Shoes upon the table
> An' a spider's been killed.
> Someone broke the lookin' glass
> A full moon shinin'
> An' the salt's been spilled.
> [...]
> And you can't tell anyone
> But y' know the devils got your number,
> [...]
> And he's knocking at your door (95–6)

When after seven years the two boys meet and, fascinated by each other's very different manners, become firm friends, Mrs Johnstone finds out and forbids Edward to see her Mickey again. But Mickey goes to Edward's house to ask him to play, so Mrs Lyons realizes what has happened and is so upset she insists on moving to another part of town so that Mickey and Edward will have no chance of meeting again. The fact that the seven-year-old 'blood brothers' are played by adult actors invariably elicits huge laughs from an audience, but it is also a Brechtian device that emphasizes the difference between actor and character, encouraging the audience to maintain a critical perspective on how the children are being represented – in this case, reminding them that the differences between the two boys are largely connected with their upbringing and environment rather than genetic inheritance. The audience perceives the difference between a working-class boy's conception of the world and a middle-class boy's view of it, laughing in immediate recognition of the boys' typically different class attitudes and behaviours.

Instead of the anticipated bad luck, Mrs Johnstone and her family are later rehoused in a more salubrious suburb, another example of Mrs

Figure 3 Twin brothers growing up in different classes – Amy Robbins (Mrs Johnstone), Stephen Palfreman (Mickey), Simon Willmont (Edward) in *Blood Brothers*, London 2011. Photograph by Eric Richmond. Courtesy of ArenaPAL.

Johnstone's tendency to interpret the events of her life superstitiously as luck or chance rather than in terms of a political understanding of her social position. In a reprise of her key song, Marilyn Monroe continues to be the yardstick against which her life as a woman is assessed:

Mrs Johnstone   The house we got was lovely
    The neighbours are a treat
    They sometimes fight on Saturday night
    But never in the week
    […]
    Since I pay me bills on time, the milkman
    Insists I call him Joe
    […]

Says I've got legs
Like Marilyn Monroe. (122)

Ironically, one of Mrs Johnstone's daughters appears to have repeated her mother's choices, a twist of the plot through which Russell emphasizes the cyclical pattern of working-class life as it recurrently denies young women the chance to challenge the 'fate' that typically determines their lives: 'Our Donna Marie's already got three, she's / A bit like me that way' (123).

Class versus chance: alternative conceptions of fate

By an odd coincidence the family's new house is located in the same part of town as that of the Lyons family, and the two brothers renew their friendship, both falling in love with the same girl, Linda:

Narrator The street's turned into Paradise, the radio's singing dreams
You're innocent, immortal, you're just fifteen.
[...]
And who'd dare tell the lambs in Spring,
What fate the later seasons bring. (138–9)

The notion that escapist pleasures blind the young to predetermined reality is likened to the optimism of youth, naively ignorant of what life has in store:

But everything's possible, the world's within your reach
[...]
and you can't understand
How living could be anything other than a dream
When you're young, free and innocent and just eighteen. (140)

When Edward goes away to university, he encourages Mickey to declare his love for Linda; Linda falls pregnant and decides to marry Mickey before Christmas but he is soon out of work. Through the songs, Russell generalizes the social significance of the action so that the audience comprehends the story of the 'blood brothers' and their families as a microcosmic representation of the global reality of unregulated capitalism.

The song 'Take a Letter, Miss Jones' poignantly indicates how Mickey losing his job symbolizes the fate of hundreds of thousands of working-class people whose unemployment is a result of the recession caused by the monetarist economic policies of Ronald Reagan and Margaret Thatcher's governments:

Mr Lyons   Take a letter, Miss Jones,
  Due to the world situation
  The shrinking pound, the global slump,
  And the price of oil
  I'm afraid we must fire you
  We no longer require you,
  It's just another
  Sign of the times,
  Miss Jones (144)

Ironically Miss Jones – the bearer of bad news to others – is obliged to type her own letter of dismissal and take Mickey's place in the dole queue.

Mr Lyons (and in an ironic sense, the Narrator) present the circumstances that create unemployment as chance – the arbitrary reaction to economic forces over which they have no control, thereby refusing to admit any responsibility for causing the economic recession that has led to mass unemployment:

Narrator   There's a young man on the street, Miss Jones
  He's walkin' round in circles,
  [...]
  Don't look at him, don't cry though
  This living on the giro
  Is only a sign of the times,
  Miss Jones, it's
  Just another sign of the times. (145)

By casting Mr Lyons in the role of the employer responsible for firing Miss Jones as well as hundreds of others, Russell identifies and personalizes the political factors that impact upon the relationships and choices of the central characters.

When Edward returns for the Christmas vacation he senses Linda's unhappiness and proposes to her, declaring that he has always been in love with her, but when Linda informs him she is married to Mickey the privileged brother ironically appears for once not to get what he wants. Interwoven within this scene is one in which Mickey's older brother, Sammy, tempts him with the promise of £50 into acting as the lookout in his scheme to rob a petrol station. The Narrator's continual commentary on the twists and turns of the narrative provokes the audience into questioning whether the pattern of a protagonist's life is shaped by societal factors (such as class) or whether the potentially tragic outcome confirms the conception of character as a genetically or randomly predetermined fate.

When the robbery goes wrong, Sammy and Mickey are arrested and Mickey is sentenced to seven years in prison, later commuted for good behaviour. Nevertheless Mickey is so depressed in gaol that he becomes dependent on medication. At this point in the story, the image of Marilyn Monroe no longer symbolizes glamour or sexual attractiveness but mental instability:

> A prescription note the doctor wrote
> For the chronically depressed.
> He [. . .] treats his ills with daily pills
> Just like Marilyn Monroe
> They stop his mind from dancing . . . (150)

Linda has secured a job for him with the help of Edward, who is now a town councillor. But when Mickey is informed by Mrs Lyons that Linda and Eddie have been having an affair, he completely loses control:

> **Narrator**   There's a man gone mad in the town tonight,
> He's gonna shoot somebody down,
> There's a man gone mad, lost his mind tonight . . . (155)

The Narrator's choric speech leads the audience to expect that Mickey will shoot Edward when he bursts from the auditorium on to the stage where Edward is addressing a Council meeting, but Mickey admits he is not even competent to kill Eddie: 'I thought I was gonna shoot y'. But I can't even do that. I don't even know if the thing's loaded.' The plot takes a surprising turn however when Mrs Johnstone enters from the auditorium and begs Mickey not to shoot:

Mrs Johnstone Don't shoot Eddie. He's your brother. You had a twin brother. I couldn't afford to keep both of you. His mother couldn't have kids. I agreed to give one of you away!

Mickey (*something that begins deep down inside him*) You! (*Screaming.*) You! Why didn't you give me away! [. . .] I could have been . . . I could have been him. (157–8)

Mickey pulls the trigger by accident, killing Eddie, then turns to the police marksmen, who shoot him dead. There is a Sophoclean irony in the way the brothers' simultaneous death appears to confirm the truth of Mrs Lyons' superstitious belief that if either of a pair of twins who have been secretly parted ever learns that he was one of a pair 'they shall both immediately die'. (95)

The Narrator's sober concluding speech casts serious doubt on this superstitious interpretation of the brothers' 'fate' ('And do we blame superstition for what came to pass? / Or could it be what we, the English, have come to know as class?') (158), the emphasis on the balanced antithesis and ultimate symmetry of their destinies a further reminder of the 'constructed' nature of the narrative, its dialectical representation of class difference. The Brechtian technique of laying out the incidents as though the audience were witnessing an experiment in the politics of class is starkly opposed to the emotional engagement with plot and character that characterizes the structure of *Blood Brothers* as melodrama. Cleverly, Willy Russell seems able to have it both ways: on the one hand, presenting the story in the popular form of a melodrama, with stereotypical characters, a stirring plot and music that encourages the audience to engage strongly with the highly emotional nature of the situations; on the other, cultivating a critical distance through the epic and dialectical strategies of Brechtian drama which continually remind the spectator that the show is an artistic construct, a story that might have turned out differently.

Mrs Johnstone's final reprise of 'Tell Me It's Not True' mournfully expresses the dual meaning of *Blood Brothers* as a melodrama that is not only 'just a story', entertaining by appealing strongly to the primal feelings of its audience, but also a sophisticated political drama that exhorts us to examine social reality to verify the truth of its dramatic representation and intervene to change that reality:

> Tell me it's not true,
> Say it's just a story.

[...]
Say it's just a show
On the radio,
That we can turn over and start again ... [158]

1.5 THE IMPACT OF *OLIVER!*

In many ways the crowning achievement of all the experiments and explorations in the creation of new types of musical theatre after the war is Lionel Bart's *Oliver!* (1960). Combining the most advanced and technically sophisticated use of moving scenery yet seen in the commercial theatre with the dramatization of an iconic English novel, *Oliver!* exploits the unlikely idea of staging Dickens' classic narrative of psychological melodrama and social protest as a musical conceived in the visual style of Brechtian theatre by Sean Kenny and its director Peter Coe, and illustrated with the theatrical panache and elaborate technology of a spectacular Drury Lane melodrama:

> The original production of *Pickwick* [1965] was designed by Sean Kenny and the staging of it was a natural extension of our work together on two other British musicals – *Lock Up Your Daughters* and *Oliver!* On the whole colours were muted – the set was in solid wood, heavy in construction and dark brown in colour [...] One of the basic principles of the staging [...] was that before putting any set on the stage, as much space should be created as possible. The flies were stripped of everything not belonging to the production including all cloths, battens, masking blacks, everything. The lamps were allowed to hang in full view of the audience so that space and light were seen beyond them and through them. The brick back wall of the theatre was painted in abstract multicolours, so that when different coloured light was thrown on it, it changed for each scene [...] In this way even the smallest of stages is made to look vast, and the mobility of scenery and action is altogether easier and more fluid [...] Adopting the principle that black-outs only make things more difficult for actors and stage staff, it means that all scene changing needs to be done in full view of the audience.[49]

Tapping into the long legacy of Victorian music hall, Dickensian cinema[50] and popular melodrama, Bart mined the cultural imaginary to create a musical

44

that for all its obvious flaws strikes to the heart of English parables of childhood injustice to create a piece of musical theatre that has become so iconic it now rivals Dickens' original work in its mythic hold on the popular imagination. Apart from being the first full-scale musical version of a Dickens novel, *Oliver!* answered a need in its time to distance popular culture from the Victorian past by representing it as mythic history. By adding songs Bart contrived a way of ritualizing elements of the 'Dickens world' to make all characters more sympathetic with the exception of Bill Sykes, and to historicize the novel so that Dickens' trenchant criticism of the pitiless attitude of authority towards the poor becomes an assumption that crime is the appropriate and inevitable result of an unjust society. In this way, *Oliver!* is probably the first musical that expresses the spirit of upward mobility that characterized British society – and especially youth culture – in the 'swinging sixties'.

Revived in the West End more often than any other musical, it was the longest-running English musical on Broadway before *Cats*, became a staple of British school productions, and was made into a highly successful film in 1968. It spawned a number of imitations – *Vanity Fair* (1962), *Half a Sixpence* (1963), *Pickwick* (1965), *The Match Girls* (1966), *Ann Veronica* (1969), *Scrooge* (1970), *Trelawney* (1972), *The Card* (1973), *Nickleby and Me* (1975) et al. – based on Victorian or Edwardian novels and plays. Many of these shows appear on the surface to be critical of the class system they represent while in fact upholding it in a muddled and genial spirit of compromise. Some were commercially successful, but none ever approached the legendary status of *Oliver!*[51]

Lionel Bart's work at the Theatre Royal, Stratford East (*Fings*) and his own experience as a working-class Jewish boy growing up in the East End during the war taught him everything he needed to know about the class stratification of British society, but it also provided him with egalitarian notions of social justice – and Bart seemed to be the figure most capable of embodying Joan Littlewood's notion of theatre as participatory entertainment for all. Bart followed *Oliver!* with *Blitz!* (1962), a musical set in London during the war, but his most overtly political musical was *Maggie May* (1964), set in the dockyards of Liverpool with a book by the playwright Alun Owen. All his shows combined a genuine feeling for the forms and styles of working-class entertainment with a flair for histrionic effect. Generous to a fault, Bart lived a recklessly hedonistic life, earning and spending enormous amounts of money until he finally lost everything as a result of investing his own money in the disaster that was *Twang!!* (1965), declaring bankruptcy in 1972.

Figure 4 A musical conceived in the visual style of Brechtian theatre – Georgia Brown (Nancy) and the gang in *Oliver!* standing on the original Sean Kenny set, London 1960. Photographs by Eileen Darby. Courtesy of Eileen Darby Images and The Billy Rose Collection of the New York Public Library.

With their ground-breaking *Stop the World – I Want to Get Off* (1961), the actor and singing star Anthony Newley and composer-lyricist Leslie Bricusse initiated a very different trend in British musical theatre. A contemporary morality play set in a circus environment, the show's powerful 'showbiz'-style numbers utilized theatre as a metaphor to present an allegory of the small man's battle with conformity. The show made the ubiquitous Anthony Newley famous in America and a number of its songs became show business standards. The meta-musical aspect of this show and its successor *The Roar of the Greasepaint, the Smell of the Crowd* (1964) – possibly a better show, which was produced on Broadway by David Merrick but never got to the West End – was paralleled by such musicals as *Oh What a Lovely War!* (1963) and *Cabaret* (1966), but the Newley-Bricusse formula soon became a cliché and their West End follow-up to these shows, *The Good Old Bad Old Days* (1972), though a moderate commercial success was critically lambasted. Most British musicals of the 1960s veered between formulaic imitations of *Oliver!* and haphazard attempts to compete with Broadway shows on their own terms.

Innovations in musical theatre are as often manifest in 'drama' as within the genre of the popular musical. The great television plays of Dennis Potter (*Pennies from Heaven*, 1978 and *The Singing Detective*, 1986) and Alan Plater (*The Beiderbecke Trilogy*, 1985–8), make innovative use of popular music to frame and signify their particular thematic concerns, their use of songs from the past resembling that of the modern 'jukebox' musical. The varied and sophisticated deployment of song and music in serious drama has been a regular feature of British theatre since the 1950s, more recent examples ranging from *Restoration* (1982), Edward Bond's harshly satirical pastiche of Restoration comedy, *Our Day Out* (1983), Willy Russell's moving depiction of a day's outing for working-class school children in Liverpool, to such diverse works as Neil Bartlett's *Sarrazine* (1990), *A Judgement in Stone* (1992) and his meta-theatrical pastiche of 1950s musical comedy, *Night after Night* (1993). Improbable Theatre's astonishing 'junk opera' *Shockheaded Peter* (1998) defies categorization, while Mark Ravenhill's *Mother Clap's Molly House* (2001) is a Brechtian fable with songs about the incremental commodification of queer culture over 250 years. Alan Bennett's *The History Boys* (2005) makes camp and comic use of a range of popular songs from the 1930s onwards to capture the 'folk' identity of a vanishing British culture, while Victoria Wood's *That Day We Sang* (2011) and Tim Firth's *This My Family* (2013) are quietly affecting depictions of the quotidian. Richard Thomas and Stewart Lee's *Jerry Springer: The Opera*, and Adam Cork and Alecky Blythe's *London Road* (2011)[52] are through-sung 'operas'.[53] In New

York, these shows are most likely to be treated as experimental off-Broadway musicals; in London, they are regarded simply as theatre.

1.6 AFTER *JESUS CHRIST SUPERSTAR*: GLOBALIZATION AND CULTURAL SPECIFICITY

British music, however, had moved away from the pop styles mastered by those such as Lionel Bart, and the musical theatre was soon to follow suit. The swinging sixties expressed itself musically in the global triumph of the Beatles, the Kinks, the Rolling Stones, Genesis, the Who, Pink Floyd and other rock and pop bands whose music knocked American rock and roll and soul off the top of the charts globally and gave birth to the idea of the rock opera as a fashionable new form that enabled Tim Rice and Andrew Lloyd Webber to achieve world recognition with the concept albums of *Jesus Christ Superstar* (1970) and *Evita* (1976), as well as giving rise to the controversial but commercially successful Ken Russell film of the Who's concept album *Tommy* (1975), while later providing the impetus for Cameron Mackintosh's development of a system of international production and licensing that created a new generation of global musicals – *Cats* (1981), *Les Misérables* (1985), *The Phantom of the Opera* (1986) and *Miss Saigon* (1989).

In the last three decades the West End has produced more than half of the most commercially successful musicals in international terms. Globally, interest in the British musical shows no sign of abating: there are continual revivals and tours of many British shows, while musicals such as *We Will Rock You* are now becoming staples of the global market, and at a local level, British musicals continue to address a wide variety of sub-cultures in very different ways. It is therefore increasingly important to study the British musical within an historical context, and to engage with individual musicals by means of both aesthetic and sociocultural analysis.

At a time when the American musical appeared to have reached its nadir, the sung-through British musical arrived on Broadway, and by the mid-2000s three British musicals had surpassed *A Chorus Line* (1975) as Broadway's longest-running show: *Cats*, *Les Misérables*, and *The Phantom of the Opera*. In the early 2000s Disney's *The Lion King*[54] (1997) and Judy Kramer's *Mamma Mia!* joined producer Cameron Mackintosh's three shows to become the most successful shows in the global marketplace. The international success of these shows and others has resulted in the development of new production companies in major cities around the world. There are now multimillion-pound musical theatre industries based in Seoul, Hamburg, Singapore and Tokyo; it will not be long before Beijing follows. While the globalization of the entertainment industry can give people around the world greater access to musicals and other entertainment forms, there is a danger that the dominant cultural economies either unwittingly or deliberately become guilty of cultural imperialism, rendering differences between one society and another invisible, and collapsing all cultures into that of the politically dominant or economically most powerful.

The journalist and critic John Lahr is guilty of such blindness to the specific contours of British culture in his review of *Billy Elliot* in *The New Yorker* in 2005:

> By nature, the musical genre deals with fantasy, not fact; it is at its most political when it delivers pleasure, not dogmatic persiflage. [Lee] Hall doesn't seem to understand this, and his prolix, repetitive book quickly loses its way. When the miners are the issue—and their story eats up a fair portion of the saga—the musical stalls; the proletariat here really *are* lumpen. When Billy dances, however, everything comes alive.

This is of course a uniquely American perspective – one that insists that the musical should celebrate the American dream of the individual's triumph over adversity as an aspect of her right to the 'pursuit of happiness' enshrined in the constitution. Workers are boring; talented individuals are stars. Lahr naturally assumes that the musical exists to celebrate the virtuosity of its star performers rather than provide a coherent narrative concerning the relationship between individuals and their community: 'When Billy is doing his twists and twirls, his youthful entrechats and jetés, the immanence of the extraordinary is credible. When he tap-dances, it isn't; Savion Glover[55] he ain't.'

What Lahr fails to comprehend is that *Billy Elliot* is not attempting to sell the American dream. Unlike 1930s musical comedy, it is not concerned with individual 'pluck and luck' – the theme Lahr sees as dominant in the Broadway musical – but with the celebration of community values as utopian. Most British musicals from the musical comedies of the Gaiety Theatre after 1892 to *Calendar Girls* (2015) celebrate community spirit and social rapprochement rather than individual success. British audiences are motivated by very different cultural mythologies to those of the United States. Cultural universalism effaces local differences, but we cannot understand individual people unless we are aware of the different cultures that have shaped their social attitudes and mentalities.

Case Study 3: *Billy Elliot*

Method of analysis

Drama is never merely a direct illustration of social and political meanings; it is a happening in time, which fleshes out these meanings in the multiple modes of human experience. As musical drama makes particularly sophisticated use of the shape and flow of experience in time,[56] my method of analysing the webs of meaning generated by this dense performance text, a product of the remarkable collaboration of Lee Hall (librettist), Elton John (composer), Stephen Daldry (director) and Peter Darling (choreographer), is to trace the accumulation of significance through the individual modes of action, dialogue, song, dance, music, and scenography and in their variety of interrelationships – both complementary and ironic. In all works of art, form expresses content, just as style articulates meaning. In a complex musical, the range of formal techniques is broad, enabling many different methods of articulating meaning. My aim in attempting a phenomenological account of the way meaning accumulates in the temporal order of the performance is to highlight not merely the signs and their signification as metaphors, motifs and tropes but the manner in which they are contextually recapitulated, paralleled, contradicted, elaborated and ironized in order to model the processes of grasping and comprehending that signification.

The musical as history play

> This is not the time to beat about the bush. *Billy Elliot* strikes me as the greatest British musical I have ever seen [...] There is a rawness, a warm humour and a sheer humanity here that are worlds away from the soulless slickness of most musicals [...] The emotion in this production always seems real and spontaneous rather than cunningly manipulated to pull at the heartstrings.[57]

What is it that inspired Charles Spencer, critic of the Conservative-supporting *Daily Telegraph*, so unreservedly to sing the praises of a musical that is trenchant in its criticism of the Conservative policies of the 1980s?

The answer surely lies in the complexity and honesty with which it represents people caught up in political events without resorting to didactic proselytizing. In the realm of commercial theatre, *Billy Elliot*'s blunt presentation of two opposing political viewpoints makes it unique. Unafraid to risk offending those of an utterly different political persuasion, the social critique in *Billy Elliot*, as in *Blood Brothers*, determines the entire structure and aesthetic of the work, linking its elements of celebratory entertainment and historical tragedy in a dialectical relationship that enacts the inevitability of the ideological conflict at stake. The musical is therefore exemplary for the way its aesthetic form enables the articulation of a complex set of competing ideologies: socialist values of community versus the Darwinian individualism of monetarist capitalism; masculine and feminine cultures; upper-middle-class against working-class cultures; queerness as a challenge to heteronormative views of gender.

From the first silent moment when a very small boy walks down the central aisle of the auditorium, the sense that he is emerging from the audience (someone's child perhaps?) connects us as a community of witnesses to what is about to be represented on the stage. Deploying Erwin Piscator's epic device of documentary film interwoven within the fabric of a fictional narrative, the show starts as a history lesson for the little boy, a reminder that the story we are watching is located within a history of socialist struggle for workers' rights. While *Blood Brothers* was both written and set in the early years of Margaret Thatcher's reactionary Conservative government (1982), reflecting upon that government's reinforcement of the gap between rich and poor, *Billy Elliot* represents and reflects upon this period as history.

Encouraging us to situate the moment of the miners' strike of 1983–4 within the historical perspective established by the Labour Government's post-war nationalization scheme for bringing major industries like coal mining under state control, the Pathé News film presents Clement Attlee announcing the birth of the nationalized coal industry in 1947 as a 'great experiment of socialism in democracy', with its communitarian values appealing to 'all our people and all our children'[58] for support. Documentary footage of miners going underground is overlaid with a heroic anthem ('The Stars Look Down') sung by mining communities in solidarity with the struggles of the pitmen[59] themselves:

> Through the fights and years of hardship,
> Through the storms and through the tears.

> We will always stand together
> In the dark right through the storm
> We will stand shoulder to shoulder
> To keep us warm.

The boy pulls down the sheet at the front of the stage on which the documentary has been projected to reveal the ramshackle municipal hall in which Easington villagers are gathered to hear news of the impending strike. In a highly effective piece of visual staging, the significance of the show as an historical representation and the meaning of 'community' for a mining town has been graphically illustrated. After the announcement that the miners are out on strike, Billy Elliot's friend Michael, who is left alone with Billy and the little boy from the opening, extends the motif of children being caught up in the political movements of history, even when they do not fully understand them, by asking: 'Billy, you know Maggie Thatcher? What's she done then?' To which Billy replies, 'Maggie Thatcher. Fucked if I know, Michael.' After Michael's exit, Billy, watched by the little boy, sings another verse of the miners' anthem to himself:

> Take me up and hold me gently,
> Raise me up and hold me high,
> Through the night and the darkness
> Will come a day when we will fly.

At this moment, Billy, closely observed by the little boy, mimes a bird or plane, while jumping from one square tile on the floor to another in movements reminiscent of dance. By copying Billy's movements, the boy reveals how values are absorbed and transmitted in a community through imitation of behaviour, a process that has been experienced by the boy since he began to watch the documentary news film.

By taking up their refrain, Billy has already identified in a subliminal way with the masculine pride of the miners, but it is pertinent that he sings lines appropriate to a child who still needs the help of fathers and brothers and that he sings about 'a day when we will fly', unwittingly anticipating the experience of being a successful dancer. The next verse similarly reveals a political identification with the downtrodden mining community, but Billy here ironically foreshadows his own situation as an individual 'outcast' from the masculine majority as effeminate because of his love of ballet:

And although we've been rejected.
And although we've been outcast
We will fight and win tomorrow
When we come to face the blast.

The sudden appearance of the miners on the picket line is the stage equivalent of a cinematic cut that changes the location in an instant; their repeated refrain of 'And the stars look down' invokes the spiritual dimension of the miners' belief in their communal way of life.

The political and the personal: class and gender

At the end of this brief episode, a scene change is effected by the emergence of a rickety staircase from under the stage powered by a hydraulic lift to create an almost filmic 'dissolve' to Billy's house, where his Grandma in her dressing gown and his brother in his underpants are getting their breakfast. We are here confronted by the image of a potentially dysfunctional working-class family in a disorderly morning routine, arguing while the transistor radio broadcasts the pontifications of Margaret Thatcher as a number of miners interrupt to hurry Billy's father and older brother off to the pickets. Grandma's apparently throwaway line, 'I can remember the General Strike' offers a sudden glimpse of what is almost a folk memory, the working-class woman's experience introducing a sense of the twentieth-century history against which these particular events are being played out.

When Billy arrives late at boxing class, which is held in the community hall where the miners had gathered, George (a middle-aged miner who is also the boys' boxing trainer) is ordering three boys, including the little one from the opening scene, to do push-ups. The humour in this scene derives mainly from the boys' unwillingness to take on a rigorous physical regime but also from Billy and Michael's timid reluctance to punch their friend. It is also notable because it introduces the audience to the habitual bad language of the children – which presumably has been learned from their parents. Much to George's chagrin, the boys' lack of enthusiasm for boxing and the way in which Billy and Michael try to avoid hurting each other comically anticipates the show's critique of traditional working-class masculinity.

At the end of the lesson, George gives Billy the keys to the hall to pass on to the ballet teacher as he leaves, and the hall fills with noisy girls rushing in to their ballet class. The traditional boys' sport of boxing makes way for the conventional pastime of girls, in which Billy finds himself caught up as Mrs

Wilkinson, the teacher, tells him to join in. The class is represented by means of a song-and-dance number, 'Shine', that interprets the notion of stars in the earlier miners' anthem in a very different way: here the 'shining' of the little girls as stars is debunked by the song as neither the teacher nor the pupils seem likely to shine, so that this number offers the parody of a stale and inept copy of the real showbiz 'razzle-dazzle' it sings about.

Bored and disillusioned, Mrs Wilkinson's instructions to the class reveal the stream of her thoughts as she mechanically goes through the motions of teaching the unappreciative girls a dance routine. Because she sings lyrics that are second-hand showbiz clichés to girls who clearly appear inadequate performers, her advice begins to seem like an ironic comment on the deluded ambition of her pupils:

> It doesn't matter if you're large or small
> Trapezeoid or short or tall
> Even if you can't dance at all
> All you really have to do is shine.

Yet somehow beneath her jaded admonition to 'Give em the old razzle dazzle / Turn on the old pizzazz' the number betrays affection for the very same showbiz sentiments it parodies. At the same time the entire musical scene offers a wry celebration of communal effort, albeit from a comic perspective: the girls represent a sizable proportion of the children of mining families, so that having seen the passion of the villagers in support of mineworkers at the start of the show, we now see a large number of their children having fun.

Although the depiction of the inadequacies of largely talentless and very naughty girls is extremely funny, it stimulates Billy's nascent feeling for movement and dance, and the clichéd white-feathered fans and smoke effects at its finale evoke in tongue-in-cheek fashion the 'magic' that ballet seriously aims to produce. Such 'magic' is a window to a world of beauty and romance beyond the dirty grey landscape of a mining town, and we see how Billy's body and imagination respond fully to its power in the shadow dancing effects he creates when he is left on his own in the dark at the end of the class.

Choreography and meaning: staging masculinities

A blackout is instantly followed by the image of Grandma at the breakfast table, another cinematic 'dissolve'. In the dysfunctional Elliot family it seems

Billy is the only one looking out for her (he has bought her a pie, partly to bribe her not to tell his father that he was late): when he reminds her that his 'mam' and her own husband are dead, she responds: 'Christ, Billy they're dropping like flies' and tells him about her marriage in a song that brilliantly stages the ambivalence of traditional gender relations in the mid-twentieth century.

> But we'd go dancing, he was me own Brando,
> And for a moment there my heart was a-glow,
> We had dust in our hair and nowhere to go
> But we were free for an hour or three
> From the people we had to be,
> And in the morning we were sober.

Peter Darling's choreography for a group of miners poetically conjures the love-hate romance of masculine men and feminine women ('women were women and men they were men'), consisting of a series of slow-motion cartwheels, jigs and athletic poses, which are extended by the use of chairs, that suggest weekends in pubs and dance halls, smoking, drinking and dancing to Gaelic folk music.[60] The pale-blue light turns the men into silhouettes, archetypal figures that haunt Grandma's memories with the glamour of dreams; she dances with them as she relives her past but her counterpointed lyrics ironically tell a tale of a strong woman, not afraid to use her fists to protect herself from her husband's drunken violence, who 'if I went through my time again / Oh I'd do it without the help of men'. Ann Emery's remarkable performance speaks of the resilience of generations of working-class women whose destinies were determined by a society that denied them educational opportunities and therefore completely restricted their freedom to choose the kind of life to which they might be suited.

Visually the performance cuts directly from the masculine recreation of the miners in a dance hall to another group of men – this time policemen Mrs Thatcher has bussed in from the South of England to 'keep the peace' in the Newcastle area. The maintenance of patriarchal authority through aggressive force is emblematized by the straight line of uniformed policemen positioned to face the audience near the front of the stage. Their surreptitious gestures of tying shoelaces, straightening ties, brushing dust off jackets, and so on, together with exaggerated behavioural tics like picking their noses, tapping their toes and scratching themselves, are wittily coordinated by

Peter Darling to illustrate the way their physical power as a fighting machine is betrayed by their anxiety as individual men, gearing up for a conflict.

From this moment in 'Solidarity' the lengthy sequence is staged as a musical scene, the interweaving of dance, mime, dialogue, song and action constituting what is probably the most complex and semiotically dense piece of musical staging in British theatre. As the policemen form their line, the ballet girls run across the stage in front of them to get to a class. The discourse on masculinity takes a new turn when Mrs Wilkinson's daughter Debbie encounters Billy and asks if he will return to the class:

Debbie   Many lads do ballet.

Billy   Ay, poofs.

Debbie   What about Wayne Sleep. He's not a poof.

The scoffing laughter of the policemen is a reminder that the virtuoso Wayne Sleep was one of the few openly gay dancers at the time. The fear of effeminacy projected by a hyper-masculinized and conventionally homophobic culture can only conceive male ballet dancers as homosexual; the Wayne Sleep joke initiates a critique of working-class homophobia from this moment on in the musical, revealing not only that the putative conjunction of ballet with effeminacy is entirely arbitrary but also challenging the heteronormative fear of homosexuality as irretrievably other.[61]

The mechanized moves of the police are paralleled with the girls' attempts at beautiful but regimented ballet steps, paradoxically demonstrating the dance-like quality of the masculine fighting gestures of policemen and miners and the muscularity of ballet steps, which require the strength and prowess of an athlete in order to evoke the lightness and beauty of swans and fairytale princes. The thematizing of gesture and dance in the sequence also poses the question of the aim of each discipline – the repression of gentleness and emotional subtlety signalled in the battle movements of police and miners side by side with the emotional liberation of the individual achieved through the physical rigour of dance. At the centre of this visual opposition of traditionally 'masculine' and 'feminine' cultures is Billy himself, who over a four-week period of classes visibly acquires the physical agility to demonstrate the poise and aesthetic beauty of a fine male dancer.[62]

Complementing the visual discourse of gender and sexuality, the lyrics of the song articulate the trope of solidarity – an idea that acquires a range of meanings when viewed within the many different perspectives of the number and the musical as a whole. On one hand, the number ironically illustrates the way in which the Thatcher government is destroying the traditional notion of workers' solidarity as developed historically through the trade union movement by appealing to individual greed in order to divide working-class people into competing interest groups, through the promise of material betterment for some at the expense of others. On the other hand, the song demonstrates the altruism and communitarian values inscribed in the socialist ideology to which the mining community is dedicated. Even the girls accompany their dance steps by singing the 'solidarity' chorus, but for them this term has more to do with keeping in step as a *corps de ballet*.

Although Mrs Wilkinson tells the girls to 'forget about what's going on outside, just concentrate', the sequence as a whole collapses the overall experience of trying to get on with life in the midst of a strike into the form of a layered musical scene. The elaborate dance is itself a vindication of the utopian value of cooperation over competition. As the policemen and miners repeatedly swap helmets, lifting, holding and partnering the girls in a surreal ballet, their machismo folk-dancing with truncheons and rolled-up newspapers in humorous counterpoint to the girls' attempts at classical grace, they all gradually become part of the process of making art. Ensemble singing and dancing requires individuals to support one another, to work together harmoniously – literally to sing in harmony – and the choreography, while dramatizing the conflict between policemen and miners, paradoxically celebrates the art of collaboration which is essential to musical theatre.

The passing of time is compressed in this sequence so Jacky Elliot at last learns from George that Billy hasn't been going to boxing for four weeks: at the end of the sequence the first big cheer from the audience for Billy's success is rudely interrupted by Jacky, who in his anger at the deception bans his son from both ballet and boxing so that he can 'stop home and look after your nanna'. The scene changes to one in the toilet where Billy has escaped, during which Mrs Wilkinson offers him free private lessons after school to prepare for an audition for the Royal Ballet School. At this juncture the conventional pattern of working-class culture that decrees boys learn boxing in order to strengthen them for a life of hard manual labour, while girls are taught ballet to acquire poise and charm as potential wives, is directly countered by the more liberal and elitist notion that the gifted individual should be allowed to develop their talent in whatever direction is best for their own personal self-actualization.

Staging difference

The trope of individuality is further explored when the action dissolves to a scene in a bedroom at Billy's friend Michael's house where Michael is trying on his sister's dresses and persuades Billy to do likewise: 'There's nought wrong with wearing lasses' dresses. Me Dad does it all the time.' Ironically, the cross-dressing Michael, like most boys in this community, thinks that ballet is weird; his only interest in it is the possibility that Billy might have the chance to wear a tutu. The ensuing song-and-dance sequence 'Expressing Yourself' is a paean to individuality. In front of a silver 'slash curtain', Billy and Michael celebrate the notion of difference in an old-fashioned showbiz-style tap dance:

> If you want to be a dancer, dance
> If you want to be a miner, mine
> If you wanna dress like somebody else,
> Fine, fine, fine.

Here, another opportunity for temporary escape from the grim realities of the miners' strike is offered – a carnivalesque fantasy of cross-dressing with an exhilarating finale in which a number of gigantic, brightly coloured dresses swirl and tap around the stage as a chorus to the two boys in drag:

> Everyone is different
> It's the natural state,
> It's the facts, it's plain to see,
> The world's grey enough without making it worse
> What we need is individuality.

From this point until the end of Act One, Billy's developing skills as a dancer are counterpoised with the escalation of the conflict between the miners and the police, articulating a dialectical discourse that tests the wisdom of fighting a hopeless but honourable collective battle for the future of nationalized coal mining against the more liberal and pragmatically motivated value of individual freedom inherent in Billy's struggle to win a place at the Royal Ballet School. Each dance number shows a development in Billy's confidence and the idea of self-expression as liberation. We see the progress of a boy towards a different image of masculine strength that includes the feminine as a vital aspect of a balanced psyche. But each stage in Billy's development towards maturity as a dancer and person simultaneously involves the acquisition of greater insight into the limitations of the patriarchal working-class culture he has been brought up to honour and obey. From the moment when his father bans him from ballet class, the trajectory of action and song/dance leads inevitably to Billy's climactic 'Angry Dance' that forms the conclusion to Act One as he gradually becomes aware that his self-realization as an individual has set him on a collision course with the traditional values of the mining community.

Staging conflict: dance and repression

When asked by his teacher to bring to his private lesson some objects that mean something to him, Billy produces a series of childish items, but when he finally shows her a letter from his 'mam' the teacher learns what truly motivates Billy: through the relationship that has emerged during the dance lessons, Mrs Wilkinson has become his surrogate mother. Like all men, Billy needs the affective experience of the feminine to balance against patriarchal repression in order to maintain a healthy emotional life.

The loss of his mother has been a crucial factor in his need to express powerful emotions in dance. Gradually all superstitions and prejudices about ballet disappear as we watch Billy's exhilarating progression with the support of Mrs Wilkinson and the burly pianist Mr Braithwaite, who progressively strips off his outer garments in 'Born to Boogie' to reveal himself comically as an unexpectedly skilful and undeniably macho dancer. Gender becomes irrelevant as Mr Braithwaite and Billy playfully compete with and support each other in the jazzy song-and-dance, which begins with boxing gloves and climaxes in a Dionysiac finale by means of the choreographic deployment of acrobatics, chairs lifted and twirled, skipping and tap-dancing. As Billy improves, we are led to imagine the passage of time; the celebration of his growth as a dancer demonstrates how dance can become the fullest actualization of the physical and emotional possibilities of human movement, completely 'natural' to men and women alike.

After this dance sequence, Mrs Wilkinson arranges to meet Billy early the next morning to attend the audition in Newcastle. She gives him a pep talk and he hugs her with great intensity, revealing how much she means to him as a maternal figure. When his father and his injured brother Tony prevent Billy from leaving the house next morning, Mrs Wilkinson is obliged to come in and get him, forming a tableau of five miners pitted against a female teacher whose explanation about the audition leaves them flabbergasted. Tony's enraged and abusive response to what he sees as her misguided middle-class patronage ('You wanna make him a scab for the rest of his life?') provokes her outraged reply: 'Don't you lecture me on the British class system, comrade.' After police sirens ring and the men hurry out to avoid a police raid, the lights turn red and Billy rushes upstairs to his room, screaming in rage against both the family's stubborn prejudice and the desperate situation of the strike.

Now all the pent-up emotion since the death of his mother seems to be unleashed in Billy's 'Angry Dance', a fiery step-dance in hard shoes that he dances in the street against a background of miners clashing with policemen who wield semi-transparent riot shields. As sirens wail, policemen march and bang their truncheons threateningly, while ordinary citizens run and jump around the stage, shouting and crying, Billy dances furiously, occasionally throwing himself at the line of riot shields and then escaping from the worst of the violence, his feet stamping out his fury in a virtuoso solo dance until he collapses, exhausted, on the ground. As the theatre audience wildly cheers his performance, Billy gets up and, ignoring the applause as the lights come up in the auditorium, walks off the stage in disgust.

For a commercial musical, the first act of *Billy Elliot* is remarkable: its large-scale depiction of an entire village embattled against the repressive force of a government dedicated to destroying its traditional way of life, presents the lifestyle and values of a specific Geordie community in terms of the broad sweep of history without excluding from view the smallest personal details of individual experience. While showing obvious sympathy for the collectivist ideals of the miners in the face of a dogmatic and insensitive political regime, the musical honestly represents the hopelessness of their cause against the global tide of monetarism.

Staging political protest

At the beginning of Act Two the theatre audience is cleverly wrong-footed as its members stroll back from the theatre bars to encounter a casual pantomime-style interplay: George and Tony Elliot appear in front of the curtain with the house lights still on, to offer us their Christmas entertainment. George is dressed as Santa Claus and Tony as a pixie, making spectators complicit in the celebratory spirit of the mining community by means of a good-natured parody of a traditional amateur concert. The fun really begins when the curtain rises on a stage within the stage, and the song 'Merry

Christmas, Maggie Thatcher' is performed. Peter Brown graphically evoked the comic horror of the experience:

> A vision of hell appeared to me last night at the Victoria Palace Theatre! A huge effigy of Margaret Thatcher, maybe twenty or thirty feet tall, stood glowering at me from the darkness. And as if that wasn't enough, dozens of smaller Margaret Thatchers gleefully pranced around [...] like crazed goblin apprentices.[63]

The effigy's surprising entrance is prepared for by an elaborately satirical puppet show on a platform stage within the stage – a pastiche of the kind of political theatre event that 7:84 might have been touring around Scotland at the time. Part pantomime, part political revue, there are puppets of well-known Trades Union Congress (TUC) leaders, a fairly large puppet of Thatcher's 'darling' Michael Heseltine, a somewhat narcissistic public school type with a long mop of blond hair he keeps sweeping off his forehead. Her gigantic crow-like effigy, with its large, greedy hands reaching out to grasp the audience in its clutches, marks the hilarious climax of the political charade. The scene is not only raucously entertaining and grotesquely funny, but it encapsulates the bitterness of left-wing political opposition to the Conservative government that was particularly vocal in the North of England, Scotland and Wales. Here again the historical moment is vividly animated, the whole show-within-a-show illustrating the mixed atmosphere of celebratory ritual and angry protest that typified Christmas in a working-class community in 1983.

A modern concept of masculinity: Billy's maturity

Amid the rowdy revelry, there are calls for Jacky Elliot to sing, one voice demanding 'Big Spender', but he shakes his head and sings a melancholy folk ballad as the revellers slowly depart.

> Oh once I had a family
> Sons to make you proud
> They have gone and left me now,
> And I count the time out loud
> For now I am an old man
> Just waiting for my turn
> Till they take me back into the ground

The song represents the typical life of a pitman, poignantly evoking the change of seasons as the young miner gradually ages, his dream of a beautiful future gradually soured by harsh experience:

> Oh once I loved a woman
> She meant all the world to me
> Saw ourselves a future
> As far as I could see
> But I was only forty-seven
> When they took her down from me
> And buried her deep . . .

When his father breaks down in tears, Billy finishes the song for him, just as he had finished the miners' 'hymn' to the community in the second scene of the show, demonstrating both personal strength and sensitivity to his father's feelings in addition to empathy for the community's plight. But as the darkness clears we notice they are alone in the community hall, and all the others have left. In a somewhat doleful mood Jacky goes home and Michael emerges from the shadows of the hall.

Now Billy demonstrates both maturity and sympathy as Michael reveals his homosexual attraction to him by tenderly putting Billy's cold hands inside his coat to warm him. Although Billy somewhat naively asks, 'You're not a poof or 'ought', he kisses Michael affectionately on the cheek before cheering him up by giving him a tutu as a gift, which Michael wears over his clothes before going home in a state of sheer delight. Billy's complete freedom from homophobic prejudice shows him in some respects to be more mature than most adult men in Easington. Another complete reversal of expectations ensues after Michael exits and Billy is alone listening to a tape of Tchaikovsky's *Swan Lake* and fantasizing about what his future could be if he were allowed to pursue a career as a ballet dancer.

Taking flight: the beauty of ballet as liberation

Billy sees what appears to be an image of his older self, grown up and fully trained. Extending the use of a chair being spun on one leg to function as ballet *barre*, he imitates the steps of the older dancer who eventually partners him until, with the aid of a cunningly disguised rope and harness, Billy takes flight above the stage in a thrilling moment that regularly draws spontaneous applause from the theatre audience. Some have opined that this is merely a second-hand *Peter Pan*-style gimmick, borrowed from other recent West End productions,[64] yet there is something extraordinarily moving about watching a talented child match himself to the virtuosity of an experienced ballet dancer and 'fly'.

The dance also presents a beautiful image of the aesthetic form that Billy has only just begun to imagine, giving concrete shape to the putative notion concerning the art of dance that has been generated by the half-hearted attempts of the girls and the rough-and-tumble of Billy's private lesson. What ensures the moment's breathtaking effect is its placement at this particular juncture in the action: its contrast with the boy's desolate situation on a cold Christmas Eve, bereft of his mother and looked after only by a depressed and drunken father who does not properly understand his son's needs. The dance is both an emotional high point of the show and its hermeneutic *raison d'être*. The transformative power of dance is expressed as both the form and meaning of this theatrical moment. Repeating the earlier moment when his father had banned him from ballet class, Billy's dance 'vision' ends when he dances until he arrives face-to-face with his father who has returned to fetch him home. Whenever the show is performed the audience enthusiastically cheers the talent of the young performer at the same time as it renews hope for Billy's future as a ballet dancer – in spite of the image of a defeated father who stands forlornly before him

A drama of environment: 'He Could Be a Star' / 'The Stars Look Down'

This time however, Jacky Elliot does not try to stop his son from pursuing his ambition but takes it seriously. As snow falls on a bare stage he trudges to Mrs Wilkinson's doorstep on Christmas day to ask her how much it would cost to send Billy to the audition. The scenic context is significant: Mrs Wilkinson says that Christmas is 'the season of goodwill and all that', but ironically Jacky is still too proud to accept her offer of financial assistance to fund Billy's audition even though he doesn't 'have enough money for the bus fare to London'; she feels obliged to recapitulate the criticism she made when Tony and Jacky stopped Billy from attending the audition in Newcastle:

> When are you going to get over your pig-ignorant working class pride? What have you got to offer him? Mining? This town has had it – it's finished. You're fighting a battle that was lost years ago. I'm not the enemy, Mr Elliot. We're all in it together . . . Let me help.

Too proud to take her offer of help, Jacky decides to break the strike and return to work in order to earn enough money to help Billy:

Dad   He could be a star for all we know
[...]
He could go and he could shine
Not just stay here counting time,
Son we've got the chance to let him live,

The witty and iconic slogan on the poster designed by the famous advertising agency Saatchi and Saatchi to help Margaret Thatcher win an election, comments ironically on the following scene at the pit: 'LABOUR ISN'T WORKING'. In the early eighties it is no longer Labour but a Conservative government that has created the economic recession which resulted in huge unemployment among working class people in the 'labour' market. The cold, snowy exterior reminds us of the harsh environment in which miners and their families exist. The stark counterpointing of Jacky's pleading chorus ('He could be a star for all we know') against his son Tony's plangent lyrics in defence of the miners' collective action pinpoints the agonizing dilemma of any mining family at this time – whether to uphold the dignity and values of their communitarian traditions or to give up the struggle in pursuit of individual success:

Tony   This isn't about us Dad
It's not about the kid
It's all of us, it's everybody's chance
It's everybody's future
It's everybody's past
It's not about a bairn who wants to dance
It's about our history
It's about our rights
Think about the sacrifice we've made

Billy's father retracts his decision to break the strike after the miners offer to collect money for his trip to London.

The word 'shine' links Billy's potential as a ballet star with the miners' integrity as well as with Mrs Wilkinson's ballet girls, each of whom wants desperately to 'shine'; the word play poses a question concerning the true meaning of a successful life,

Miners   We will go and we will shine
     We will go and seize the time
     We will all have pride in how we live

Metropolitan and regional: high culture and working-class manners

After a brief scene in which Tony and Jacky debate whether it is ethical for Billy to accept money from a 'scab' to make up the shortfall in the amount the miners have collected, the backdrop is replaced by a pseudo-classical safety curtain at the front of the stage as Billy and his dad wait for the audition on the stage of the Royal Opera House, Covent Garden. The plush and exotic décor of the opera house is in dramatic contrast to the previously grey and scruffy images of working-class Easington, a vivid emblem of the foreign nature of the elite culture in which Billy and Jacky somewhat awkwardly find themselves.

The scenes that follow comically underline the tension between high culture and working-class manners experienced by both Billy and his father. The rather effete upper-middle-class boy and his patronizing father, who are also in attendance for the audition, are like creatures from a different planet, while Billy's behaviour as he hands over his audition fee in notes and coins and provides the technician with a wonky cassette tape of his music is comically out of place in this artistic milieu.

What has at first seems like a vast cultural gulf between the world of the Geordie and the high culture of the Royal Ballet is dissolved because it appears as a much a workplace as the mines of County Durham; despite their posh accents, its denizens are fairly left-wing workers who, at the end of the audition process, wish Jacky 'good luck with the strike'. A further irony can be observed in Billy's uncharacteristically violent overreaction when after the audition Billy seems despondent and Thomas, the posh boy at the audition, puts his arm on Billy's shoulder in an effort to comfort him. Insecurity causes Billy to retreat to a conditioned reflex of masculine behaviour and to bang the boy's head against the wall, shouting, 'Piss off, you bent bastard.'

When Billy is asked at his interview at the end of the day, 'What does it feel like when you dance?' he starts to sing his answer, which culminates in the climactic song-and-dance solo 'Electricity' in which he triumphantly demonstrates the power of dancing in enabling him to liberate his deepest instincts.

Tragedy and utopia: society and the individual

The following scene in the Elliot's kitchen positions Billy's success in getting into the ballet school in dialectical opposition to the collapse of the strike: a minute after Billy and his family whoop with delight while reading his letter of acceptance, a number of pitmen arrive to bring the sad news about the return to work. Typically, the good news about the success of a talented individual is followed by the sad news of the miners' collapse. In a Broadway show it would happen the other way around. Even in this scene there is a slight variation on the theme of masculine homophobia when Billy misreads the envelope addressed to 'Billy Elliot Esquire' as 'Billy Elliot is queer'. The anxiety that links male ballet dancers with homosexuality remains in Billy's unconscious in spite of his own lack of prejudice.

As he and his father pack Billy's suitcase in preparation for his journey to the Royal Ballet School, the miners sing 'Once We Were Kings' in recognition of the tragic failure of their ideals of equality for all:

> Once we built visions on the ground we hewed
> We dreamt of justice and of men renewed
> All people equal, in all things
> We once were heroes,
> Once were kings
> [. . .]

Visually, we witness Billy's triumph as an individual in shocking contrast to the defeat of the collective. Their song is both a tragic lament for the communitarian values of their lost way of life and a proud, if perhaps hopeless, call to arms:

> And in the ground we may be lain
> But a seed is sown to rise again
>
> We saw a land where wealth was shared
> Each pain relieved, each hunger fed
> Each man revered, each tyrant killed
> Each soul redeemed, each life fulfilled

As the miners are lowered into the ground by means of a hydraulic lift, the image of their helmet lights going on and shining directly into the audience achieves an extraordinary visual poetry. As they slowly sink beneath the stage, the pathos of the many-times repeated refrain becomes overwhelming:

> So we walk proudly
> And we walk strong
> All together
> We will go as one
> The ground is empty
> And cold as hell
> But we all go together when we go

When they have disappeared into the ground, we hear the metallic clang of the lift gate closing deep down in the earth: symbolically, a way of life that has persisted for two hundred years is buried, and the miners are left without a livelihood. Billy leaves Easington by jumping off the stage and beginning to exit through the centre aisle of the theatre. He has grown up. This powerful image reverses that of the little boy who came from the auditorium on to the stage as the show began. As Billy progresses up the aisle Michael rides his bike on to the stage, stops and shouts, 'Oi, dancing boy!' and Billy returns to the stage to kiss Michael goodbye. The pathos is almost unbearable; as Billy leaves again the stage picture of Michael on his bike reminds us of what we know with the benefit of hindsight would soon become a derelict village in a broken society.

Finale: A ballet carnival

The drama itself ends with the final image of Michael, but the extended curtain call is a coda in which the performers present a carnivalesque extravaganza of tap-dancing and ballet, led by Billy himself. By fast-forwarding to the present day, the show celebrates the contemporary liberation of working-class masculinity from its macho and homophobic past and enables the audience to indulge in the sheer pleasure of watching all gender boundaries dissolved by having husky miners don tutus over their orange boiler suits as they join in the outrageous carnival of cross-dressed dancing. For a drama that ends simultaneously in tragedy and triumph, this conclusion necessarily achieves a dialectic between the failure of the miners' strike in 1984 and the values of a postmodern, post-industrial Britain as a result of the progressive break-down of both class and gender/

sexuality barriers. There is no question here of making a choice between an *either* which required the freezing of culture and society in the status quo of 1983 and an *or* that embraced the heartless promotion of a monetarist economy by ignoring the financial plight of whole towns filled with unemployed ex-miners. After mourning the death of a tradition of working-class life, we celebrate the personal and cultural liberation concomitant on the achievement of a postmodern social dispensation.

But *Billy Elliot* is a musical. So we also participate in the utopian dream of a world where not only stars but a huge chorus sing and dance together to make moments of joy in the sheer sensual pleasure of being fully alive.

1.7 GLOBAL AND LOCAL: THE FAMILY MUSICAL

The blockbuster British musicals of the 1980s from *Cats* to *Miss Saigon* were a product of the monetarism of the Reagan/Thatcher years in which British and American culture moved closer together and new forms of postmodern cultural domination of global markets seemed possible within a late capitalist system. Often – but not always – reliant more on visual and theatrical means of expression than on specifically contextualized social behaviour and wit, these shows were aggressively marketed around the world and proved to be easily transferrable to European and Asian countries. It was only a matter of time before Disney saw the scope for adopting the model pioneered globally by Cameron Mackintosh and marketing their own stage musicals abroad, just as they had done for so many decades with their animated film features. The simpler such shows are in linguistic terms, the more easily they can be marketed globally, and in the past two decades musicals have been accused of both 'dumbing down' and becoming 'McTheatre' products – like a Big Mac.[65] Some Disney shows (e.g. *Tarzan*) have failed on Broadway but succeeded in Holland and Germany; others have succeeded on Broadway and failed in some European countries (*Beauty and the Beast*); and still others have been performed in Europe (*The Hunchback of Notre Dame*) but have never been produced on Broadway – producers have been learning to test different markets for different shows and to realize that artistic taste is culture-specific.

Although a number of British musicals have enjoyed great critical acclaim and some measure of commercial success on Broadway in the past decade (*Billy Elliot, Matilda*), some others have been interesting failures (Sting's *The*

Last Ship, 2014), while the British-authored *Finding Neverland* (songs by Gary Barlow, book by James Graham) that mainly received poor reviews on Broadway in 2015 appears to be a commercial hit. Production standards for musicals originating in London are now as high – often higher – than they are on Broadway, a result of the large-scale development of training facilities for musical theatre performers that followed in the wake of the success of Lloyd Webber and Macintosh in the 1980s. A number of international production companies (Disney, Weinstein Live Entertainment, et al.) are actively attempting to globalize the values and internationalize the reach of Anglophone musicals. Yet popular theatre stubbornly resists attempts to become wholly assimilated to a globalized identity, reflecting the particular circumstances and attitudes of individual cultural and social traditions. British audiences love American movies and stage musicals, but they still see them as uniquely *American*. Just as no one would regard the new musicals *Bend It Like Beckham* (2015) or *Calendar Girls* (2015) as anything other than British, so it would be foolish to view *Chicago* (1975) or *Legally Blonde* (2007) as anything other than American.

The 'family musical' has since the 1980s become a phenomenon peculiar to West End theatre. Since 1981 a number of family musicals have succeeded in the West End: the best known have been *Cats* (1981), *Starlight Express* (1984), *Chitty Chitty Bang Bang* (2002), *Mary Poppins* (2004), *Matilda* (2011), *The Wizard of Oz* (2011), *Charlie and the Chocolate Factory* (2013), and two highly successful revivals of *Oliver!* (1994 and 2009).

Unlike children's theatre, the notion of the 'family musical' is an off-shoot of the British tradition of Christmas pantomime[66] in which parents and their children are simultaneously entertained by different levels of humour or meaning, and both play along with the age-old conventions of live interaction between the stage and auditorium. In its witty appeal to both parents and their children (who, when I saw the show tended to laugh at each gag three seconds after their parents, possibly for different reasons), *Matilda* transforms many of the components of traditional pantomime into a family musical.

Case Study 4: *Matilda – The Musical*

Subsidized theatre and artistic collaboration

Musical theatre is a supremely collaborative art form. One of the glories of the British theatre since Trevor Nunn and John Caird's production of *Les*

Misérables for the Royal Shakespeare Company in 1985 has been the way subsidized theatres such as the RSC and the National Theatre have sponsored the writing or production of musicals that are usually more experimental than the average Broadway or West End fare. The collaboration of great directors, scenographers, choreographers, librettists, composers and lyricists made possible by the more generous working conditions of subsidized theatres has enabled complex forms of artistic integration in which the interaction of the key components of narrative, numbers and visual spectacle has often produced a whole that is greater than the sum of its parts. The great critical and commercial success of *Matilda* (2010) as a West End musical is attributable both to its extremely sophisticated staging by the creative team at the Royal Shakespeare Company and to its conjuring of the dark ironies and facetious tone of Roald Dahl's story, without slavish adherence to its narrative structure.

All elements of Matthew Warchus's ingenious production help to articulate *Matilda*'s leitmotif of reading and story-telling. Rob Howell has designed a framework of books, picture frames and alphabet blocks in the surreal style of a grim, old-fashioned book of fairy tales. Flying in from above, popping up from beneath the floor or pushed around by actors like toy building blocks are school desks and chairs, tall and rickety bookshelves, banks of television screens, picture frames, swings and school gymnastic equipment from which children suspend themselves or on to which they climb in kinetically exciting ways devised by Peter Darling as an extension of his comic and eccentric dance steps. Matilda's story of the acrobat and the escapologist is illustrated by projections in the manner of an old magic lantern show, and the overall visual effect suggests the way in which a child's imagination plays variations upon the bare objects of material reality, rearranging them into the desired shapes of fantasy.

Dennis Kelly's book and Tim Minchin's songs capture the anarchic spirit of Roald Dahl's story with delicious wit and gleeful bad taste. The musical appeals to the child in all of us because it presents a child's-eye view of the world and therefore does not resist giving the villains a bad time. Slapstick entertainment co-exists with witty self-reflection and the overall moral scheme of the piece, although entirely coherent, never appears didactic or preachy.

The family musical and British children's literature

Many 'family musicals' actually take the family as their principal subject. Since the late Victorian era, English literature and drama for young people and their families has been virtually obsessed by the idea of the family. As a matter of course, most of these novels and plays explore various ideas of what constitutes a dysfunctional family:

> Children of the empire would often find themselves separated from their parents for long periods of time – sometimes years at a stretch – at a crucial stage in their development [. . .] [T]he empire also created a huge market for stories: the kind of consoling and enthralling make-believe that would assuage the terrible isolation of its orphans, alone at school in England while their parents were away on 'colonial service'.[67]

J. M. Barrie's *Peter Pan* is the iconic example of an Edwardian play (rewritten by Barrie as the novel *Peter and Wendy* in 1911) that has become a 'family' favourite. In the Victorian era, the patriarchal family is the most significant emblem of an ordered society, its dysfunction viewed as a disruption of that order. A child's isolation from or even within their family might have many causes: some stories – such as Edith Nesbitt's *The Railway Children* – treat the subject of the broken family as a matter of the separation of one or either parents from children who are obliged to learn self-sufficiency. Others, such as *Peter Pan* and the *Mary Poppins* novels, view the Edwardian family as seriously, sometimes irretrievably, damaged, the emotional inadequacy or detachment of parents (particularly fathers) a result of extreme emotional repression suffered in their own (Victorian) childhood. Many of Roald Dahl's children's stories have recourse to this archetypal psychic pattern, in which the children 'rescue' their parents from their own dysfunctional family relationships.

Much children's literature since the late Victorian period has pictured childhood as a 'golden age', its Eden-like state inevitably giving way to the harsh realities of the world of work:

> [Frances] Burnett's and [Kate] Greenaway's visions of childhood as innocent and blissfully gay would dominate until late in the century, when some adults began to wonder whether childhood with its special access to the emotions and play, was not in fact a better way of being; for adulthood with its curtailment of imagination and renunciation of play, left humans undeniably diminished.[68]

At the onset of the Edwardian period, the playfulness began to be invested with intrinsic value, and childhood acquired new significance as a special time in human development:

> Reliving childhood through playing at it and giving children permission to be mischievous and imaginative were steps towards throwing off the social fetters that had bound Victorian society. It was a playful, mildly anti-authoritarian impulse that opened the door to irony. Stories began to emerge in which children looked at adults and found them lacking.[69]

The significance of this for Dahl's *Matilda* is obvious, but there is also irony involved, as Matilda behaves better as a potential adult than her own corrupt and stupid parents. Matilda does not wish to destroy authority; she wishes to restore an unjust and decadent society to its proper order and thereby improve the status quo. In this, her story incorporates the irony that operates in *Peter Pan*, yet moves beyond it:

> When the Darling children follow Peter Pan to Neverland they immediately reconstruct and re-enact the domestic routine they have just left behind, revealing in the process their thorough acceptance of the bourgeois mores and conventional gender roles embraced by their parents.[70]

For in her effort to rewrite her 'story', Matilda chooses to join Miss Honey and form a single-parent family, thereby experimenting with life in a different type of unit than the nuclear family she has been born into.

The postmodern family: narcissism and bullying

The show opens with a gang of precocious children, each trumpeting their parents' grotesquely inappropriate pride in their offspring in an elaborate sung scene that culminates in the birth of Matilda. A girl and boy boast:

Lavender and Eric   My mummy says I'm a miracle!

Reginald   My daddy says I'm his special little guy.

Alice   I am a princess.

Bruce   And I am a prince.

All Girls   Mum says I'm an angel sent down from the sky.[71]

The narcissistic self-esteem promoted by contemporary parenting is satirized in this brilliantly witty song: it portrays the competitive individualism of a neo-liberal society. The vanity that motivates such deluded parents is ironically exposed by a teacher:

> It seems that there are millions of these
> One-in-a-millions these days.
> 'Special-ness' seems de-rigueur.
> Above average is average – go figueur.

In an example of the musical's dramaturgical economy, the scene scrolls forward five years in time and we witness Matilda reflecting on her parents' selfish and uncaring attitude to their own child.

Matilda's parents, Mr and Mrs Wormwood, regard their children as fashion accessories, extensions of their warped self-image, who should ideally reflect their values back at them. Because Matilda's precocious intellectual abilities and her surprisingly adult knowledge of books directly challenge the Wormwoods' ignorant philistinism, they resent her:

> My daddy says I should learn to shut my pie hole.
> No one likes a smart-mouthed girl like me.
> Mum says I'm a good case for population control.
> Dad says I should watch more TV.

Matilda's imaginative way of challenging injustice constitutes a bold stand against the prevalence of bullying in contemporary society:

> Nobody but me is gonna put it right for me,
> Nobody but me is going to change my story.
> Sometimes you have to be a little bit naughty.

The first time Matilda takes the law into her own hands, she switches her father's oil-of-violet hair tonic with her mother's platinum-blonde hair dye, causing his hair to turn green; the next is to punish him for destroying a library book by applying superglue to the inside of his hat, making it stick fast to his head.

When we see Matilda at school, we understand that it is not just within families that injustice and bullying occurs but that whole institutions may be in the charge of bullies, who abuse and persecute those at their mercy. In an ingenious song that puns with all the letters of the alphabet, the older schoolchildren explain the twisted logic of the school to the new recruits:

> So you think you're A-ble
> To survive this mess by B-ing
> A prince or a princess, you will soon C,
> There's no escaping trage-D.
> [...]
> Cause your life as you know it is H-ent history.

As a stage villain, Miss Trunchbull is a comic masterpiece: an English champion hammer-thrower who whirls children in the air by their hair as she once threw hammers, she is not merely a sadistic bully but one who champions the most conservative idea of education. Miss Trunchbull believes in rote learning administered with iron discipline, being wholly opposed to encouraging or rewarding students in order to enhance their creativity or self-esteem. Instead she terrorizes pupils through arbitrary bullying and punishes them horribly for minor infractions of petty school rules: appropriately the school motto is 'Baminotomus Est Maggitum' ('Children Are Maggots').

Pop culture: 'telly'

Since both Mr and Mrs Wormwood hate reading and have little imagination, their values and attitudes to life are ready-made by 'telly'. As Mr Wormwood tells the audience at the beginning of the second act, 'Somewhere on a show I heard that a picture tells a thousand words, so telly, if you bothered to take a look, is the equivalent, of like, lots of books!' The commodification of contemporary culture is wickedly satirized in his song 'Telly', which teases the audience by unapologetically voicing its own guilty philistinism:

> All I know I learned from telly –
> What to think and what to buy.
> I was pretty smart already,
> But now I'm really, really smart – very very smart.

Tim Minchin captures precisely the insidious way in which television itself reflects and produces the 'society of the spectacle':[72] in selling both goods and ideas by means of glamorous images that promise material plenitude to fill the emptiness of shallow lives, television both reflects and reinforces the domination of life by images that subsumes all other forms of domination:

> Endless content, endless channels . . .
> Endless chat on endless panels . . .
> All you need to fill your muffin,
> Without having to really think or nothing!

The song wittily echoes Guy Debord's idea that the spectacle is 'capital to such a degree of accumulation that it becomes an image' and that images are the currency of contemporary society.

Mr Wormwood's veneration for the mind-numbing pleasures of 'telly' is complemented by his wife's passion for ballroom dancing, another pastime made fashionable by television. When Miss Honey comes to tell her that Matilda should be moved to a more advanced class because she is extremely gifted, Mrs Wormwood mocks her for her lack of worldliness, scorning her interest in intellectual pursuits as naive. Her verse introduction to 'Loud' advises Miss Honey to show off her body rather than cultivate her mind in order to compete with the vulgar majority:

> Somewhere along the way, my dear,
> You've made an awful error.
> [. . .]
> You seem to think that people like people what are clever.
> It's very quaint. It's very sweet. But wrong.
> People don't like smarty-pants what go 'round
> Claiming that they know stuff we don't know.
> Now here's a tip.
> What you know matters less
> Than the volume with which what you don't know's expressed.
> Content has never been less important, so
> You have got to be . . .
> LOUD!

This number is staged as a parody of television dance competitions such as *Strictly Come Dancing* and demonstrates the obsession for style at the expense of content in a three-dimensional comic illustration of Debord's conception of the history of social life as 'the decline of being into having, and having into merely appearing.'[73] The Latin-American rhythm of the number enables

Mrs Wormwood and her louche dance partner to mimic the exhibitionism of TV dance shows, in which the performers willingly commodify their own bodies to 'sell' themselves to studio audiences and television viewers:

> No one's gonna tell you when to wiggle your bum-ba!
> No one's gonna love you if you don't know the rumba!
> The less you have to sell, the harder you sell it!
> The less you have to say, the louder you yell it!

'Loud' exemplifies in word and action Debord's conception of the postmodern condition as the 'historical moment at which the commodity completes its colonization of social life.'[74]

A story about stories: changing the narrative

> Many Edwardian authors [...] were convinced that 'doing something for the intrinsic enjoyment of the thing ... is one of the ultimate ends of art and perhaps of human existence.'[75] Reading joined physical activity as a form of play, both thought to involve the imagination.[76]

Roald Dahl exploits the conception of reading as a form of play in a postmodern fashion: *Matilda* is a story about an exceptionally gifted little girl who, in spite of an appalling upbringing, has learned to read, write and think for herself. Dennis Kelly doubles the idea of a story about a child who loves stories by having Matilda invent her own tale of an acrobat and an escapologist, which, by a mysterious quirk, turns out to be the biography of her kind teacher Miss Honey.

In the musical, Matilda reflects and acts upon the assumption that life is a story, which can be altered to provide a more satisfactory outcome:

> Like Romeo and Juliet
> 'Twas written in the stars before they even met.
> That love and fate, and a touch of stupidity
> Would rob them of their hope of living happily.
> The endings are often a little bit gory.
> I wonder why they didn't just change their story?
> We're told we have to do what we're told, but surely
> Sometimes you have to be a little bit naughty.

Figure 5 A story about a child who loves stories – Kerry Ingram as the title character in *Matilda*, Courtyard Theatre in Stratford-upon-Avon 2010. Photograph by Nigel Norrington. Courtesy of ArenaPAL.

There is something extremely liberating in observing an abused child insisting on her right to improve her own conditions by being 'a little bit naughty'. The repressed id in all of us is unleashed as we spur on Matilda to exact an appropriate revenge against her father's unfairness. And Matilda has the ability to rationalize her 'naughty' behaviour as an act of poetic justice that might lead to amelioration of injustice in the future:

> Just because you find that life's not fair, it
> Doesn't mean that you just have to grin and bear it.
> If you always take it on the chin and wear it
> Nothing will change.

This bouncy refrain represents a call to arms repeated a number of times in the show. 'Naughty' is the obverse of the ruthless individualism portrayed in 'Miracle', identifying the confidence engendered by the postmodern construction of self as courage to challenge corrupt authority and alter one's personal 'story':

> Even if you're little, you can do a lot, you
> Mustn't let a little thing like 'little' stop you
> If you sit around and let them get on top, you
> Might as well be saying
> You think that it's ok and
> That's not right.
> And if it's not right
> You have to put it right.

The most important event in Matilda's everyday life is her regular visit to the local library. Reading feeds her imagination, allowing mental freedom from the oppressive constraints of her domestic existence. In the musical, the story of the acrobat and her escapologist husband, which Matilda invents for the benefit of the librarian Mrs Phelps, has a mysterious connection with the real events of Miss Honey's life, offering a metaphor for the transforming power of art. When Miss Honey confides in her pupil the details of her own childhood, Matilda understands that the acrobat and the escapologist were Miss Honey's parents. Matilda's exercise of imagination not only provides a fantasy of escape from the prison of her circumstances but, by exposing Miss Trunchbull as the acrobat's wicked sister who murdered the escapologist, actually promotes a change that makes life bearable.

Both the child's invented story and the musical itself deploy certain structural elements of pantomime. Miss Trunchbull is an archetypal character deriving from the pantomime tradition of the dame – usually played by a rather butch man in drag. Like the witch or an ugly sister in pantomime, Miss Trunchbull is the embodiment of evil, whereas Miss Honey is both a good fairy and (as revealed later) a Cinderella character who remains kind and virtuous through all her travails. Within the pantomime scheme of *Matilda* it is the child who plays the role of fairy godmother to her teacher Miss Honey, helping her to take control of her own life.

Teachers and children: growing up

According to Debord, the spectacle is the inverted image of society, replacing relations between people with relations between commodities: 'The spectacle is not a collection of images, rather, it is a social relationship between people that is mediated by images.'[77] At one end of the spectrum, Matilda's parents represent this passive approach to contemporary education as a commercial transaction. Like the parents who believe that each of their children is a 'miracle', they are products of a culture of entitlement that conceives talent and intelligence as commodities possessed by people in the form of 'goods', rather than faculties that can be cultivated through practice and schooling.

At the opposite end of the spectrum, Miss Trunchbull's top-down system of training eschews the notion of education as self-actualization in favour of a mechanical method of drilling and repetition:

> If you want to make the team
> You don't need happiness or self-esteem,
> You just need to keep your feet inside the line.
> [...]
> And if you want to teach success
> You don't use sympathy or tenderness
> [...]
> You have to force the little squits to toe the line.

One of the reasons why Miss Trunchbull was particularly funny and pertinent in 2010–11 was that this was precisely the moment at which the Conservative Secretary of State for Education, Michael Gove, was engaged in aggressively promoting an Education Act, which became law in early 2011. This Act replaced a liberal British secondary school system that had supported the teaching of creative arts, by a reactionary approach that stressed the old-fashioned virtues of 'Reading, Writing and 'Rithmetic', yet was paradoxically designed to allow the principles of free-market capitalism to further undermine the state-sponsored comprehensive system.[78]

Between the two extremes of consumer entitlement and neo-Fascist bullying lies Matilda's creative approach to learning as a form of self-motivated questioning and active discovery. Matilda does not need to be taught for she knows how to learn. Like the Edwardian stories in which children find the adult world inadequate, Roald Dahl and Dennis Kelly make it clear how much wiser and more moral Matilda is than most of the adults she encounters. Matilda is appalled at the way Mr Wormwood cheats his customers by interfering with the odometers to reduce the mileage that appears on the used cars he sells. Although her gormless brother Michael is impressed by their father's dishonest scheme, Matilda has an intuitive sense of right and wrong – and lets her father see her disapproval.

There is a moment near the start of the second act when, in stark contrast to the grotesque world of self-obsessed parents and sadistic teachers, a number of children on swings voice their utopian vision of adult life in song. The pastoral image of simple pleasure involves a wry and double-edged comment on the way children view adulthood both as a fantasy of total liberation from parental control and as a solution to all the mysteries childhood prevents them from comprehending:

> And when I grow up,
> I will be smart enough to answer all
> The questions that you need to know
> The answers to before you're grown up.

Sung at times in the form of a round, the repeated cycle of sweet children's voices evokes the continuous flow of the life cycle and the idyllic nature of freedom, to which we all at times, somewhat unrealistically, aspire. The mood of wishful reverie is both genuinely moving and wryly funny in its observation of the circularity of the children's perception of adulthood as a form of childhood without restriction:

> And when I grow up,
> I will eat sweets every day,
> On the way to work, and I will
> Go to bed late every night.
> [...] and I
> Will watch cartoons until my eyes go square,
> And I won't care 'cause I'll be all grown up.

Putting it right: 'Revolting Children'

The reprise of sections of 'Naughty' at significant moments during the musical creates a leitmotif which serves as a constant reminder that freedom and justice must be fought for and earned, as Matilda demonstrates after Miss Trunchbull's cruel treatment of Miss Honey's class during a punishing session of Phys Ed (Physical Education). Lavender, a girl in the class, has put a newt in the headmistress's water jug, and when Miss Trunchbull discovers the newt and accuses the first child in her sight of being the culprit, Matilda stands up and reprimands her for bullying. As the headmistress screams abuse at her, Matilda is able to focus her mind on a place away from the incessant noise of 'my dad and my mum / And the telly and stories':

> And suddenly, everything, everything is
> Quiet.
> Like silence, but not really silent.
> Just that still sort of quiet
> Like the sound of a page being turned in a book,
> Or a pause in a walk in the woods.

In antithesis to 'Loud', her mother's celebration of noise, Matilda discovers during 'Quiet' that by achieving the mental concentration to shut out this cacophony she acquires the power to move objects, and is able to make the jug spill both the water and the newt over Miss Trunchbull. This quasi-mystical experience is a poignant symbol for the transformative power of imagination, the strength of 'mind over matter', which elevates the capacity Matilda has demonstrated earlier to use stories as an escape from an untenable reality to the level of magic that can change the arrangement of the material world. However one interprets it, this moment of sheer slapstick delights children and adults alike as they watch the unjust headmistress get her well-deserved comeuppance.

Matilda's defiance of Miss Trunchbull's bullying has effectively taught the schoolchildren to fight for their rights and they later celebrate the rebellion that forces their headmistress to flee in a song that ironically admits that their own bad behaviour is a consequence of the 'revolting times' they are living in:

> We are revolting children.
> Living in revolting times.
> We sing revolting songs
> Using revolting rhymes.

The self-reflexiveness of the song at once draws attention to Minchin's talent for clever rhyming and gleefully dramatizes the overcoming of oppression in a carnivalesque outpouring of joy.

Dennis Kelly and Tim Minchin have written a book and score that is entirely up to the minute in its outlook on the world in which we live: in the spirit of Dahl they make no patronizing attempt to protect young audiences from the cruelty and vengefulness of human nature but appeal uncompromisingly to the 'id' in all of us, devising a genuine 'family musical' that gives children and adults an equal share of anarchic fun. But musicals usually generate an impulse towards Utopia, and Matilda herself evinces a deeply utopian idea of social justice that threads through the narrative: the power of *not* doing what you're told.

PART II
BRITISH POPULAR CULTURE AND MUSICAL THEATRE
Millie Taylor

The impact of jazz, blues, rock'n'roll and later reggae, soul, punk and bhangra, which all found their way into British popular music, cannot be underestimated, but it was only very gradually that they began to feature in musical theatre. Alongside the transformations that were occurring in the pop charts in the 1960s musical theatre continued to speak to its white middle-class audiences using the musical and theatrical languages of historical entertainments; pantomime, pierrot show, music hall and operetta. These theatrical forms and musical genres gave creators a short-hand to communicate characters and situations whose attributes and atmospheres, locations and histories could be understood immediately and intuitively by audiences imbued with those traditions. As Britain's cultural mix changed, resulting from American influences in the Second World War and after, the musical innovations arriving with immigrants from Britain's former colonies, and an increasingly mobile global culture, so too did the musical and theatrical structures through which Britain represented itself.

The aim in this part of the book is to begin to document the diverse ways in which musical theatre responds to the popular cultures of its communities. It does not attempt to provide a comprehensive account of the relationships between popular culture and musical theatre or document the developments of the form chronologically. Instead it is split into three sections that introduce aspects of popular culture, each illustrated by one or more case studies that exemplify the arguments and document a work of significance. The first section identifies the influences from pantomime, music hall and operetta that have informed character stereotypes and narrative structures in some mainstream works. The second section will acknowledge the important work of Britain's black and ethnic minority communities that provides an extraordinarily dynamic substrate in the community, regional and subsidized sectors. This work only rarely features in the commercial West End, with the important exceptions of *Bombay Dreams* and new arrival *Bend It Like Beckham* (2015), and offers the prospect of new directions for the future. The third section focuses on the ways in which particular types of music signify at different times and places as popular music is constantly revivified by each new generation. The link between these three is that popular culture is multifarious and constantly transforming to represent and entertain its increasingly diverse audiences, and that different communities are developing their practices in different ways simultaneously.

2.1 NOSTALGIA IN CHARACTER AND DRAMATIC FORM

The popular theatre forms of the Victorian period, such as music hall, burlesque and more especially pantomime, provide a theatrical context for some aspects of musical theatre in the twentieth century. In Britain pantomime is a musical theatre work that uses a well-known fairy story or legend as the basis around which to build a show that contains song, dance, comedy, spectacle, audience interaction and sometimes other types of entertainment.[1] It is a uniquely British form, though it has been exported to some parts of the former colonies including, as we will see, Jamaica.[2]

Pantomime in contemporary Britain continues to transform, but its structures remain quite consistent, deriving from the late-nineteenth- and early-twentieth-century form.[3] It offers an opportunity for audiences to join in with the performance, albeit in strictly codified ways, and includes comic cross-dressing by men as aging female grotesques (the Dame) and by women as young men (the young male hero or principal boy) – though this latter role is now often played by a man and sometimes combined with the comic, knockabout character.[4] Since pantomime is still one of the most popular forms of theatre in the UK, with which a wide audience demographic is familiar, its characters, structures and exchanges have become a lingua franca through which to communicate, and it has influenced the style, structure, characters and events in other musical theatre works.

The clearest example of the way the form of pantomime has been adapted for political commentary is *Poppy* by Peter Nichols and Monty Norman (1982). *Poppy* employed the framework of British pantomime in a tale about the opium wars, with the word 'Poppy' being both a slang word for 'money' and a reference to the opium poppy trade. Act One opens with a prologue in rhyming couplets – a style that, at the time and until very recently, was common to the metaphysical characters in pantomime, good and evil, fairy and demon. In pantomime the fairy enters from Stage Right, the demon from Stage Left, so that audiences can be in no doubt as to which is which. In *Poppy* good and evil are Queen Victoria and Tao-Kuang, Emperor of China, and they don't enter from Left and Right, but the Emperor flies in from above and the Queen rises from a trap. By the end of the show these entrances have been reversed, reflecting the relative power of the two empires at the end of the opium wars; a visual symbol that critiques Britain's high-handed and ethically unsound role in these wars.

While *Poppy* discusses the politics of imperial expansion, the story, just like in pantomime, is told through the experience of individuals. It focuses on the experience of a working-class family in straitened circumstances but with contemporary topical and political reference. *Poppy's* opening sets the scene and involves the audience through direct address by the good and evil characters, and contains theatrical pyrotechnics, all features of opening scenes in contemporary professional pantomime. Since one of the most popular British pantomimes is the story of Dick Whittington, the setting of Scene Two at Whittington Manor, where the audience will be introduced to Idle Jack, Dick Whittington, the heroine Sally and the Dame, Lady Dodo, is also typical of pantomime, which contains these character types and whose exposition takes place very quickly and clearly during Scene Two. In this case, Scene Two opens with happy villagers singing about their idyllic country village in a reflexive manner: 'What more could you ask for an opening scene? / The heavens so cloudless, the meadow so green.'[5] But this verse is contrasted with one sung by the boys who are leaving to join the industrial revolution – an unusually conflicted opening chorus for a pantomime, but one that provides the usual clear catalyst for action. Jack Idle is the comic character who enters with his pantomime horse, Randy – a double act that performs the anticipated comic business. In this case, the double entendres and libidinous sexuality of pantomime are much more overt and pervasive; Jack's horse, Randy, attempts to mount Sally's horse, Cherry, with attendant sexual commentary, while the names, Dick, Randy, Cherry and Upward all feature in comic sexual innuendo.

Pantomime's features are mercilessly and playfully parodied in this work, much of which is in verse. It includes a speech in rhyming couplets spoken by Queen Victoria in Act One, Scene 6 that describes pantomime to the audience. The Queen describes the interventions of immortal characters (fairy and demon) before continuing:

> A man, for instance, always plays a Dame
> Yet he may have a son who by the same
> Perverse tradition struts on high-heeled shoes

Figure 6 Randy by name and Randy by nature – Pantomime's comic sexuality and lack of verisimilitude in the Royal Shakespeare Company production of *Poppy* by Peter Nichols. Photograph by Conrad Blakemore. Courtesy of ArenaPAL.

> And flaunts an ample bosom but can't lose
> An urge to meet some girl he can convince
> That he's her long-awaited Fairy Prince.[6]

In Act Two, Scene 2, when the Commissioner to Canton and the Viceroy of Kwuantung first meet Dick and Dodo, they can see the cross-dressing that the British characters appear not to notice. Whereas the comedy in a British pantomime links the audience and performers in a shared knowledge of theatricality, in this case it is the Chinese characters and the audience who share knowledge, which, in this scene, presents the grotesque comic caricatures of the British family. In *Poppy* the Chinese characters have fun at the expense of the British through the absurdities of the cross-dressing pantomime convention. This allows a greater level of empathy between the audience and the Chinese characters than would be normal for the 'villain' of pantomime, and makes the critique of Britain's imperial role much more obvious, even despite the attraction of the comic pantomime characters. The grotesque pantomime Dame features in British comedy elsewhere, but is most notable in recent musicals in the character of Miss Trunchbull in

Matilda (Dennis Kelly and Tim Minchin, 2010).[7] But as we will see in the case study below, the sexuality and gender ambiguity of pantomime also feeds into *The Rocky Horror Show* (Richard O'Brien, 1973).

Other features of pantomime are direct address and self-reflexivity. In *Poppy* Sally and Jack speak directly to the audience, and use one of pantomime's interactive devices: Sally asks the audience for help – they are to shout 'Whoa, boy' if Randy attempts to mount Sally's pantomime horse, Cherry. Later Jack addresses the audience and conductor (here referred to as 'professor') directly, both features of pantomime's self-reflexivity. The involvement in pantomime of performers from music hall and variety who performed specialty acts is also targeted here when Jack says to the audience and his horse Randy:

> But look, old sport, they've left us all alone
> A chance for me to play my xylophone.
>
> *He pulls a xylophone from behind a tree and nods to the orchestra conductor.*
>
> Thank you, Professor.[8]

Luckily the Chorus and Sally return before he actually begins to play. It is possible that this is a parody of an event that occurred when Issy Bonn is reputed to have said in pantomime:

> Now that I am all alone, I think I'll play my xylophone.[9]

This event becomes a standing joke as, with attendant diabolical rhymes, Jack attempts to play the spoons:

> Perhaps you'd like to hear me sing some tunes
> Accompanying myself on the spoons?[10]

the mouth organ:

> Well, now at least we've shook off the old Gorgon.
> It's time for me to play on my mouth-organ[11]

and an ocarina:

> Randy, do you realise it's been a
> Long time since I played my ocarina?[12]

before he finally manages to sing a song:

> The sun is setting and time is nigh
> For me to sing your favourite lullaby.[13]

The same self-reflexivity, along with a valorization of a working-class and rough theatre aesthetic, could be argued in relation to *Spamalot* (Idle, DuPrez, Innes, 2006), a musical based on a British film that seems to retain many features of pantomime even though it opened on Broadway. It is set in medieval England and approximates to a version of the King Arthur legend, but always from the perspective of the poor working-class outsiders. It is nostalgic, irreverent, anachronistic and self-reflexive. During 'You Won't Succeed on Broadway', characters from many other musicals appear on stage; Sir Galahad and Lady of the Lake sing 'The Song That Goes Like This', which describes the features of musical theatre songs even while those features occur. Later, the Lady of the Lake bemoans the fact that her part is no more than a cameo in the song 'Whatever Happened to My Part'.

One of the most significant features of pantomime, and of *Poppy* and *Spamalot*, is that there is no attempt at realism or verisimilitude. Stories are enacted for audiences by performers who engage in a critique of the form, their characters and the production. These are all conventions that allow the performers and audience to identify with each other and to critique aspects of the story and the performance. In fact in pantomime and these musicals the performers promote the impression that anyone can 'do it', even as they engage in perfectly timed physical comedy or slapstick routines with appropriate percussive buttons, stings and crashes.[14]

The lack of realism is particularly useful in promoting awareness of multiple frames for the performance which distance the audience to engage with the political commentary. In pantomime, generally, there are topical references and localized political criticism but not a biting satire, whereas in *Poppy* the same form and techniques are used with a much harsher satirical intent. A similar political intent can be seen in *The Cheviot, the Stag and the Black, Black Oil* (McGrath, 1973), discussed below, and in the case study of *Oh What a Lovely War!* (Littlewood and Theatre Workshop, 1963). It is this potential in pantomime to be purely entertaining or for the form to be used for satire that is most interesting when considering the relationship between pantomime and British musical theatre.

The Cheviot, the Stag and the Black, Black Oil was written by John McGrath with his company 7.84 (Scotland) for performance in local communities around Scotland from 1973. It tells the story of the exploitation of the Scottish Highlands by wealthy English landowners who cleared the land of subsistence farmers. The highland crofters and subsistence farmers were first replaced by cheviot sheep, and later the sheep were replaced by large estates providing shooting for the rich; deer and grouse. The story ends by identifying a contemporary new clearance that was occurring at the time the work was written that resulted from the discovery of oil off the Scottish coast. This work, in common with much small scale, regional and community theatre in Britain, is not usually described as musical theatre, though it contains many songs. However, the narrative structure of pantomime and the use of stereotypical characters, recognizable musical genres, intertextual references and a nostalgic emotional atmosphere all contribute to a popular form that can be widely understood. Songs are used in similar ways in musical theatre, pantomime and in this type of community performance. In the case of *The Cheviot* the performance of an opening and closing song in Gaelic was the opportunity to document the demise of the language and to create community with the audience in small village halls around the highlands and islands.

As John McGrath documents in the introduction to the play text, the form of the play is based on a ceilidh – a gathering at which most of those present play, sing, or tell a story, and at which the dancing continues far into the night.[15] He continues: 'In the past, these gatherings had also had their political side, particularly at the time of the Land Leagues, and stories of Highland history and oppression had been passed on. In the West, they were also one way of keeping intact the Gaelic culture.' McGrath wanted to use this form because of its popularity and so that everyone would get the chance to have a talk, a dance and a good time, but it's also true that the actual performance by the company contains many of the features of pantomime and draws on the same cultural references as musical theatre. The audience is asked to join in the songs and a dance at the end of the performance, but is also the recipient of direct address as the facts of the clearances are read to them by narrators or MCs. There is the opportunity for audience participation using the same formula and sexual innuendo as pantomime; the audience is asked to let the Sturdy Highlander know when the Red Indians attempt to attack from the rear. The characters, other than the Gaelic singer with whom audiences are expected to empathize, are gross caricatures and stereotypes, especially the English characters; the audience is expected to identify with the performers behind the characters, and the Scottish working-class position they are articulating in opposition to the English who are the villains.

Queen Victoria and Granny were played as female grotesques, in the tradition of the pantomime dame, while all the other characters were also larger-than-life stereotypes. Texas Jim, for example, in a ten-gallon hat speaks nostalgically and sentimentally of his great-great-grand-pappy who left these 'calm untroubled shores' to an audience who has just been told of the horrors of the clearances. He sings using a highland tune, before breaking into a hoedown that reveals his true affiliation and economic intention:

> Take your oil-rigs by the score,
> Drill a little well just a little off-shore,
> Pipe that oil in from the sea
> Pipe those profits – home to me.[16]

The combination of story-telling through physical action, stereotypical characters, coarse comedy and the swift one-liners of music hall along with song and dance and a lack of verisimilitude became hugely influential in political theatre of the 1970s. A similar aesthetic, derived from pantomime, is evoked in the commercial West End production of *Spamalot* in the costume, minimal set, the use of coconut shells for horses' hooves and many other features. Although here it is used for comic effect, this aesthetic continues to pervade aspects of British musical theatre, where, for example, characterization and theatricality are often prized over vocal perfection, dance technique, or indeed linear narrative to signify working-class roughness.

Aletta Collins' choreography for *Made in Dagenham* (Arnold, Thomas and Bean, 2014) exemplifies this aesthetic in a different way. The chorus of workmen are actors of different sizes and shapes who move together as a community, when, for example, they are sweeping the factory, but they always maintain a modicum of difference and individual characterization even while performing steps in unison. The gross comic parody of former Prime Minister Harold Wilson fits this aesthetic too; an aesthetic that perhaps first spawned *Spitting Image* and its puppet caricatures. This aesthetic in dance can be seen in the British film version of *The Full Monty* (1997), in the musicals *The Hired Man* (Melvyn Bragg and Howard Goodall, 1984), *Billy Elliot* (Lee Hall and Elton John, 2005)[17] and *Betty Blue Eyes* (Daniel Lipman, Ron Cowen, George Stiles and Anthony Drewe, 2011). A politics that explores the plight of the working classes is mixed in these works with the grotesque in an aesthetics of idiosyncratic movement and actorly individuality rather than singing or dancing uniformity. It is interesting to note, therefore, that some of these works were not very successful in the West End, let alone on Broadway where a different aesthetic pertains.

More recently, in *Soho Cinders* (Anthony Drewe, Elliot Davis and George Stiles, 2008) pantomime is updated in a contemporary love story. The value of a widely known theatre form is in the fixed points it generates around which it can weave its points of difference, its satire or comedy. The greater the disjunction between the popular or comic aspects of the work and its serious intent, the more extreme is the range of emotions generated for and in the audience, and the more telling is the political effect. This is perhaps best exemplified by *Oh What a Lovely War!*

Case Study 5: *Oh What a Lovely War!*

History and development

Oh What a Lovely War! was first performed at the Theatre Royal, Stratford East on 19 March 1963. It was directed by Joan Littlewood and devised by Littlewood with her Theatre Workshop company based on a range of materials and sources including Charles Chilton's *The Long, Long Trail*, a radio programme utilizing the songs of the First World War to tell the story of the 35,942 men who fell in the Battle of Arras, and a play he was commissioned to write by Joan Littlewood's partner, Gerry Raffles. How much of Chilton's writing remained in the 1963 Theatre Workshop production is debatable, though the idea of using the songs to counterpoint the story remained a key feature. In fact it was Littlewood's usual process to gather supplementary materials and adapt the play texts on which she worked. She and the company conducted their own research, gathered and adapted factual materials, but Chilton was credited as the writer along with 'The Members of the Cast' and Raymond Fletcher as the Military Adviser.[18] What is interesting, however, is that subsequently the order of authors has been altered so that the Theatre Workshop has become the first recorded author. In any case, Joan Littlewood records that she and the company had found the radio play 'terrible', 'sentimental' and 'pure nostalgia'.[19] To supplement the play text Littlewood and the company 'raided the local libraries, dug out facts and figures. A neighbour brought in a little tin box, with Princess Mary's profile stamped on the lid.'[20] What is very clearly established in the programme and all the published ephemera is that the performance is based on 'factual data in official records, war memoirs, personal recollections and commentaries' – a very early type of verbatim theatre – and the programme provides a list of some of the sources of material.[21] The final Author's Note in the 1963 programme is reproduced here in full:

> Everything spoken during this evening either happened or was said, sung or written during 1914–1918.
>
> *Everything presented as fact is true.*
>
> In 1960 an American Military Research Team fed all the facts of World War I into the computers they use to plan World War III. They reached the conclusion that the 1914–18 war was impossible and couldn't have happened. There could not have been so many blunders nor so many casualties. Will there be a computer left to analyse World War III?

The show was slightly adapted before it played for a week at the Sarah Bernhardt Theatre, Place du Châtelet in Paris (11–15 June) where it won the Grand Prix of the Théatre des Nations Festival. The adaptation is movingly described by Murray Melvin[22] in the programme of the 2014 revival at Stratford East. Most importantly the ending was adapted to reflect the French context. The French Soldiers, who were told that if they refused to obey they would be shot, agreed that 'We follow you – like lambs to the slaughter' and so advanced towards the footlights saying 'Baa' until, with a burst of machine-gun fire, they collapsed and fell silent.[23] This scene remained in the West End production, followed only by finale songs, news and slides. For, despite some misgivings from the official censor (at this time all plays still had to have official approval from the Lord Chamberlain's office) and due in part to the approbation of Princess Margaret who saw the production at Stratford, the show transferred to the West End in June 1963. The following year it transferred (via Philadelphia) to the Broadhurst Theatre, Broadway[24] where it played 125 performances. Henry T. Murdock in the *Philadelphia Inquirer* wrote: 'This is not a conventional show in either material, playing or staging, but it is a potent one. … [W]e think it will stand out in the memory and perhaps the conscience of almost any adult audience.'[25] The production was adapted for BBC radio and a film was made in 1969.

Production and design

Oh What a Lovely War! uses popular entertainment forms and characters to reach out to the local community in Stratford East, referencing *commedia dell'arte* stereotypes, circus and music hall. The design for the original production was by John Bury and contained the following essential elements: a large screen on which could be projected slides of wartime photographs; a 'Newspanel' on which the names of battles, numbers killed and wounded, and numbers of yards gained or lost could be displayed in lights; and furniture in the form of four truncated cones to be used as seats.[26] Lez Brotherston, who designed the revival, wanted to use elements of this design in his version. He described it as 'very minimal but it had a showbiz touch'. There were steps from the auditorium to the stage and a balcony that looked rather like a light-entertainment variety show in the early days of television.[27] The stage itself, though, was open and had no scenery. Nadine Holdsworth describes it as being like a traditional seaside entertainment 'complete with red, white and blue fairy lights'[28] around the proscenium arch. Instead of scenery, projected slides created the backdrop for the action. So, for example, a slide of 'dead Germans lying in a shallow trench in a peaceful-looking country field' is projected during the lyrics 'Down in your dugouts and say your prayers'. This is followed by a slide of 'A young French soldier, obviously on burial duty, laden with wooden crosses' at the words 'Hush, here comes a whizzbang'.[29] Later the song 'I Want To Go Home' is accompanied by a series of slides in sequence of Highland infantrymen around a small camp fire; two captured wounded German infantrymen; a trench of Tommies at ease; three Tommies walking through a rain-soaked muddy field; two captured Germans; a group of Tommies skylarking with an old horse-drawn coach on which they've chalked 10 Downing Street.[30]

In contrast with the real photographs projected on the screen, the company decided that there should be no khaki on the stage and no represented deaths. Instead the actors were dressed as pierrots and pierrettes.[31] Joan Littlewood records that 'Pierrots were all the go in those days. They'd perform on a platform set up on the beach, seats 3d. and 6d.... They could all sing and dance and make you laugh. They were the great joy of the seaside.'[32] These seaside variety shows became end-of-the-pier shows[33] and were the remainders of the once ubiquitous music hall tradition. This format, that was somewhat nostalgic even in the 1960s, offered Littlewood a framework that referenced popular entertainment at the time of the First World War. It was also a distancing device through which to achieve a Brechtian alienation from the chaos, death and destruction of the trench warfare and provided the opportunity to juxtapose the light-hearted commentary and popular songs with the black comedy of the blundering generals, and the documentary facts and figures.

Figure 7 Clowns and Soldiers – a stark commentary on the wisdom of war in the 2014 revival of *Oh What a Lovely War!* by Joan Littlewood at Theatre Royal, Stratford East. Photograph by Nobby Clark. Courtesy of ArenaPAL.

Although the scenes and events of the First World War are in chronological order there is no causal relationship between them so that, rather than a linear narrative, the show proceeds as a series of isolated incidents in the manner of Brecht's Epic theatre, each of which contains internal juxtapositions between the photo montages, the songs and the scenes. The style of performance was constantly shifting too, between black comedy, stylized and naturalistic acting, direct address to the audience and song and dance so that the mood switched from satire to pathos and anger. As Robert Leach notes of all Littlewood's work, the use of minor and illegitimate forms of drama such as music hall and the pierrot show 'oppose the dominant naturalism of the contemporary stage, and give the plays a flavour of rebellion, or subversion, even in their form. This is compounded by the use of meta-theatrical devices.'[34] He argues that the productions of Theatre Workshop were carnivalesque in their attempt to break down the hierarchies and subvert authority through parody, in asserting the values of community and affirming the primacy of action and the body. 'The plays demystify or challenge accepted narratives, especially historical narratives which explain current society'[35] and in this case the accepted narrative of the First World War was subverted by dramatizing the experiences of ordinary soldiers naturalistically or humorously while presenting the officers as grotesque stereotypes, as for example in the contrast between the naturalistic Christmas Day football match and the black comedy of the meeting of the generals without translators.

Musical dramaturgy

The show opened with an overture of well-known period songs including 'Oh It's a Lovely War', 'Goodbye-ee' and 'I Do Like to Be Beside the Seaside' before the company strolled on, chatting to each other and the audience, and the M.C. began proceedings by welcoming the audience and announcing the opening number.[36] At the same time a Newspanel displayed events from the summer of 1914. The combination of materials opens a gap through which audiences can read the critique of government policy and official bureaucracy, a strategy that Brecht described in his discourse on epic theatre.[37] When interwoven the music and songs extend the range of material presented, hook into the nostalgic and emotional memory attached to them, and provide a rhythmic punctuation and tempo change, all of which increase the capacity of the show to reach a wide popular audience and to entertain.

The use of existing songs in a musical is now loosely termed a 'jukebox musical', but this phenomenon existed long before jukeboxes were invented and was much more satirical or political than contemporary jukebox musicals tend to be. It was a feature of burlesques of opera and theatre from John Gay's *The Beggar's Opera* (1728), which interpolated melodies from popular songs of the time with ironically contrasting lyrics to satirize the Italian opera of Handel and his contemporaries, right through the nineteenth century and into the present. This process relied on audiences' memory of the original context so that it is subverted or challenged by its new context. It is this possibility that Joan Littlewood exploited in *Oh What a Lovely War!* by tapping into the memory of war that was retained in the British psyche. Although the memories of the First World War were somewhat distant, the impact of the Second World War was very recent, so that the show can be seen as a pacifist commentary on the futility of war in general as much as a specific depiction of the First World War.

In terms of the music, the hymns in the church scene are a prime example of the juxtaposition of musical texts. To the tune of 'Onward Christian Soldiers' the men sing 'Forward Joe Soap's Army', which includes the lyrics 'but the men who really did the job are dead and in their grave' in contrast with the old commander who is 'safely in the rear'.[38] To the tune of 'The Church's One

Foundation' the men sing 'Fred Karno's Army', which contains the lyrics 'We cannot fight, we cannot shoot, What bleeding use are we?', and to the tune of 'What a Friend We Have in Jesus' the men sing 'When This Lousy War is Over'.[39] These are replacement lyrics created by soldiers in the trenches, but they rely on awareness of both sources so that the juxtaposition has its effect. Rather than the 'schmaltz' that Littlewood had perceived in Chilton's original drama, the combination of tune and altered lyric, or song, photograph and Newspanel facts makes a strong political statement. The first act ends with the lyrical 'Goodbye-ee' being disrupted: the words 'Don't cryee, don't sigh-ee, there's a silver lining in the sky-ee' are followed by the sound of a shell exploding so that the last line of the song is inaudible, even as the Newspanel reads 'welcome 1915 . . . happy year that will bring victory and peace'.

The first act was relatively optimistic and patriotic, even as it demonstrated the confusion and chaos that informed the war planning. The second act 'compresses the final years of the War and deals with the scale of death, destruction and maiming on the Western Front' through appropriate juxtapositions of unrelated material.[40] For example, the lyrical 'Roses of Picardy' follows a black comedy scene in which the officer insists that a leg sticking out of a parapet should be removed, leaving the Sergeant to wonder what he will 'hang my equipment on. . . . Heads, trunks, blood all over the place, and all he's worried about is a damned leg'.[41] The song follows, but is further subverted by the Newspanel announcement 'Easter 1916. . .rebellion in Ireland' both of which are performed as the scene is set for an officers' ball during which Sir Douglas Haig is introduced as a somewhat surprising choice to lead the army.

In a later scene Haig announces that 'everything points to a complete breakdown in enemy morale', which is juxtaposed with a nurse reading her letter home: 'It is beyond belief, the butchery; the men look so appalling when they are brought in and so many die.' She then sings 'Keep the Home Fires Burning' while the Newspanel announces: 'average life of a machine-gunner under attack . . . four minutes', and 'Sept 20 . . . Menin Road . . . British loss 22,000 men Gain 800 yards . . . Sept 25 . . . Polygon Wood . . . British Loss 17,000 men Gain 1,000 Yards'.[42] These juxtapositions of naturalistically presented lyrical songs with black comic stylization and Newspanel facts meant that the audience's emotional memory of the songs was disrupted and the combined effect was highly political. The final song in the show is 'They'd Never Believe Me', with the lyrics sung as they were sung in the trenches:

And when they ask us, and they're certainly going to ask us,
The reason why we didn't win the Croix de Guerre,
Oh, we'll never tell them, oh we'll never tell them
There was a front, but damned if we knew where.

Set against this are slides of Canadian infantrymen; Tommies trying to pull a field gun out of the mud; French infantrymen marching past with rifles at the slope; two weary British officers, one with a bandaged head; two Canadian soldiers leaning against spiked boards, one writing a letter; a long line of Tommies walking away from the camera following the direction of a trench.[43]

Impact and influence

The impact of this production was felt immediately and has continued to resound in British theatre. The show opened the way for a new form of political theatre that influenced a generation of directors and writers. Richard Eyre and Nicholas Wright summarise Littlewood's achievement: 'she [. . .] revolutionised the way that plays were presented, the way that they were written, and the way directors and actors and writers collaborated.'[44] Holdsworth notes the influence on John McGrath (whose 7:84 theatre company is discussed above) and Peter Brook as the show's 'provocative theatricality and anti-war stance continues to speak to us in the here-and-now as the "war game" maintains potent resonance in the twenty-first century.'[45] Carol Ilson notes Littlewood's influence on Harold Prince, who discussed with Sondheim her improvisatory technique and free style, her irreverence and looseness,[46] while Robert Leach described her influence as 'pervasive.'[47] He notes the spread of influence through the later careers of John Bury and many of the other Theatre Workshop alumni, including David Scare (especially at the Manchester Library Theatre), through the E15 acting school, in the work and writing of Clive Barker, the Radio Ballads of Ewan MacColl, Peter Cheeseman's use of community and verbatim in productions at the Victoria Theatre, Stoke-on Trent, and the continuing work of the Theatre Royal, Stratford East. Harold Hobson, drama critic of the *Sunday Times* remarked that Littlewood 'began an internal revolution in the theatre in the way plays were produced and the sort of plays that were produced, in the way that they were written, in the way the director and the players were operating with the author, and this has gone through the whole British theatre.'[48]

Whether *Oh What a Lovely War!* is a musical or not is often debated, but as was noted in Part One, there is a strand of plays with music in the history of British theatre that have been highly influential in the development of both dramatic theatre and musical theatre. Certainly the response to the Philadelphia performance demonstrates that the work was unexpected when considered in the context of other Broadway musicals, but its importance cannot be doubted. In the UK it influenced subsequent political music theatre works, such as those by McGrath, Osborne, Heneker, Nichols and Goodall. The meta-theatrical reference to popular forms, the use of stereotypical characters, range of performance styles and the incorporation of songs or musical genres from popular culture all tap into a sense that this work spoke to and for a wider working-class community using the signifying strategies with which they were familiar, while using sharp juxtapositions for parodic or satirical effect and to comment on contemporary politics.

2.2 REFLECTING MULTICULTURALISM[49]

Partly influenced by British popular theatre forms, and as a response to decades of immigration which began to alter the ethnic character of British cities and by second- and third-generation British minority ethnic communities who wanted to represent their own experiences of living in Britain, new companies and new types of performance began to emerge alongside the mainstream musical theatre world.

From the 1970s onwards, small-scale touring companies, community theatres and companies based within ethnic or immigrant communities began to create works representative of their audience constituencies. Black and Asian theatre often practised a greater interaction between audiences and performers than was common in mainstream white theatre other than in pantomime, and theatres of African and Asian derivation tended to incorporate dance, drama, music or visual arts 'within the same piece of theatre, [where] meaning is made as instinctively and readily from movement as from spoken text.'[50] Dimple Godiwala comments on the way black and Asian theatre producers and directors use different systems of signification that includes 'their own group's cultural and social codes, in the verbal and non-verbal elements of the performance text'.[51] This often includes music, dance, visual imagery and the use of other forms of English or indeed other British minority ethnic languages, producing what Jatinder Verma refers to as 'Binglish'. The result of this is that black and Asian theatre uses a very diverse range of signifiers drawn from a combination of source cultures in many countries of origin alongside British theatrical and cultural traditions, but always influenced by popular culture.

British African and Caribbean performers have a long history on the British stage in popular music and in the production of Carnival,[52] but it is only since the development of Dark and Light (1969), which became the Black Theatre of Brixton in 1975 and whose participants spawned the Black Theatre Co-operative and the Black Theatre Forum, that black writers and performers have begun to move from the fringe into the British theatrical mainstream.[53] Interestingly, among the first musical productions were versions of Jamaican pantomime and Carnival. *Play Mas* (1974) by Mustapha Matura used carnival, while *Anansi and Brer Englishman* (1972) written by Manley Young and Gloria Cameron and directed by Yvonne Brewster may have been the first Jamaican pantomime in Britain.[54] *Anansi* is a national folk hero of Jamaica, part spider, part human, whose identity is here developed as a metaphor for the outsider status of black Britons. The pantomime features include male drag, topical references (to Enoch Powell and Edward Heath, the local council and the Royal Family).[55] The show was revived the following year and then began a series of *Anansi* pantomimes that included *Anansi and the Strawberry Queen* (1974) again written by Manley Young, with music by Ilona Sekacz[56] and directed by Norman Beaton.

Somewhat earlier, Norman Beaton,[57] who had been a Guyanan calypso champion, wrote the musicals *Jack of Spades* (1965) for Liverpool Everyman and *Sit Down Banna* (1968) for the Connaught Theatre, Worthing. By the time the Black Theatre of Brixton folded in 1978 it had produced 'the world's first reggae opera', *Jericho* by Jamal Ali.[58] Other musicals produced by Keskidee included Ali's earlier musical *Black Feet in the Snow* and *The Father and the Child Reunion*, which were performed at the Roundhouse Downstairs in 1976.

Another of the early black British theatre companies was Temba, which was established in 1972 and sought to promote new black writing from the UK and South Africa.[59] One of its founders, Alton Kumalo, had performed in the township musical *King Kong*, which played in Britain as early as 1961.[60] This company, too, was influenced by Jamaican pantomime as a format that offered the opportunity 'to appropriate the culture of their parents and infuse it with their new, hybridised cultural identities'.[61] *The Pirate Princess* (1986, co-directed by Alby James and Paulette Randall with music by Felix Cross) was part of the 1986 Black Theatre Season as a production by the Temba Theatre Company, and was in the tradition of Jamaican pantomime.

Despite the long tradition of Jamaican pantomime (since 1941) and its different narrative framework, Randall recalls that the combination of influences from Jamaica, British pantomime and British realist theatre meant that the work ended up as a musical.[62] There was a lot of underscore to ease the transition from speech to song, and the characters went through a consistent emotional journey. The music was 'a mix of R & B, reggae, Mento music, Jamaican soul and some other rhythms from Jamaican folk music'.[63] But in Jamaican pantomime the influences are just as diverse as those in British pantomime, and choruses similar to those in Gilbert and Sullivan were also incorporated, so Cross comments that, in that sense, 'it is very English'.[64] The audience, though, was raucous in a way that went beyond the well-rehearsed patterns of British pantomime, and required the performers to 'become an ensemble and work with one another and with the audience'.[65] This new hybrid format, which reflected something of the condition of post-colonial Britain, had been successfully established and was later used by Talawa in the production of *Arawak Gold* (1992) by Carmen Tipling and Ted Dwyer; it is a format that has influenced contemporary multicultural pantomime, especially at venues such as Stratford East, Watford Palace and Hackney Empire, where Clive Rowe first played Dame in 2004.

Talawa was established in 1985 by Yvonne Brewster and remains one of the most important black British theatre companies.[66] The company was not greatly interested in musical theatre, but in 1988 Derek Walcott's *O Babylon!* with music by Galt McDermot (composer of *Hair*) was produced, and later musicals included *Arawak Gold* (mentioned above) and the Rastafarian musical *One Love* (Kwame Davies 2001).[67]

One of the most important contemporary companies when discussing black musical theatre (perhaps because of the leadership of Felix Cross) is Nitro – formerly the Black Theatre Co-operative, 1979. As Nitro records on its website, it collaborates with leading and emerging black artists and performers to create dynamic music theatre events 'exploring the contemporary black British experience, celebrating the wealth of black music from reggae, calypso, salsa, soul, jazz and hip-hop to contemporary opera'.[68] Its production of a hip-hop musical *Slamdunk* (2004) outsold the company's previous work, and it continues to develop new music theatre projects under its new name Nitrobeat.

The Theatre Royal, Stratford East became a very important collaborator, commissioner and developer of new multicultural work under the artistic directorship of Philip Hedley from 1981 to 2004. He remarked that he was simply serving the theatre's local community, 'drawing from it and giving back in that continuous process'.[69] At first there was 'a sprinkling of black work, the occasional invited show, a co-production', and these shows were in the lower quarter of the box office. But very soon there was a leap in the commercial success of black theatre, and those productions are increasingly directed and written by black and Asian artists.[70] Since 2004 the theatre, under its new artistic director Kerry Michael, has continued to develop jukebox style musicals such as *The Harder They Come* (2006, by Perry Henzell, based on his film of the same name)[71] and annual pantomimes, as well as collaborations with companies from the British minority ethnic communities that are among its audiences.

Britain's Got Bhangra (Kumar and Chopra, 2010) resulted from such a collaboration, this time between Rifco Arts (The Reduced Indian Film Company) and Stratford East, in association with Warwick Arts Centre in 2010. It was conceived and directed by Pravesh Kumar with lyrics by Dougal Irvine and original music by Sumeet Chopra. The story, set amid the Asian music scene in multicultural Britain, follows Twinkle, who goes from being a van driver to becoming a Bhangra star in a Bollywood-style performance. It won the People's Favourite Musical Award in the Off West End Awards and was nominated as Best Musical Production in the TMA Awards, Best New Musical in the What's On Stage Awards and Best Musical in the Off West End Awards.[72]

Michael Billington opines that 'Sumeet Chopra's score is a delight that brings the audience to its feet and introduces a new sound into the stale world of the British musical'.[73] Although he has some reservations about the book, he continues: 'But the score, ranging from traditional bhangra to Bollywood and hip-hop, is dance-based, energizing and mercifully free of the soulful wailing of so much Western pop. It is also smartly executed and vividly performed by the on-stage band, making use of the dhol drums (while lifting you out of them)'.[74]

The company, whose artistic director Pravesh Kumar was influenced by Bollywood film, first came to notice with its second production *Bollywood: Yet Another Love Story* (2000). This is 'a sideways and firmly tongue in cheek look at the gaudy, glitzy and glamorous world of Bollywood'.[75] Lyn Gardner's review of the 2003 revival at Riverside Studios is decidedly mixed, pointing to the frenetic narrative, clumsy stagecraft and lack of structure, but she remarks that 'the evening is saved by its sheer good humour, the lively songs, some wit ... and the film component'.[76] This show appeared at a time of burgeoning interest in and influence from Bollywood film. More recently the same company, now based at Watford Palace Theatre, presented a combination of Bollywood and street dance in *Break the Floorboards* (Khan and Chopra, 2013), which tells the story of a teenage boy who just wants to dance and escape into his Bollywood fantasies.

By the mid- to late 1970s, South Asian theatre companies in the UK had started to perform their cultural heritage, to creatively explore the phantasmagoria of Bollywood movies and to investigate the anti-realist traditions of the sub-continent. Whereas black music had become hugely influential within mainstream music charts, perhaps because of the intervention and cultural imperialism of American artists who share many similar roots and experiences, Asian music and language has largely remained outside the British mainstream. A significant factor that may account for this in some part is the predominance of rhythm and bass in Caribbean, African American, British and American popular music in contrast to the predominance of ornamented and partly improvised melody in South Asian music. This has an effect on the timbres, resonance and aesthetics of Asian musical theatre performance, which relies on a musical language that has been much less influential or even audible in the Western mainstream. Another possible reason for the difference between black African/Caribbean and South Asian communities is explored by Colin Chambers, who speculates that many British Asians initially fled to Kenya and Uganda and were then forced to migrate again to Britain.[77] The fact that they could not return may have affected their response to living in Britain, and their double removal also contributed to the diverse influences on their cultural practices. Second, Bollywood was at first perceived as a clichéd and second-rate derivative of Hollywood musical film rather than fully acknowledged as a popular form in its own right with its own aesthetic in narrative, music, dance and design. All these factors and other cultural factors may have contributed to an earlier visibility for British African and Caribbean musical performers and companies than their South Asian counterparts. The most visible cross-cultural musical theatre production of the period is *Bombay Dreams* (Rahman, Black, Syal, 2002). It has been considered somewhat controversial, especially on Broadway, but it had a successful West End run and will be discussed in a case study below.

At first some of the South Asian companies performed in a number of South Asian languages, as recorded in a 1976 report by Naseem Khan for the Arts Council and the Commission for Racial Equality.[78] But very soon companies sprang up, at first in London, through which minority communities were able to create work for and about their own lives. It is not surprising that the works incorporated influences from diverse cultures, since many of the creators and performers had a mixed heritage, which included growing up in the UK alongside parental and cultural influences from elsewhere.

The first British Asian theatre company was Tara Arts, founded by Jatinder Verma in 1977 in response to the murder of a Sikh teenager in Southall in June 1976.[79] By the early 1980s the company had become professional, with grants from the Commission for Racial Equality (CRE), the Greater London Arts Association (GLAA) and the Arts Council of Great Britain (ACGB) among others, and very soon afterwards they secured a permanent building. They described themselves at that time as an 'Asian community theatre group, presenting original plays, in English, about Asian life in Britain today'.[80] What is interesting about these early works is that stylization and the use of music and dance very soon replaced naturalism and became commonplace.[81] For example, *Lion's Raj* (1982) contains a speaking chorus, while *Sapno Kay Ruup* (*The Shape of Dreams*) (1982) (a play loosely derived from *Scenes in the Life of . . .*) 'incorporates some familiar Hindi songs and simple dance sequences'. In this respect, the company very quickly returned to an Indian aesthetic that it had at first rejected.[82]

In 1981 workshops were given to Tara members by Kirti Jain on movement patterns in Indian folk theatres, and Jatinder Verma recalls discussions among those members at the Millan Centre in the same year about how 'the narrative was pushed along by song and dance' in Bollywood films.[83] Between July and November 1982, and again in early 1983, workshops were held in movement, voice and classical Indian vocal music.[84] Certainly Shobana Jeyasingh, a classical Indian dancer of Bharatanatyam,[85] was partly responsible for the idea of bringing traditional forms of music and dance into collision with naturalism. Her influence, which stimulated an increased stylization alongside the use of dance and movement techniques, may also have been responsible for an increased use of music. For Tara's production of *Miti Ki Gadi* (1984), a Sanskrit play by Sudraka, a musician was employed who 'may be an "ironic commentator" or act as a "vehicle" to support the characters, functions which were both realised by Baluji Srivastav'.[86] The production was later revived as *The Little Clay Cart* (Verma, Srivastav and Khan) in 1985 and again at the National Theatre's Cottesloe studio in 1991.

Anuradha Kapur was invited to provide skills workshops in 1985, and she continued to work with the company on developing a mode of presentation using Indian folk theatre styles to represent the tensions between traditional epic fables and stories about contemporary British life for Asians. The programme for *This Story's Not for Telling* describes the process as one where 'traditional stories were improvised on and traditional elements were used to present these stories, because these offered the best means for the Company to come to terms with a subject that was also itself'.[87] So Kapur incorporated elements from street performance, especially music because of 'the way that it intervened, obstructed, sometimes stopped the performance, then actually sped it on'.[88] Verma also developed 'Binglish', a term for the textual transposition of texts to an Indian setting using accent, inflection, tone, gesture and stance derived from Asian theatre and the use of several languages in a predominantly English text. The theatrical forms included 'Brecht; Bunraku; Indian folk forms such as Bhavai or Bollywood film conventions; and *commedia dell'arte*'.[89] The effect was to decentre the English language and culture, presenting it as one in a group of languages and cultures rather than the sole authority, and realism as one of a group of theatre traditions that informed the production. In 1991 *This Story's Not for Telling* was revised again for performance at the National's Cottesloe Theatre, a performance 'that emphasized the stylized, physical expression of character and used song, dance, and music played live on Asian instruments throughout'.[90] This was followed by productions of *The Little Clay Cart* and *Cyrano* (1995), which represented a radical transformation of what might be meant by a national theatre.

Jatinder Verma summarized what he felt were the key features and skills that might define a British Asian theatre for Tara in the late 1980s and 1990s: the chorus, the story-teller/narrator (*Sutradhar*), the curtain (*Yavanika*) and masks, and the accompanying skills were those of singing, dancing and mime as well as acting.[91] A third professional production of 1985, *Anklets of Fire*, was not so well received. The play was a reworking of a Tamil epic *Cilappathikaram*, into which were incorporated Tamil and other songs from Indian film to which English lyrics were added. Hardial Rai, who had been working with the Hounslow Arts Cooperative, questioned whether the move of Tara Arts into the mainstream circuit should require it to conform to the theatre practice of an elitist British class structure.[92] It is this question that underpins the difficulty faced by British Asian creators and performers as they began to move into the mainstream in subsequent years. Once again we discover that a more diverse aesthetic pertains from that promoted in the commercial West End and on Broadway.

From 1980 to 1991 the Hounslow Arts Cooperative had a brief life, and Actors Unlimited was in operation for an even shorter period, from 1981 to 1983. Both these companies were trying to redress discrimination in politics, on the streets and in the theatre. Actors Unlimited, in particular, promoted multiracial collaborations and casting, and there were many overlaps among members of this company with the mainstream British theatre. Several of its productions had music composed by John Mayer, and many included music and dance, but more importantly, 'the company had offered a model for multi-cultural theatre and contributed much to the promotion of Asian arts and theatre in the UK'.[93]

The British Asian Theatre Company was also short-lived, running from 1982 to 1988. This company began by training young Asian runaway youths and was very influenced by Bollywood film, both in the incorporation of song and in the use of flashback. The work of this company was multimedia, containing dance and music, and multilingual; it reflected the linguistic culture outside the theatre. An ideological split emerged between those who wanted to maintain a strong Indian idiom derived from Bollywood, which the wider mainstream audience might consider clichéd and amateurish, and those who wanted to present work in the style of the largely white mainstream, changing its politics from within.[94]

The Asian Co-operative Theatre (ACT) lasted from 1983 to 1989 and was responsible for the early exposure of writers Hanif Kureishi and Meera Syal, among others. It had links with the Black Theatre Co-operative (now Nitrobeat) and produced six plays, four of which were original and dealt with the life and history of Asians living and working in Britain. ACT's second production was an adaptation of *King Lear*, named *Film, Film, Film* (1986). It was set in the Bollywood film industry with music composed by Baluji Srivastav and song and dance that reflected the Bollywood aesthetic.[95] It is a similar aesthetic that will be discussed in the case study below in relation to *Bombay Dreams*, whose script was written by former ACT member Meera Syal. The narrative of *Film, Film, Film* attempts to parody the Indian film, echo the Shakespearian story and reflect contemporary British life. Shobana Jeyasingh was employed as choreographer for the final production by ACT, *Blood Wedding* (1987), which was inspired by the links between 'Rajasthani dance, music and itinerant culture and Spain's gypsy culture'.[96] Music was composed by Akintayo Akinbode and incorporated flamenco, Indian and African music, with Baluji Srivastav playing sitar.

Tamasha appeared as this earlier group of Asian companies were fading in 1989, founded by Kristine Landon Smith and Sudha Bhuchar. It had a much more professional organization, gained revenue funding from the Arts Council in 1997 and is still in operation. The company does extensive research for performances using a realist aesthetic, but music remains important, with, for example, John O'Hara composing songs for *Women of the Dust,* which had movement by Shobana Jeyasingh.[97] In 1997 the company developed *A Tainted Dawn,* a realistic production by Bhuchar and Landon-Smith, which nonetheless featured an original score by Nitin Sawhney,[98] before in 1998 developing a Bollywood-influenced production, *Fourteen Songs, Two Weddings and a Funeral.*[99] The story was adapted by Sudha Bhuchar and Kristine Landon-Smith from the film *Hum Aapke Hain Koun* (1994), which has a romantic plot that revolves around matchmaking. In Bollywood cinema the songs are not sung by the actors but by specialist playback singers, who are just as celebrated as the actors. However, for this production English song lyrics were supplied by Sean McCarthy and Felix Cross, with musical arrangements made by Barrie Bignold, so that the songs could be performed by the actors to backing tracks. The stage version contains moments of comedy using stock characters and enjoys the camp clichés of Bollywood, but it also contains melodramatic moments of high emotion with songs and dances that fit into the story at all the key moments – rather like Western musical theatre. These include Prem and Nisha (hero and heroine) dancing by the poolside (reflecting Fred Astaire and Ginger Rogers in Hollywood films) and the song 'Jute Dedo Paise Lelo', which Landon-Smith describes as 'the climactic number right at the heart of the piece', in which the young people from both sides come together en masse (as in *West Side Story* and *Grease*).[100] The English song lyrics have to capture the reference to family and tradition that are so important to the source culture and yet still be relevant to a contemporary British audience, while at the same time having the wit and rhyme of musical comedy. More importantly, as Landon-Smith argues, the playing style must demonstrate affection for the genre – it mustn't be sent up.[101]

One of the potential criticisms levelled at British theatre companies who use Bollywood conventions is that they seem amateurish and clichéd, when in fact what these criticisms sometimes demonstrate is a lack of understanding of the dramaturgies of Bollywood film and the cultural sensibilities of its British Asian audiences. The influences on Bollywood film are already multicultural, since the reference to Indian folk plays and myths and Parsi theatre are combined with imported British theatre traditions. This results in productions that are designed for end-on proscenium viewing, whose song and dance sequences are staged frontally to break the fourth wall, and whose form and narrative mirror the conservatism of Hollywood musicals.[102] By using this popular form Tamasha made a connection with a British Asian audience, but also potentially with a much wider audience from within and without the British Asian community and within and without a theatre-going audience. Although the company and therefore its audiences were often focused around British Asian communities, this production, perhaps because of its titular reference to the British film *Four Weddings and a Funeral*, also played in some more conservative, largely white cities including Guildford as well as Manchester and Bristol. In fact, Jen Harvie argues convincingly that the Asian cast and music in *Fourteen Weddings* drew attention to the fact that *Four Weddings'* 'unabashedly whitewashed, racially exclusive British identity was latently racist'. The similarity of title alongside the difference of cast and aesthetic drew attention to the dichotomy, though this is not to deny the potential marketability of the title.[103] What this burgeoning of British black and Asian theatre has done is similar to what Harvie argues in relation to *Fourteen Weddings*; it succeeded in privileging British Asian identities, audiences, characters, and forms of address; it provided professional and highly visible work for British Asian performers and creators. As Harvie concludes, 'The production affirmed British Asian cultural difference and implicitly posited intrinsic *British* cultural difference.'[104]

Figure 8 A Yorkshire story relocated to Rajasthan highlights British cultural diversity – *Wuthering Heights* by Tamasha Theatre Company. Photograph by Pete Jones. Courtesy of ArenaPAL.

The company has continued in the intervening years, and in 2009 produced its biggest production, *Wuthering Heights*, which relocates Emily Bronte's story to Rajasthan.[105] The concept and book were developed by Deepak Verma, and the music was by Felix Cross and Sheema Mukherjee with lyrics by Felix Cross and additional text by Sudha Bhuchar. The musical supervisor was John Rigby, and orchestrations and arrangements were by John Rigby and Chandru of Bollywood Strings. As is traditional in Bollywood film practice, the songs were pre-recorded, and in this case they were sung by stars of Bollywood film who would be recognizable voices to the Bollywood audiences. Author Deepak Verma comments on the importance of Bollywood traditions in an interview with Claire Allfree for *Metro*: 'Bollywood isn't just a fad anymore: it's part of the fabric.'[106] Other companies formed in the 1990s include Kali Theatre Company, whose *Moti Roti Puttli Chunni* (1993) 'captured the spirit of Bollywood on stage',[107] as happened again in *River on Fire* (2000).

Colin Chambers argues that 'in asserting a new aesthetic, British-Asian theatre offered a self-assured reply to the constraints of British naturalism and its concomitant style of subjective acting that mistrusts theory and dedicated training'.[108] Companies such as Nitro, Rifco, Tara Arts, Talawa and Tamasha continue to use the musical languages of their communities within a diverse range of works, while Stratford East continues to represent the borough of Tower Hamlets, which boasts a multicultural population speaking over 100 languages. As the work of these local, small-scale companies grew, the ethnic diversity of the mainstream began to change – a change reflected in works such as *Bombay Dreams*, *The Harder They Come*, *Britain's Got Bhangra* and most recently *Bend It Like Beckham*, the musical version of which arrived in the West End in 2015. This increasingly multicultural theatre was not without problems or detractors, but it has altered the representation of diversity within what was even in the 1970s an almost exclusively white mainstream theatre. As Chambers notes, artists incorporated an African, Asian and Caribbean heritage 'that did not separate drama from music and dance. The thrust of this diasporic theatre carried the potency of participatory, multi-genre forms as found in Carnival, resisting the idea of culture as a unified given and seeing it rather as a changing and interconnected set of varied practices.'[109] It is the consequence of multiculturalism that seems to have had the most pervasive and vibrant influence on contemporary British musical theatre, even though its effects have rarely reached the commercial West End of London.

Case Study 6: *Bombay Dreams*

History and development

Bombay Dreams opened at the Apollo Victoria Theatre on 19 June 2002. It was the product of an international collaboration between Bollywood and British musical theatre produced by Andrew Lloyd Webber through his Really Useful Group. The show was composed by the internationally famous A. R. Rahman, who had already sold over 100 million albums and written the music for many Bollywood films. He worked in collaboration with his usual group of Indian musicians to create and record the music that would be played live for the show by, among others, percussionist Kuljit Bhamra.[110] Some of the composition was adapted or created in a collaborative process in the rehearsal room, a practice that lyricist Don Black found 'unexpected'.[111] The book was written by Meera Syal,[112] who was already well known in the UK for her work on the ground-breaking radio and television programme *Goodness Gracious Me*.[113] The lyrics were supplied by Don Black, who is perhaps best known for writing the lyrics for the James Bond theme songs 'Thunderball', 'Diamonds are Forever' and 'The Man with the Golden Gun', but who has also written lyrics for many musicals.[114]

The director was Steven Pimlott, who had worked at the Royal Shakespeare Company, English National Opera and Opera North as well as in the West End. According to resident director Lucy Skilbeck, Pimlott 'understood that the show was about making a third way; a blending of Bollywood and Western/West End traditions', hence the need for him, Anthony Van Laast (co-choreographer) and Nichola Treherne (assistant choreographer) to spend time in Mumbai ahead of the rehearsal period.[115] Assisting Pimlott was associate director Indhu Rubasingham, who had worked at Stratford East, Tricycle and the Old Vic, among other places, and is now artistic director of the Tricycle Theatre – so on the directing team there was a combination of mainstream and subsidized-sector experience. The cast was a multicultural mixture of dancers and British Asian actors, some of whom had performed in the West End; others were from the subsidized sector and some were from Bollywood – including Dalip Tahil, who played Madan in the first year, and who had performed in 'more than a hundred Bollywood films'.[116]

There were two choreographers: one an established Bollywood choreographer and another imbued in the West End traditions and practices. Anthony Van Laast trained, danced and choreographed for London Contemporary Dance Theatre before developing a hugely successful career in musical theatre. Highlights before *Bombay Dreams* included the 1993 reworking of *Joseph and the Amazing Technicolor Dreamcoat* and *Mamma Mia!* (1999). The other choreographer responsible for bringing Bollywood traditions in choreography to the mix was Farah Khan, who had already choreographed many Bollywood films, including *Monsoon Wedding* (1999) and *Dil Se* (1998), from which the interpolated song 'Chaiya Chaiya' is derived. By the time of *Bombay Dreams* she had already won four Filmfare Best Choreography awards including one for *Dil Se*. The wealth of experience and success in the team was quite remarkable, but perhaps more noteworthy was the diversity of that experience in different media and genres and in two different cultural traditions; British commercial theatre and Indian popular film. However, resident director Lucy Skilbeck notes that the production was not really different in rehearsal from other musicals in that the same problems needed solving in order to tell the story in the best way possible.[117]

This is a reverse-gendered Cinderella story – a love story between Akash and Priya. Akash is a poor slum dweller who wants to become a famous Bollywood star and escape the poverty that surrounds him. He meets Priya, a budding film producer and the fiancée of the lawyer who is trying to prevent the destruction of the slum, ironically called Paradise, in which Akash lives. She is also the daughter of the very Bollywood producer that Akash hopes to meet to start his acting career. Akash becomes successful in the film industry and begins a relationship with Priya, but his success comes at the price of his own cynical change of character and his estrangement from his friends in the Paradise slum. He returns to the slum, but finally he and Priya re-establish their love and successful careers while he retains a more grounded awareness of the importance of his roots.

Reactions in London and New York

The work appealed to a British Asian audience who knew the Bollywood films from which it derived, recognized the musical and choreographic styles, and essentially understood both British and Asian cultural signifiers and aesthetics. The world premiere took place in London's West End in 2002, and the show closed two years later. This was a different audience than usually attended West End performances, attracted by the marketing of Dewynters with Hardish Virk and Suman Bhuchar. Bhuchar had also worked on Tamasha's *Fourteen Songs, Two Weddings and a Funeral* and many other subsidized productions specifically aimed at British Asian audiences.[118] Altogether every aspect of the London production offered opportunities for a cross-cultural exchange 'from music production to choreography, casting and directing.'[119]

The show was less successful on Broadway, where it ran for 284 performances from April 2004 to 1 Jan 2005. Susan Bennett records that the reviews in New York were mediocre and sales soon fell.[120] Lucy Skilbeck remarked that it was a different show in America, with some really good work and some new songs, but that you can't underestimate the different audiences. Even before it opened there was concern that New York audiences would not have sufficient familiarity with South Asian culture to understand the pastiche behind the narrative. The producers had anticipated this and the script had been adapted for New York by Thomas Meehan, but when Ben Brantley reviewed the Broadway production, he wrote: 'For a Broadway show set in Bombay that has arrived by way of London, this musical winds up suggesting another provenance altogether: Las Vegas, land of the flashy floor show and simulacra of foreign metropolises.'[121]

The British reviewers were much more positive about the show. Robert Gore Langston for the *Daily Express* noted that 'it's as subtle as panto, but then so is Bollywood, which this show joyfully echoes. Great fun, great costumes, and a refreshing change from every other West End show'; and Georgina Brown for the *Mail on Sunday* added that 'it brings a new sound, new choreography, a whole new style and vibrancy with it'; while Michael Billington noted that 'the acting honours are stolen by such familiar British-Asian performers as Raad Rawi as the white-coated Mafia boss and Shelley King as an astringent gossip columnist'.[122] Altogether the show received a much more positive response – and my own memory of it is of a family-friendly, singing, dancing, colourful spectacle.

Academic responses to the show have questioned its ability to critique the position of British Asians, while focusing on whether the show represents a commodified cultural brand that is simply jumping on a new bandwagon to attract an audience and make money, and as such has become deracinated or white-washed.[123] Of course, a commercial product in London's West End that cost £4.5 million to mount must have confidence in its ability to attract more than the core musical theatre audience, but perhaps there is a misconception about Bollywood film at the root of this disquiet. Bollywood films are essentially melodramatic romances using character archetypes – heroes and villains like those recognized from Victorian melodrama, musical comedy and pantomime. The characters and stories promote traditional conservative family values and modes of behaviour even among modern Westernized young people like Akash and Priya, and to some extent they allow Asian audiences to see some of their own cultural practices, though, indeed, the stories fail to address contemporary British Asian issues. More importantly, though, in a musical or musical film, the characters use song and dance as metaphors for the excesses of emotion they portray, which allow for transformational and utopian moments of entertainment. This emotional content may be seen as excessive in British culture beyond musical theatre, which is perceived as feminized in comparison to the more masculine literary drama, and Bollywood could be argued to be excessive even in Asian culture. However, there are moments of irony, self-parody and kitsch in *Bombay Dreams* that are also present in recent Bollywood movies,[124] and there are opportunities for performers, characters and audiences to perceive a different cultural aesthetic being prioritized in this most public of places.

Where the musical is particularly successful is in the visibility it provides for Asian characters and Asian performers in a large commercial production in London's West End. *Bombay Dreams* offered audiences the opportunity to celebrate and enjoy a new hybrid cultural event that reveals something of the creative potential in a multicultural Britain. For the first time, British Asian performers, voices, music, characters and story were being presented on the commercial West End stage in a story and using an aesthetic with which the British Asian audience identified, rather than seeing British Asians as supplementary or stereotypical characters in a white/Western story or medium. It gave opportunities to British Asian performers, who have since achieved a greater presence in British and American theatre and television. Although it did not in any way represent contemporary British life, the creative teams attempted to create a genuinely hybrid product in which the music, the dance and the voices effected a transformation as exciting as the presence of these performers.

Multicultural music

In *Bombay Dreams* there are two main types of music. The songs that are sung diegetically, as Indian film clips in the show, are sung in Hindi and with an Asian vocal placement, and are familiar from their original performance in Bollywood films. They are effectively 'jukebox' moments embedded within the show and reference the practice in Bollywood films of employing star performers to sing backing tracks to which the visual stars lip-sync. These moments create an intertextual juxtaposition or parody, since the choreography, the singing style and, of course, the music and orchestration reference the source film live in a Western context. The slight alteration to the choreography and design that moves the song 'Chaiya Chaiya' from a single wide shot of dancers on the roof of a moving train crossing a ravine to a moving staircase (with a hand rail for reasons of health and safety) provides a parodic and reflexive moment of camp, and an affirmation of Bollywood as a mainstream cultural form in the West. These songs tend to have a more nasal vocal placement and a particular type of ornamentation that is culturally identifiable and references a classical tradition. In 'Chaiya Chaiya' the melodic pattern, rhythm, orchestration and atmosphere has an Indian feel, which is not surprising since it was written and orchestrated by an Indian composer and is written within his cultural language (which derives from a global amalgam of Western pop, American film and Western musical theatre, as well as classical Indian music). The significant differences from Western musical theatre are the lack of drum kit and its replacement by Asian percussion. There is a concentration on higher pitched and higher frequency sounds, rather than the regular bass beat of Western music, and the incorporation of sweeping strings and the mirroring of melodic lines in the accompaniment are features of much Asian vocal music.

By contrast 'The Journey Home', which is sung when the hero Akash, who has been on a 'rags-to-riches' journey, realizes that wealth and fame need to be balanced by remaining true to his home and background, is a non-diegetic song. It is acted in a Western 'realistic' style and produces a much more complicated hybrid sound incorporating a rounder (more Western) tone, a more breathy timbre, less ornamentation and more vibrato; the vocal set-up is generally closer to Western musical theatre. The melody and vocal tone is arguably the most Western musical theatre sound in the show, but the orchestration retains the sounds of Asian music. There is also the interjection of a cry from the Qawwali singer. Qawwali singers are traditional Sufi singers who perform at weddings to bring luck to the marriage, but they are so popular that they are also used at Hindu weddings. None of the singers in the show was able to reproduce this vocal sound, for which the best singers train from childhood. What 'The Journey Home' contains is the rising ornamentation more characteristic of Indian than Western music and, for those who recognized it, the presence of the Qawwali singer also symbolized the cultural background and the potential for future happiness. It could be argued that the vocal cry is purely atmospheric rather than significant, but the combination of vocal tone, technique, ornamentation with orchestral timbres demonstrates a musical interculturalism that contributes to the way the performance might be perceived as a genuine hybrid.

There is a slightly less obvious feature in 'How Many Stars' that contains an unusual (to Western ears) ornamentation on the word 'stars'. In musical theatre we have become accustomed to the ornamentation derived from American-influenced Blues and R'n'B, so these small vocal features locate the work, and give it atmosphere, but also derive from the composer's and performers' shared histories.

Influences and impact

Bombay Dreams is an interesting intercultural collaboration that draws on diverse influences, incorporates the performance of hybrid voices, and speaks directly to a particular diasporic community whose voices and musical references incorporate this range of musical genres. The music feeds atmospherically into the escapist Bollywood narrative, but simultaneously suggests the hybrid influences of Bollywood itself and speaks to the diverse British Asian communities, thus empowering a contemporary British identity within a narrative of utopian escapism. Far from being deracinated, the music explores the diverse voices and sounds of a British Asian diasporic community in the heart of the British equivalent of the 'great white way'. And what happened to *Bombay Dreams* bears this out – it had a successful two years in London but didn't play well in New York. This hybrid interplay of British and South Asian voices and music has a very clear and specific local audience rather than a global audience.[125]

Whatever we might feel about intercultural practice and hybridity in musical theatre performance, music is a globalized phenomenon, and from cassette recorders to the internet, technology has made music much more accessible across most of the world. Rahman, himself, was somebody with diverse influences and a broad international career. What the globalization of the music industry has done is to increase the influences on any composer or form and to create a multiplicity of hybrid forms that can communicate to some extent to diverse groups of people, but the specificity is also apparent in music's timbres and voices. While the stories and characters can be perceived to have universal resonances, the music and the voices locate the work in a very particular locality.

British musical and vocal identities are complex and diverse, and the performance of voices and music can add complexity to the narratives they accompany. Such intercultural performances may 'gradually lead to the creation of a world culture in which different cultures not only take part, but also respect the unique characteristics of each culture and allow each culture its authority'.[126] So do the hybrid voices of Indian composer Rahman and the performers of *Bombay Dreams* avoid the charge of cultural imperialism? I would suggest that this performance is, in fact, representative of a changing cultural environment in which respect for difference has stimulated a diverse, original and spectacular performance that occupies the borderlands between a universal story and locally specific hybrid cultural practices. Certainly I found the performance provocative on an intellectual and an emotional level, raising questions about British voices and identities: who's speaking, and to whom?

2.3 CHANGING SIGNIFICATION IN POPULAR MUSIC

Alongside the increasingly diverse music of community, regional, subsidized and fringe productions, the West End continued largely as a Western musical environment, but gradually its musical styles have changed to reflect developments in popular music. First, jazz, blues and ragtime arrived from America, and then in the 1950s rock and roll with its drum kits, guitars and amplification provided a new sound to represent youth and modernity. As each new musical style – rock, soul, punk, hip hop, bhangra, and so on – appeared, a new group of young people or a new community identified with that musical genre and its characteristics. Each new phase represents the rebellion of a new generation and signifies within the codes of that generation or cohort of people, and so is interpreted differently by those who were young when it appeared and those for whom it was a challenge. Thus there is a cycle within which certain genres appeal to the mainstream as others decline and still others are being developed, and in this way signification and the way meaning is created constantly shifts in time and as it is received by its listeners.[127] A rock riff means something different now that it is familiar – and even somewhat nostalgic – than it did in the 1960s when it was new, urgent, noisy and rebellious. It also means something different to those born in the 1950s, to whom it was fresh and exciting, and those born in the 1980s, for example. The use of musical genres allows composers to create a sound world that has cultural significance and so produces an easy understanding of time, location, character and dramatic style, but that understanding is dependent on cultural context, and using the latest fashion has a narrow audience. Hence, mainstream musical theatre has tended to incorporate new musical genres only as their signification can be understood by its large audiences; often somewhat belatedly.

The vocal inflections of jazz and crooning relied on one of the most important developments in popular music during the first half of the twentieth century – the invention of microphone and amplification technology – innovations that influenced a whole range of new styles of singing, new musical instruments and new forms of musical expression. Innovative genres developed as a result of the new technology such as rock and roll, soul and, much later, rap, and featured in musicals initially aimed at and featuring a younger generation, such as *Expresso Bongo* (David Heneker and Monty Norman, 1958), *Jesus Christ Superstar* (Tim Rice and Andrew Lloyd Webber, 1970), *Blood Brothers* (Russell, 1983), *The Commitments* (Doyle and various, 2013), and *Into the Hoods* (Prince and various, 2006), as well as a host of jukebox musicals. Some of these musicals contained narratives of dispossessed youth expressing themselves through their music, thus making connections between the continuous development of pop music and the expression of adolescent disaffection.

The majority of musicals rely on widespread understanding of popular music genres. This can be seen in musicals as diverse as *Betty Blue Eyes*, *Billy Elliot*, *Matilda* and *Made in Dagenham*, which are comic or dramatic, presented in realistic, melodramatic or symbolic styles. The important feature that they share is that they tell stories as linear narratives, and they speak most clearly to audiences from the same or similar cultural backgrounds, who share the same popular musical references. So, for example, the story of *Billy Elliot* and the emotional atmosphere created around the line of policemen in riot gear is likely to be different for people who lived through the miners' strike of 1984–5 and especially those from mining communities affected by the strikes than for those for whom those events are a distant memory or the stuff of history. Nonetheless, the music Elton John wrote in the early 2000s derives from what was by then a widely understood pop music aesthetic in songs like 'Born to Boogie', whose refrain and verse are each 12-bar-blues sequences. The verse has a walking bass accompaniment, and the refrain a boogie-woogie style piano 'left hand', which derives from an African American tradition that has come to characterize joyfulness or happiness, upbeat emotions within working-class cultures, and which is recognizable through the imperialism of white US pop culture. 'Merry Christmas Maggie Thatcher' derives from a much harder-hitting punk aesthetic with its solid four heavy beats in the bar, and the high, almost-shouted melodic line, which follows the same rhythmic structure as the bass and represents protest and disaffection.

However, long before *Billy Elliot* (which is commented on much more fully in Case Study 3) arrived in London, *Jesus Christ Superstar* marked what seemed to be a sudden and dramatic shift in the musical style and content of musical theatre, though it simply reflected changes that had been occurring gradually in popular music over the previous decade and a half. For most of the 1960s, the music of musical theatre had remained nostalgic, drawing on stereotypes that had become safe and easily recognizable. As contexts changed, the musical signifiers changed, but always with a significant delay reflecting musical theatre's nostalgia as well as its reliance on the understanding of and appeal to a wide mainstream audience. Even though jazz and ragtime harmonies, rhythm and style had influenced British composers like Noel Coward and Noel Gay in the 1930s, and had subsequently become pervasive, more-recent American imports in popular music, such as rock and roll, were less easily assimilated into musical theatre. An example of a nostalgic story and the use of locally recognized musical and theatrical signifiers is *Oliver!* (1960) by Lionel Bart, which will be discussed in a case study below. However, there were exceptions as popular music fed into musical theatre especially in fringe and regional theatres.

In the late 1950s rock and roll became hugely popular, using electric guitars, drum kits and amplified voices, and it was probably David Heneker who first incorporated these influences into a British West End musical in *Expresso Bongo* (David Heneker and Monty Norman, 1958). *Expresso Bongo*, which was introduced in Part One, presented a rather more cynical or 'realistic' narrative than was common in musical theatre. It satirized the music industry in a tale of a predatory agent and an older actress, both of whom prey on the somewhat limited talents of the young pop star, singer and bongo player Bongo Herbert. The actress wants to revive her career by association with the young star, while the agent wants to make money. The singer and bongo player is, of course, in a band playing the popular rock and roll music, supported by groups of Teddy Boys. This music, which was played by an onstage diegetic band, was widely popular among young people as an expression of their difference from their parents' generation.

A number of other shows of the 1960s contained songs that were successful in the pop charts, including Leslie Bricusse and Anthony Newley's *Stop the World – I Want to Get Off* (1961), whose 'What Kind of Fool Am I'[128] was widely covered by other recording artists in the UK and United States. But musical theatre didn't really reflect the fact that the Beatles and the Rolling Stones were changing British popular music until Andrew Lloyd Webber and Tim Rice burst on to the scene.

The second performance of *Joseph and the Amazing Technicolor Dreamcoat*, which took place at the Methodist Central Hall, Westminster, in May 1968, had the accompaniment augmented by the rock band The Mixed Bag, and caught the attention not of a theatre critic, but of a pop critic.[129] The music was recorded by Decca and only later extended as a theatre production. Rice and Lloyd Webber were young men who were writing music and lyrics that felt fresh and exciting and that reflected what was current in pop music, as pastiches or stylistic copies. Most notable is the Elvis pastiche 'The Song of the King', sung by the Pharaoh, which, according to John Snelson, combines 'the opening of the refrain of Presley's "All Shook Up" . . . with the middle-eight of "Don't Be Cruel" or "Teddy Bear", but the I-IV-V chord patterns derived from the twelve-bar blues'.[130] Other songs that stand out as popular pastiches in the later West End version are the country rock of 'One More Angel in Heaven', the pop ballad and 12/8 rhythm of 'Joseph's Dreams', and the calypso of 'Benjamin Calypso', while right from the start the score contained the energetic electric guitar and vocal harmony of 'Go, Go, Go Joseph'.

As pop music has changed over the period of *Joseph*'s popularity, accompaniments, instrumentations and rhythms have been adapted and the show reinvented for each new generation.[131] Snelson uses the example of 'Go, Go, Go Joseph' to illustrate the changes that occurred as the song moved from the all-male pop group sound of 1969 to the faster rhythm-and-blues-influenced version of 1973, the addition of funkier overtones in 1974 and the introduction of gospel, funk-gospel and disco by the time of the 1991 version.[132] The musical, and especially the music, has continued to speak to audiences in contemporary popular languages. The constructions of pop music, with short melodies, simple melodic and harmonic direction, repetitive rhythms, and association with memorable lyrics, demonstrate the relationship of this work with contemporary pop music,[133] but until this point and with the exception of the American *Hair* (Galt McDermot, Jerome Ragni and James Rado, 1967) pop and rock music had not really been seen as appropriate for musical theatre. Musical theatre, which appeared to be moving in the direction of increasing 'integration', seemed to require something very different from the repeated verses and choruses of pop and rock music.[134]

While *Joseph* had begun life as a pop cantata using the language of pop and rock and roll, *Jesus Christ Superstar* was influenced by the heavier rock of bands such as Led Zeppelin, Deep Purple, the Who[135] and the Rolling Stones. These bands were incorporating amplified and distorted guitar sounds and increasingly complex and strident solos, over heavy drum rhythms in extended works. 'Heaven on Their Minds', 'Damned for all Time' and the scene in the Temple all contain hard rock riffs, and the tonic/subdominant relationship that features in blues and rock music is heard throughout this score.[136] Another feature of rock is the descending bass line, which can be heard in parts of 'Gethsemane' (the section beginning 'But if I die'). The vocal style is also influenced by rock music, in which the female voices tend to be pitched lower in a chest voice; consider, for example, the vocal range of Mary Magdalene in 'I Don't Know How to Love Him' as an example of this change. The tenor range is extended upwards to falsetto, and both male and female voices employ ornamentation to develop and express their emotional interpretations.[137] The male voice in particular can be extended into shouting and even screaming (think of Freddie Mercury's vocal range), as can be heard in the later DVD of *Jesus Christ Superstar* in which Jesus is played by Glenn Carter.[138] The orchestration, too, demonstrated inventive ways to integrate orchestral instruments with an electronic rock group or to contrast their sound worlds.[139] Clearly there is a musical and vocal language at work here that is completely at home within its contemporary context, and which interprets Jesus and Judas as countercultural figures promoting an alternative morality and politics – a representation signified by the urban rebellion of rock music at the time. The signification of rock music will be further expanded on in the case study of *The Rocky Horror Show* below, while *Jesus Christ Superstar* will also be the subject of Case Study 9.

Lloyd Webber's early works were significant for the way they used genre pastiche to signify character using a combination of genre signification and motivic association. As John Snelson argues, pastiche was an important part of Lloyd Webber's earlier works, including *Jesus Christ Superstar, Evita, Cats, Joseph and the Amazing Technicolor Dreamcoat* and *Starlight Express*.[140] The musical origins and the generic associations and signification must be obvious to the listener for pastiche to work, and a pastiche based on American-influenced popular music proved to be widely understood, entertaining and appealing. Ben Macpherson has identified a dramaturgy in *Cats* that arises from the juxtaposition of musical pastiches such that, for example, the character of Rum Tum Tugger, whose song relies on a musical reference to Elvis and Mick Jagger, signifies rebellion against social order, freedom, fun and sexuality, which thus suggests a character type that is mischievous, disruptive and anti-establishment.[141]

Lloyd Webber's later works are increasingly nostalgic, using novels or films as the source and music that increasingly alludes to familiar signifiers from the classical and operatic traditions as well as popular culture, rather than using pastiche. Allusion stimulates cross-reference that provides a background of connections in a similar way to pastiche, but is a less specific reference, less cartoon-like or stereotypical, and it relies less on audiences recognizing the source. Allusion may result from melodic style, rhythm, harmony, orchestration or texture, all of which create a connection between the new work and the material to which it alludes, creating a sense of familiarity and a level of signification through which audiences perceive meaning. Such intertextuality, and the classical sources from which they are drawn, make the work widely accessible in a global commercial market. In Lloyd Webber's later works this type of practice is more apparent than pastiche: works such as *The Phantom of the Opera* (Hart, Stilgoe and Lloyd Webber, 1986), *Aspects of Love* (Black, Hart and Lloyd Webber, 1989) and *Sunset Boulevard* (Black, Hampton and Lloyd Webber, 1993). As Snelson concludes, 'Throughout his output, Lloyd Webber's references to a variety of musical genres, styles, and even specific works have been used as a method of allowing the audience to relate to what is heard by providing a sense of the familiar that can then be shaped in unexpected ways.'[142]

However, back in the 1970s, other shows that were experimenting with electric-guitar-based pop and rock include *The Rocky Horror Show*, which opened in June 1973 at the small Theatre Upstairs above the experimental Royal Court Theatre. It won the *Evening Standard* Award for best musical that year. It is the subject of a case study below, so suffice it to say here that it incorporated a glam rock aesthetic that was at odds with the hard rock of *Superstar*, almost simultaneously reflecting a different aspect of the contemporary popular music scene. Also in 1973 the English characters in *The Cheviot, The Stag, and the Black, Black Oil* drew on the musical genres popularized in music hall and Gilbert and Sullivan operas. Importantly the Gilbert and Sullivan operas were intended to satirize the conventions of late nineteenth-century British society, but by this time had come to represent a particularly mannered and stereotypical upper-class Englishness. So, in a style reminiscent of English folk song, at the pitch and pace of speech, and in a jaunty 6/8 rhythm, English lawyers sang that they would 'teach you the secrets of high industry' and that 'the price of a culture is counted in gold'.[143] In this context the musical style is English (regarded as alien by the Scottish village communities for whom it was performed), and the words were foregrounded by the pitch and style so that the politicized lyrics could be understood as deriving from stereotypical villainous characters.

What began to happen from the late 1960s, perhaps influenced by the ubiquity of radio and television, was that an increasingly diverse selection of musical genres could signify to audiences at any one time, and musical theatre began to reflect this variety. From this point on, and including the Asian- and black-influenced musical theatre performances that were introduced in the last section, musical theatre continued to reflect popular culture and to seek new audiences, especially outside the West End of London.

Caribbean music influenced one of the only black shows that made it into the West End in the 1970s. *The Black Mikado* (1975) adapted Gilbert and Sullivan's libretto and score and set the action on a Caribbean island. The music was rearranged into rock, reggae, blues and calypso by Janos Bajtala, George Larnyoh and Eddie Quansah and was performed by an almost entirely black cast. As John Bush Jones remarks, only Pooh-Bah was played by a white performer giving the impression of a 'lone scheming westerner "condescending" to serve an emerging black nationalist country for his own grafting purposes'.[144] This contrasts with the 'sexy, exuberant Caribbean islanders', who are portrayed in a much more exciting, contemporary and popular musical language.[145]

Soul appeared much more recently in the West End when the film *The Commitments* was adapted for the stage (Doyle and Various, 2013), while hip hop and street dance were introduced in *Into the Hoods*, a dance musical commissioned by Sadler's Wells, created by ZooNation Dance Company in 2006 and performed at the Peacock Theatre before being extended for runs at the Edinburgh Festival (2007) and the West End in 2008. *Into the Hoods* alludes to the story of Stephen Sondheim's *Into the Woods* and features street dance performed to music by artists such as Kanye West, Massive Attack and Black Eyed Peas. This success has been followed by *Some Like it Hip Hop* (2012), *Groove on Down the Road: A Journey to Oz* (2014) and *The Mad Hatter's Tea Party* (2014) – all created and choreographed by Kate Prince for ZooNation, and all containing some original music and lyrics. What these shows demonstrate is that, despite the variety of music around the country and the vibrancy of the pop music scene, the pace of musical change in musical theatre is slow. Nonetheless, there is a continual broadening of the variety of music that can be relied on to signify character and create meaning within the commercial mainstream of musical theatre.

Outside London, popular music had been used widely to speak to local people and especially young people. In the early 1980s, folk and blues were the musical genres Willy Russell employed to write a 70-minute youth theatre project for Merseyside Young People's Theatre Company, with a cast of five performers and one song 'Marilyn Monroe'. The piece was then

Figure 9 The vibrancy and acrobatics of hip hop speak to a younger generation – Andry Oporia dancing in *Into the Hoods* by ZooNation at the Novello Theatre 2006. Photograph by Francis Loney. Courtesy of ArenaPAL.

extended into a full-length show, *Blood Brothers*, which opened at Liverpool Playhouse in 1983.[146] Case Study 2 expands on the story.

Russell was already well established as a playwright and had already written a musical that incorporated popular music in the form of a jukebox musical that used existing pop songs to tell a new story. *John, Paul, George, Ringo . . . & Bert* (1974) featured a number of songs by the Beatles, but unusually they were not played by the band – nor did the actors who played the Beatles sing them; Barbara Dickson, a folk singer, sat at the piano and sang the songs, thus placing them in a new context.[147] The show is set at a Wings concert that Bert is attending. He is a fan and someone who had played with the Quarry Men before they became the Beatles. The plot then becomes something of a fantasy as Bert recounts the history of the Beatles to a youngster who really just wants to go and see a punk rock band. As Bert recounts the story it is re-enacted with songs interpolated as they fit the plot rather than in chronological order. The story traces the rise and fall of the band, while also commenting on the changing society in which they lived. As Herbert Kretzmer remarked in his review of the London show, 'It depicts without sham, for example, the mounting dislike and eventual feud between the irascible, aggressive Lennon and the quick, compromising Paul McCartney.'[148]

Much more significant than the use of contemporary pop songs to speak to the Liverpool youth – from where the Beatles had emerged a decade earlier – was the presentation of those songs using a female voice, thus distancing the songs and lyrics from any mimetic sense of impersonation, and re-articulating them so that the songs are heard anew in their new contexts. This was to be a feature of some of the later 'jukebox' musicals, especially *Mamma Mia!* (Catherine Johnson, Benny Andersson and Björn Ulvaeus, 1999), which will be considered further in Case Study 12.

Still outside London this format began to be used more widely and a greater range of musical genres and contexts was employed. At The Everyman Theatre in Liverpool in the 1980s, a series of musicals sought to represent and entertain the local community, and to do it using contemporary popular music. In some of these musicals, actor musicians were employed to act as well as sing and play the music. Among these shows was an annual rock and roll pantomime each Christmas whose director, Peter Rowe, continued the practice when he moved to Theatr Clwyd, and then to The Wolsey Theatre, Ipswich. *Return to the Forbidden Planet*[149] is an example of an actor musician jukebox musical by Bob Carlton that began life in a London community venue, the Theatre Bubble. It toured and played in the regions before finally arriving in the West End in 1989. Bob Carlton and Peter Rowe[150] have continued to experiment with jukebox musicals and actor musicianship throughout their careers in regional theatres. In addition, and as seen above, in recent years a number of musicals and pantomimes incorporated black and Asian music, especially at the Theatre Royal, Stratford East, Watford Palace Theatre and Hackney Empire in Greater London.

One example is *Five Guys Named Moe* (Clarke Peters and Louis Jordan, 1990), which began life at Stratford East before transferring into the West End and to Broadway. It used the music and lyrics of 1940s jazz and blues saxophonist Louis Jordan to tell the story of Nomax. Nomax has split up with his girlfriend and is feeling sorry for himself, but five guys named Moe appear out of the radio – No Moe, Little Moe, Four-Eyed Moe, Big Moe and Eat Moe. They help Nomax get his life back on track, teaching him that he needs to change himself if he wants to have a successful relationship. The show includes opportunities for audience participation and a show within a show by the five guys before the Moes disappear and a wiser, more sober Nomax leaves to meet his girl. All these jukebox, actor musician and popular music shows demonstrate the vibrancy of the subsidized sector at this time, whose successes generated income from West End runs that fed back into their local theatres. This perhaps enabled a greater level of experimentation in musical genre than was possible in the commercial West End, not for its own sake, but to speak in the musical languages of its local communities.

Meanwhile in London's West End the biographical musical *Buddy – The Buddy Holly Story* (Alan Janes, Buddy Holly, Laurie Mansfield, Paul Jury, 1989) incorporated the songs of Buddy Holly, Chuck Berry, Ritchie Valens and others, with additional new songs written by musical director Paul Jury, to tell the story of Buddy Holly's life chronologically. The show was a long-running success and spawned many other biographical and jukebox musicals building on back catalogues of pop music composers. One example of the many shows in this category is *Jolson* (1995), a show by Francis Essex and Rob Bettinson, which tells the story of Al Jolson, accompanied by a score of songs from the glory days of Tin Pan Alley.[151] Another example is *Our House* (2002),[152] which has a book by Tim Firth and songs by Madness. It tells two parallel stories in which a young boy who commits a petty crime chooses either to run from the police or to stay and face the music. The show follows both courses to see how his life would continue. *Taboo*, which also opened in London in 2002, was written by Mark Davies Markham with lyrics by Boy George (George O'Dowd) and music by George, John Themis, Richie Stevens and Kevan Frost. It is partly biographical about Boy George's rise to fame, but, although George did know the central characters,[153] there is some artistic licence in the time frames and relationships, and a number of new or composite characters appear in the musical. It is the closest, in this category of musicals, to an autobiographical musical. Another jukebox musical returns us to some of the features of pantomime. In *We Will Rock You* (Elton and Queen, 2002)[154] the music of Queen is used to tell the story of a dystopian future in which there is no music. The character names are contemporary pop star names, though applied across genders, and there are frequent references to pop lyrics throughout the script.[155] The show is littered with reflexivity and references to contemporary popular culture. Here, as in the pantomimes discussed at the beginning of this part, is the nostalgic combination of a score of popular music alongside contemporary topical reference that is constantly updated to retain its currency.

Whether the music of British musical theatre uses pastiche, allusion, or is a compilation of extant music, it refers to the popular musical history of these islands. Because of that geographical specificity the web of signifiers it draws on is local, and in the course of this chapter we have seen a greater diversity of music and musical theatre outside the West End than in it, speaking to local and regional communities. Through its signification music locates shows geographically, historically and culturally, but in order to do so, the musical genres must have achieved sufficient currency to be understood by its diverse audiences, and account must be taken of the ways in which the reception of musical genres changes over time. This will be discussed further in the case studies of *Oliver!* and *The Rocky Horror Show* below. What this section has demonstrated is the diversity of musical genres in use in contemporary British musical theatre, and the variety of ways in which that music is used to create meaning, to attract audiences and to entertain.

Case Study 7: *Oliver!*

History and development

Lionel Bart,[156] composer, lyricist and book-writer of *Oliver!*, began his theatre career at Unity,[157] where he began writing songs and sketches with Jack Grossman.[158] The first complete show Bart and Grossman wrote was the Christmas show *Cinderella* (1953). The songs for this show included 'Be a Man, John Bull, Be a Man', which was recycled as 'Be Back Soon' in *Oliver!*, and Bart also performed as an Ugly Sister in this show. Bart continued to write songs and work with Unity, and it was there he learned about stagecraft and dramaturgy. Meanwhile he began writing rock and roll songs, influenced by the music arriving from America. The first song he sold was 'Oh For A Cup Of Tea', for which he was paid 25 guineas. He formed a short-lived band with Tommy Steele[159] and Mike Pratt, with whom he wrote 'Rock With The Cavemen'. In both 'Rock With The Cavemen' and 'Oh For A Cup Of Tea', the most important feature is Bart's ability to write witty lyrics with internal rhymes, colloquial language and topical references. In 'Oh For A Cup Of Tea' Bart bemoans the fact that 'The whole place has gorn Italian' 'I've tramped all round London Town / Without any dillyin' or dallyin'',[160] while in 'Rock With The Cavemen' he comments on the cavemen's tendency to club a girl 'right off her feet' and then in a reflexive reference continues 'You know the lyric writers never lied / 'Swhere they got the saying "starry-eyed"'. The trio continued writing rock and roll songs, and for the film *The Tommy Steele Story* Bart and Pratt wrote twelve songs. By now (1957) Bart was a successful songwriter, but he was still interested in the theatre, and so for Unity Theatre he wrote his first complete musical, *Wally Pone, King of the Underworld* (1958), an adaptation of *Volpone*.[161] Colin Chambers describes the show, which Bart had set in the contemporary Soho world of coffee bars and 'vice barons', as 'provocative and original', but audiences and reviewers were not impressed.[162]

Meanwhile Bart was working on some songs for a show, originally called *Petticoat Lane* but which were later transported into an adaptation of Charles Dickens' novel *Oliver Twist,* in which he tried to interest various managements. Through this process he met Oscar Lewenstein (of the Royal Court), who introduced him to Gerry Raffles and Joan Littlewood, who were then running the Theatre Royal at Stratford East. At the Theatre Workshop Bart began work writing songs for a play by Frank Norman called *Fings Ain't Wot They Used T'Be.* In Littlewood's usual fashion the original conception of the play was 'developed' during the company research. Improvisations and more and more songs were added in what appears to have been an exceptionally creative process for actors and writers, and the show was a huge success. There were three productions at Stratford in 1959, and then it transferred to the Garrick Theatre in the West End in 1960.[163] In the meantime Bart had written a number of other pop songs including 'Living Doll' for Cliff Richard and lyrics for the musical *Lock Up Your Daughters* (1959)[164] in collaboration with Bernard Miles (book), Laurie Johnson (music), Peter Coe (director) and Sean Kenny (designer). It opened at the Mermaid theatre in 1959, and in 1962 was restaged at the Mermaid before transferring to Her Majesty's Theatre.[165]

Bart was, by now, hugely successful both in theatre and pop music; he had learnt his trade in theatre through his work at Unity, Theatre Workshop and the Mermaid, and he had a group of collaborators in director Peter Coe and designer Sean Kenny, with whom he moved on to develop *Oliver!* After twelve rejections by London managements, Donald Albery agreed to produce the show, providing he could cut the costs to just £15,000 or less.[166] Rehearsals began in early May, but because of the scale and complexity of the design by Kenny, moved to the Prince's Theatre (now the Shaftesbury) where a mock-up of the set was available. The show opened for a two-week try-out on 10 June 1960 at the Wimbledon Theatre. The sets were so large that an out-of-town tour was not deemed possible. Instead, at the end of the two weeks in Wimbledon, the show went straight into the New Theatre (now the Noel Coward Theatre) on 30 June 1960. The show ran for six years (or 2,618 performances in London and 774 on Broadway), holding the long-run record for a musical in London (until overtaken by *Jesus Christ Superstar*) and the record for the longest-running import to Broadway (until overtaken by *Evita*).[167]

Production and design

Sean Kenny's set, which consisted of multi-level scaffolding built on a revolve with two rotating side pieces, was hugely important because it gave the production a fluidity that allowed scenes to 'tumble onwards'[168] as characters moved from one scene to the next turning up in different places; Fagin's hideout, the funeral parlour, the misty streets of London's East End or the bedroom at Mr Brownlow's. Kenny had been influenced by the Berliner Ensemble designs of Karl von Appen, and blacks and greys dominated his sets and costumes; his designs had abandoned the pictorial approach of painted cloths and flats in favour of stylized and symbolic structures. Apart from the moving structures, Kenny added three symbols to each scene to depict a specific place. Examples include a shopkeeper's counter, an undertaker's shop sign, and coffins that flew in from above for the Undertaker's shop, and for the tavern scene a table, a large oil lamp and a lot of smoke. This influenced the dramaturgy of the work; locales shifted frequently and fluidly through the use of the revolving stage and Kenny's innovative set design, making it possible for a long novel to be reduced to less than three hours of stage time.

Ethan Mordden remarked of the later Broadway production that *Oliver!* 'was like a children's show put on by radical experimentalists. It was Piscator's idea of a musical, Artaud's.'[169] Milton Shulman in *The Evening Standard* attributes much of the triumph of *Oliver!* to the 'ingenious timbered sets of Sean Kenny which were manipulated like some gigantic jig-saw puzzle and could wondrously conjure up for us the cavernous depths of the workhouse, the rollicking gaiety of a Cockney dive, the claustrophobia of Fagin's den and the eerie loneliness of London Bridge at night.'[170] *The Independent London News* reported that the set was 'at once multiple and divisible, that manages, in its complicated timbering, to suggest both the lost recesses of the thieves kitchen and the high-flung, gas-lit London Bridge of the ultimate (and very sudden) naphtha-flare of melodrama.'[171] The reviewer for the *Observer* noted that Kenny's 'spare, eloquent, workable settings have the advantage of the architect's comprehensive eye'.[172]

But the scenery, however important and influential in the development of set design,[173] cannot succeed alone. Lionel Bart adapted the book from Dickens' novel or, perhaps more likely, the David Lean film,[174] and wrote the music and lyrics.[175] The novel was already well known, perhaps more so because of the David Lean film, and so the show, like many musicals adapted from films today, had an immediate appeal to a nostalgic audience who already knew the story. The story, though, has a political edge and reflects a left-wing social conscience in its awareness of the inequities of wealth and poverty, its focus on the most vulnerable in society (orphaned children) before the introduction of the welfare state, and its foregrounding of working-class or underclass lives. To some extent, though, the politics is undermined by the presence of a troupe of singing and dancing children, the challenge to Dickens' anti-semitism in the character and actions of Fagin found in the novel,[176] and the happy ending in which Oliver is restored to his family. As the reviewer in the *Tatler* noted, 'Some of Dickens's most sinister creations lose much of their menace when set to Lionel Bart's music.'[177] On the other hand, perhaps Bart had learned from the critical reaction to *Wally Pone* in making the show much more direct and appealing so that its messages were much more widely disseminated.

Characters were suggested in action, dialogue and music reducing the need for novelistic description. Scene changes were integrated into the action allowing greater tension and momentum to build. Although many details in the novel were cut, and a particular focus established, the musical version managed to contain the main elements of the plot, including drama, comedy, a flavour of London and of the period through clear musical and lyrical articulation of character and a strong sense of the social inequities that drove Dickens' politics and later inspired Bart in his adaptation of this work. Although it followed *Expresso Bongo*, *Fings*, *Make Me an Offer*, and some of the other experimental musical plays mentioned in Part One above, it remains a radical step forward in the development of British musical theatre, perhaps partly as a result of its enormous popularity: it was not only innovative but successful and therefore noticeable enough to be influential.

Musical dramaturgy

Bart used musical genres and motifs to define characters and to illustrate, as he put it, 'people's walks'.[178] The *Oliver!* theme was a reflection of the Beadle's walk, while Fagin's music was described by Bart as 'like a Jewish mother-hen clucking away'.[179] Aside from illustrating walks, the music and lyrics do much more than provide tunes to hum on the way home.[180] Nancy is introduced in the rather ironic song 'It's a Fine Life', whose sentiments are epitomized by the opening words of the chorus 'If you don't mind having to go without things, / It's a fine life!'[181] The music is an upbeat music hall song that the boys join in, singing 'It's a fine life!' in a rousing repetition, but the reality of Nancy's life is revealed as she sings of the upper-class ladies who with their 'Fine airs and fine graces / Don't have to sin to eat'.[182] Already one can perceive the paradoxical layering of a bleak reality in the words with a superficially upbeat and singable tune whose musical 'hook' and atmosphere belies the content of the song. This gives the actress a real complexity of character to explore.

The same paradox is evident in the waltzing singalong in a music hall style that is 'Oom-Pah-Pah'. Each verse tells a story of drunkenness, debauchery or prostitution, concluding with the tale of 'Pretty little Sally' who allowed men to 'see her garters, / But not for free and gratis'.[183] Naively she 'let a feller feed 'er, then lead 'er along'. Nancy concludes her tale of Sally, singing 'She is no longer the same blushing rose. / Ever since Oom-pah-pah!'[184] Nancy might equally have been referring to herself, demonstrating character not only in music and lyrics but also through the raucous delivery of this song.

The vocal aesthetic and vocal ranges of characters in the show might be regarded as democratic, drawn from music hall and pub singalongs in contrast with, for example, the operatic ranges required in *West Side Story*, or the light operetta vocal style of *Salad Days*. Song delivery used the raucous vocal character of popular variety and music hall, and even in ballads the musical range often focused around the pitch of speech rising to belted notes at the end, as can be heard in 'As Long As He Needs Me'. Although written at the pitch of speech, this song is not in any way ordinary, as it requires technique to deliver the belted notes at the climax of this song night after night, and it is constructed beautifully using the tools of popular songwriting.

Georgia Brown, in the original cast recording, achieves a deep husky and emotional quality throughout, helped by the low vocal range.[185] The words of the opening line 'he needs me' are sustained on low A3s, while the lowest note in the song is a passing F3. The first climax is in the middle bridge section on the words 'I'll play this game his way', which rises to a sustained A4 and leads into the second chorus. After the second chorus there is a key change to A-flat triggered by the words 'when someone needs you / You love them so'. This is the perfect key change to raise an audience to its feet; the note G4 is sustained as the orchestra swells into the new key and the voice resolves into the new key of A-flat for the start of the new phrase. This leads into the big finish 'I've got to stay true just / As long as he needs me' whose highest belted note is C5 on the word 'needs'. Bart is using all the tricks of popular songwriting here with a vocal range that allows an emotional sob and husky quality in the voice, belting for climactic notes, and the key change to raise hairs on the back of the neck just before the end of the song, as well as repeated notes, lyrics and choruses to enhance recognition. 'I'd Do Anything' is very different as it sends up the politeness of the gentry in a gavotte – a musical form and performance designed to pastiche the archaic manners the boys and Nancy see being demonstrated by the upper classes. These two songs give audiences the opportunity to understand complex nuances in the character and so empathize with Nancy.

Fagin isn't a good character, but his situation is presented in a nuanced and complex way in the musical through the three songs he sings (two with the boys), while his Jewishness is revealed only through musical motifs, keys and ornaments. In his first song, 'Pick a Pocket or Two', Fagin and the boys perform a comic demonstration of the tools of a trade that will allow Oliver to earn bed and board with the gang.[186] The minor key (F minor), the strong emphasis on the opening beat of the bar (e.g., 'In this life' – which could be compared with 'If I were a rich man' from *Fiddler on the Roof* (Jerry Bock and Sheldon Harnick, 1964)), the chromaticism of the title phrase ('you've got to pick a pocket or two') are all reminiscent of Jewish traditional music, as is the opportunity for a little cadenza by Fagin on the word 'boys', just before the final line of the song. Fagin's second song, also with the boys, is 'Be Back Soon'. This is a much more cheery song with open diatonic harmonies and a marching-pipe-band sound as the boys leave for work, almost turning Fagin into a pied piper or community band leader. Both of these give Fagin opportunities for comedy, and are upbeat and attractive, allowing audiences to be engaged by and with him and his paternalism.

Fagin's final song, his soliloquy 'Reviewing the Situation', is not at all paternal and is the most overtly Jewish in style. It is in F-minor again, but more importantly it goes 'from free tempo to a slow *boom-chick* that accelerates in typical Klezmer fashion'.[187] Klezmer is used at weddings throughout the diasporic community and is the clearest signifier of Fagin's ethnic background in the show. This is particularly interesting as the pace changes are used here to represent Fagin's indecision rather than for choreography – mental rather than physical action. Each acceleration occurs as he gets carried away with a fantasy building to a climax that he suddenly realizes is impossible for him, and he backtracks in the descending phrase 'I think I'd better think it out again.'[188] In a sense this extends Bart's own observation that he created music based on the way people walk and applied it to the way they think – this scene of indecision sees Fagin thinking slowly, developing an idea and then getting carried away. In parallel the music speeds up before the pause and descent/decline of the final phrase.

The company songs have a simple and direct quality at the pitch and pace of speech and tend to be predominantly in unison apart from the ensemble street scene 'Who Will Buy' whose street criers provide almost the only polyphonic singing in the show. The other example is the double chorus of Fagin and the boys in 'Be Back Soon'. The predominance of direct address in unison with repeated choruses means that melody and words are clear and easily remembered; a style that draws on the characteristics of audience participation songs in variety and music hall.

Impact and influence

Milton Shulman's review in the *Evening Standard* described Bart's music as 'a zestful, unabashed blending of Tin Pan Alley, Yiddish folk melodies and the rhythms of the Old Kent Road. They not only button hole you; they practically slug you', adding, with remarkable prescience, that the show could 'stimulate an avalanche of Dickens musicals', which, as noted in Part One above, it did. The *Independent London News* summed it up as a 'grand theatrical business, and one that arrives at an hour when the British "musical" needed something as downright and as likeable'.[189] In this show Bart used musical genres and styles derived from popular culture in ways that illustrate and signify character and action, opening the way for later developments in musical dramatization and pastiche. The show itself is built on a nostalgic adaptation of a well-known story told from a working-class perspective using the musical language of popular culture, while incorporating the scenic and working-class aesthetics of contemporary European theatre. It transformed the potential of British musical theatre both as a commercial vehicle and an aesthetic form, and influenced a generation of theatre makers.

Case Study 8: *The Rocky Horror Show*

History and development

In 1968 the Theatres Act removed the power of the Lord Chamberlain to censor plays, and almost immediately (27 September 1968) the American musical *Hair* opened at the Shaftesbury Theatre in London's West End. *Hair* had been developed at the Public Theatre in New York through a devising process, and it portrayed a contemporary American world of hippies in a story about the Vietnam War draft. More importantly the score was contemporary and featured a series of pop/rock songs, several of which made it into the pop charts. It also attempted to break down the barriers between audience and performers, partly by distributing participatory 'kits' to the audience at each show.[190] Many of the performers who later worked on *The Rocky Horror Show* were also in the UK production of *Hair*, including

Tim Curry, who then became the first Frank'N'Furter, and director Jim Sharman, who worked on the Sydney production of *Hair* before arriving in London to direct *Jesus Christ Superstar* in 1972. A new kind of music had arrived in the pop charts and was just beginning to be heard in musicals.

Meanwhile The Royal Court theatre had been acquired by George Devine in 1956 to start his English Stage Company as a subsidized theatre committed to the development of new writing, and famously John Osborne's *Look Back in Anger* (1956) was the third play to be produced there. In 1969 the Royal Court opened a small black box studio seating just 63 people. It was here, in the home of new writing rather than in the West End, that *The Rocky Horror Show* began its journey.

The music, book and lyrics for *The Rocky Horror Show* were written by Richard O'Brien, who also created the role of Riff Raff in all the early productions and the film version. It was developed as a one-act entertainment in collaboration with producer and director Jim Sharman, and, after two previews, it ran for the planned month (19 June–20 July). Tim Curry played Frank'N'Furter in this, the film and many subsequent productions. The show was sufficiently successful critically and commercially that it was transferred to the 230-seat Chelsea Classic Cinema from 14 August to 20 October, and then in November to a 500-seat venue, the King's Road Theatre. Interestingly, given its subsequent life and its narrative content, both of these venues were cinemas. The show was awarded the Evening Standard Award for Best Musical (1973), and the first of many cast recordings was made by record producer Jonathan King of UK Records, who had seen the show on its second night. He and theatre producer Michael White promoted and backed the show, which ran at the King's Road Theatre until 31 March 1979. When the King's Road Theatre was threatened with closure, the show was finally transferred into the West End, to the Comedy Theatre, where it ran from 6 April 1979 until 13 September 1980. The Comedy was the first theatre that the musical had played at with a traditional proscenium arch stage, and for the first time, the musical was broken into two acts with an interval.

The show has had repeated regional productions and UK tours, especially since the 1990–91 West End revival, including a new production in 2012 to celebrate the show's 40th anniversary. At the time of writing, tickets for a new tour beginning in December 2015 are already on sale with dates through to August 2016.[191] There have also been many successful performances and cast recordings all over the world, including in Australia, New Zealand, South America, Europe, Singapore, South Korea and Japan.[192]

Audience interaction

At some point during the early years *The Rocky Horror Show* became an interactive event, and this probably began in the United States, though it is also feasible that Jim Sharman's experience of promoting audience interaction on the Sydney production of *Hair* fed into this development. At the Royal Court a sign greeted audiences reading 'The Sloane Cinema regrets the inconvenience caused to patrons during renovations. A modern 3-screen cinema centre will open shortly'.[193] This provided an already disconcerting context for theatre audiences, who were further unsettled by ushers in 'fright masks and heavy black shades, who creep around like androids from the back lot, crooking their little fingers at you and leering behind their torches'.[194] It is clear that such environmental estrangements, the presence of entrances through the audience and the intimacy of the early venues all contributed to the overall experience being like an immersive event.[195]

However, a much greater level of interaction was to develop in the United States. In 1973 the show was seen by producer Lou Adler, who transferred the show to the Roxy Theatre in Los Angeles where it ran for ten months from March 1974. It was during this run that members of the audience began dressing up as characters in the show.[196] Raymond Knapp suggests that one of the many possible influences on this trend was the way in which audiences and performers interacted at rock concerts, and dressed up for punk rock concerts.[197] In the meantime a contract was secured with Twentieth Century Fox to make a film of the show, which consequently closed in Los Angeles in January 1975 to prepare for filming in the UK and for the Broadway opening. The New York theatre production at the Belasco Theatre was not well received, however, and lasted just 45 performances, so that the planned boost to the film distribution from the Broadway success failed to materialize.

The film was made in the UK in 1975 and opened in London in August 1975. It then had its US premiere at the Westwood Theatre, Los Angeles, on 26 September 1975 before its general US release date on 29 September 1975. Given the lack of success of the live show in New York, Fox decided not to distribute the film on the mainstream circuit. Instead the company first attempted to attract audiences in college venues and then tried it out with midnight cult-film audiences in New York. The film opened at the Waverly in Greenwich Village in April 1976, and it was here that audience participation and conversation with the screen really took off.[198] The soundtrack was played to 'warm up' the audience before the film, and gradually a regular audience developed who booed the villain and cheered the heroes. During 1976 members of the audience, who, by this time, had seen the film many times, began to interject lines of dialogue between lines of the script. By 1977, many audience members were dressing up, most of the props, such as rice, newspaper, cards, torches, and so on, had appeared, and fans occasionally performed mini-floorshows before the film was shown; the whole evening took the form of an event or live 'happening'.[199] And this feature of the show quickly transferred back to London, where not only the film but the live show became interactive.[200] In 1983, a 2 LP[201] audience-participation version of the film was released.[202]

But, of course, the UK already had another popular theatre tradition in which audience interaction was part of the performance event. As noted above, British music hall and pantomime had long traditions of audience participation and interaction with the stage, so in terms of the theatricality of the event, and whenever and however the interactions began, *The Rocky Horror Show* could be argued to have tapped into an existing theatrical tradition. The direct address of the concert-style performance and the Narrator's presentation would have lent itself to the perception of audience involvement right from the start, even if audiences were not actively participating at this time. In fact the relationship to pantomime goes further. The *New Musical Express* (*NME*) reviewer described the show as 'basically a pantomime – AC/DC Babes in the Wood with cunnilingus',[203] while Tim Curry remarked in an interview at the time the show transferred into the West End that the role of Frank'N'Furter was 'really an absurdly masculine role, in the tradition of the pantomime dame . . . you need to make theatre as close to the circus as possible – to try for a dangerous performance . . . Frank is a perfect role because you can behave badly and the audience loves you for it.'[204]

The production and its politics

The story of *The Rocky Horror Show* is a pastiche of the science fiction and horror B-movies that had grown out of Mary Shelley's novel *Frankenstein* (1818) and Bram Stoker's *Dracula* (1897). A young all-American couple, Brad and Janet, break down outside a mysterious gothic castle. When they knock on the door to ask to use the phone, they are drawn into a hedonistic world dominated by the transvestite Frank'N'Furter. Frank has just created a perfect being who is brought to life in the course of the evening. Rocky (in contrast with the monster created by Frankenstein) is the beautiful, muscular man that results from this experiment. In the course of the night the couple stay at the house, Frank 'deflowers' both Brad and Janet, Janet then has sex with Rocky, and all end up, with the Narrator, in what appears to be a drug-induced 'floor show' stimulated by the 'sonic transducer'. The servants, Riff Raff and Magenta, realize things have got out of control and decide to beam the entire house back to the planet Transsexual in the galaxy of Transylvania. Riff Raff then kills Frank, Columbia and Rocky with a 'laser capable of emitting a beam of pure anti-matter'. The song 'Super Heroes' ends the journey for Brad, who 'down inside is bleeding', and Janet on whom 'still the beast is feeding'. Both are much more worldly-wise than when they arrived.

The rise of science fiction in the 1950s is often regarded as an allegorical response to a cultural paranoia resulting from the two World Wars, and the development and dropping of the nuclear bomb. The Campaign for Nuclear Disarmament began talks in 1958, but the non-proliferation treaty was not signed until 1968 and came into force in 1970. In the UK, British troops were sent onto the streets of Londonderry in Northern Ireland in 1969 and Direct Rule from London was enforced in 1972. Britain joined the EEC in January 1973, and by November the miners had begun an overtime ban that led to fuel shortages and the three-day week. American bases in the UK and the rise of communism in Eastern Europe behind the Iron Curtain also brought the sense that the British government was no longer in control of the country's destiny. Technological developments included first the nuclear bomb and then nuclear energy, but also space exploration resulting in the first moon landing in 1969. Although technological development was also responsible for many of the tools that released women from the kitchen and brought entertainment into the home, there was a widespread feeling of paranoia, of being out of control, that was allegorically expressed from the 1950s in the rise and popularity of science fiction films that identified the 'other' as an alien from outer space. In these films the alienation of the modern world and the fear of being out of control is given outward expression in a clearly fictionalized fantasy, and as the alien is contained and suppressed, the paranoia is momentarily released.

The Rocky Horror Show not only expressed the political alienation of young people, but related that alienation to the depiction of the transgressive sexuality of the creatures from outer space. The first wave of feminism sought equal voting rights, but once that was achieved a second wave began concerned with other issues of women's rights. This movement led into the development of identity politics and ultimately the achievement of gay rights, too. Although this wave is usually argued to have begun with the publication of *The Second Sex* by Simone de Beauvoir in 1949, it really gathered pace as a result of the development of the birth-control pill and the sexual freedoms of the 1960s epitomized by bra-burning, the fight for equal pay, and the publication of *The Female Eunuch* by Germaine Greer in 1970. In the mid-twentieth century the media promoted the ideal 'nuclear family' and a normative heterosexuality. In *The Rocky Horror Show* the alien was not only an allegory for a paranoid feeling of alienation as a response to contemporary politics, but the aliens embodied and subverted normative sexuality. Frank is dressed as a transvestite from the start, wearing sexually encoded versions of women's underwear, a basque, stockings and suspenders, but displays an authoritative, assertive and butch male sexuality in performance reinforced by strutting to the glam rock music. For the birth of Rocky, he adds a surgical gown and a pearl necklace – the pearl necklace being a signifier of a middle- or upper-class conformity to normative values, but this is juxtaposed with a homoerotic relationship with Rocky, the seduction of Brad and an unquestionably heterosexual relationship with Janet (and earlier Columbia). Riff Raff and Magenta also appear to have some type of incestuous relationship and, until the end, support the liberal expression of non-conformity.

Theatrically there are two framing or distancing devices in the production. The show opens with Magenta, as the Usherette, introducing the 'Science Fiction Double Feature' that the audience is about to see – building on the fiction introduced by the sign posted outside the Theatre Upstairs during the initial run that the show is the replacement for a film that cannot be screened because of renovations. She refers to Flash Gordon, Claude Rains as the Invisible Man, Fay Wray and King Kong before describing in the refrain how in this show 'Dr X will build a creature / See Androids fighting Brad and Janet'. At the end of the song the scene switches to the 'real world' of the show where Brad and Janet are attending a wedding.

The second distancing device is the intervention of a Narrator, a 'staple of low-budget British thrillers … clutching a large book and intoning the smooth, sepulchral clichés of an Edgar Lustgarten'.[206] He interrupts events several times addressing the audience directly, and in a complete breaking down of the fourth wall interjects lines in a number of songs. The Narrator winds up the inner story with the lines

And crawling on the Planet's face
Some insects called the human race

136

> Lost in time and lost in space
> And meaning.

Magenta, dressed once again as the Usherette, winds up the outer story singing

> Frank has built and lost his creature
> Darkness has conquered Brad and Janet
> The servants gone to a distant planet
> At the late night double feature picture show.

These frames contribute to the theatricality of the event, creating layers that act as prisms through which to view the show, and contributing to the layers of reference to contemporary popular culture in the performance.

Figure 10 Subverting heteronormative sexuality – and using 1970s microphone technology – Tim Curry as Frank'N'Furter in *The Rocky Horror Show* by Richard O'Brien at the Theatre Upstairs, 1973. Photograph by Johnny Dewe Mathews.[205]

Musical dramaturgy

The musical signification too is both referential and meaningful. In the decade from the mid-1960s to mid-1970s, rock music was a genre associated with the macho posturing of performers such as Mick Jagger and the Rolling Stones, and with counter-cultural youthful subversion, resistance and left-wing communities even as it existed in the mainstream. Within rock, sub-genres emerged that included, in the early 1970s, glam rock performed by artists such as David Bowie (in his Ziggy Stardust and Aladdin Sane periods), Marc Bolan and Annie Lennox. The music and its performance have enormous sexual energy, with performers using alternative and androgynous identities and high levels of sensuality. Glam rock regards as 'authentic' music that focuses on experimentation, progress, technology and the elitist positioning of the artist.[207] *The Rocky Horror Show*[208] draws on both these categories of authentic rock performance in its characterizations.

Frank and the Transylvanians might be participants in a glam rock concert. Frank indulges in sexually provocative posturing while wearing women's underwear, and has bisexual romps with Janet and Rocky. This, alongside Magenta and Riff Raff's possibly incestuous relationship and their deliberately mysterious and grotesque presence, could be seen as extensions of the glam rock personas of the early 70s. Eddie, on the other hand, is a leather-jacketed, motorbike-riding character whose music contains the nostalgic folk or country blues-influenced rock and roll of 'Whatever happened to Saturday night'. This is regarded as passé within glam rock, and he is killed and hidden in the fridge. Janet and Brad are associated with the pop sound of 'Damn it Janet', which from a rock aesthetic might be regarded as more superficial. Brad is made to appear insignificant and foolish, while Janet's musical language adapts as the plot develops. Rocky's 'The Sword of Damocles' draws on associations of sensuality through the use of rumba and prefigures his overwhelming sexual drive.

The guitar rhythm of 'Time Warp' introduces the aggressive and distorted sound world of the Frankenstein place as the young couple arrive, making an association between the distorted guitars, the rock music and the strange, aggressively sexual and disturbing world at the castle. This sets up a relationship between the musical style, the location, and its inhabitants. The place has 'rock music' credibility. Frank, who enters to a much heavier, slower drum pulse, becomes the star performer at the rock concert in 'Sweet Transvestite'. The glam rock performance with its connotations of youthful subversion and sexuality reinforce the character and his credibility with the culturally aware rock fan audience.

Musical genres are being used to underpin characterizations, but the perspective from which they are read is that of a glam rock music aesthetic, which looks for experimentation and progress. This is apparent in the transformation of Janet from a conformist virginal female 'just like Betty Munro' looking forward to a dull marriage to Brad, into a sexually liberated woman. This is represented by her musical development from the pop sounds and clear soprano tones of the refrain of 'Damn it Janet' to her solo 'Touch-a, Touch-a, Touch Me' with its rock-rumba rhythm, introduction of a lower vocal register, and a throatier, full-bodied vocal sound. The plot here draws on a perception that rock music can release the uptight from societal restrictions.

Intertextuality and the performance of anarchy

Neither in performance style, nor in narrative content is this an integrated musical theatre show. Rather it draws on the style and imagery of science fiction and B-movies in its narrative and its imagery, and distances audiences from attachment to the characters through the theatrical layering and multiple popular references. Frank represents Victor Frankenstein, while the Gothic castle with its strange staff derives from the Dracula films. Rocky is, of course, the promethean monster who dies saving his master in a pose reminiscent of Fay Wray and King Kong. The sonic transducer and the references to other scientific devices are characteristic of this group of B-movies, including *Flash Gordon*. The Time Warp is a reminder of numerous dance crazes of the 1950s, including the Madison (to which Brad refers), or 'Ballin' the Jack'.[209] The pastiche and the intertextual referencing is comic in its own right, especially when performed with the melodramatic seriousness of the genre. Associated with the mostly very camp music and dancing and the audience participation, this becomes hugely entertaining, but it is also postmodern in its aggregation of signifiers and its potential for the deconstruction of all forms of normative politics.

Overall, the show contains a combination of elements from popular culture combined, not in a politically resonant juxtaposition, as Littlewood had achieved in *Oh What a Lovely War!*, but in a postmodern amalgam whose intertextual associations clash. The work spoke allegorically to the alienated young people using the language of popular music, of growing sexual freedom and of popular movie culture. It was anarchic both in content and form and encouraged the audience to perform its own anarchy in the theatres and cinemas in which it played by interacting and joining in, speaking back to the authority figure, Frank, who is seen to be entirely hedonistic and self-interested. It reflected a time of dissatisfaction with politics and authority and offered an outlet to challenge, albeit in the safe space of a theatre or cinema, the status quo.

Conclusion to Part Two

This part has identified some of the diversity of British musical theatre by exploring the stories, characters and music through which it relates to its various audiences. British musical theatre is not only the work that arrives on the commercial stages of the West End of London, but includes community, regional, fringe and small-scale productions all over the country, and this part has only touched the tip of the iceberg as far as such work is concerned. Local community practices generate new ways of thinking and performing, and gradually these developments feed through to changes in the mainstream commercial sector. Equally the constant reinvigoration of pop music through the different generations of creators feeds into a dynamic process of signification in music. Commercial musical theatre, though, can be conservative, relying on musical genres, narrative forms and dramaturgical structures with which a broad audience is comfortable, so developments in the mainstream can be slow. Nevertheless musical theatre has changed and continues to develop to reflect the diversity of the cultural backgrounds of British people.

The aim in this part was not to provide a comprehensive account of the relationships between popular culture and musical theatre, but to begin to document the variety of ways in which musical theatre responds to the popular cultures of its communities. Thus we can begin to recognize its diversity and the way it transforms in response to a popular culture that is influenced by a global music scene, increasingly mobile global citizens and many local diasporic communities. It is therefore possible to argue that its diversity arises from the quality and character of the creative teams, the performers and the people British musical theatre entertains.

PART III
NARRATIVE AND STORY-TELLING IN THE BRITISH MUSICAL SINCE 1970
Olaf Jubin

Preamble

Many of the musicals discussed in this and – to some degree – the other chapters have repeatedly been categorized as 'megamusicals', a label that is highly problematic as well as misleading, which is why we have tried to avoid using it.

The term 'megamusical' was coined by American journalists in response to what they perceived in the 1980s as a 'British invasion' of Broadway, and describes certain globally successful shows coming over from the West End entirely from an American perspective. This approach persists in the most extensive and serious study of the so-called subgenre, Jessica Sternfeld's *The Megamusical* (2006). The book has many virtues – the most notable being that it deems its subject worthy of unprejudiced analysis, another its intelligent in-depth reading of the musicals in question – however, the definition of the term 'megamusical' as offered by Sternfeld (based on a scrupulous account of its use in US publications) confirms that the concept of the 'megamusical' is severely flawed.

On the one hand the list of features ascribed to the subgenre is so general that it tends to obscure rather than illuminate the subject. When the megamusical is summed up as 'epic, sweeping tales of romance, war, religion, redemption, life and death' that 'tend to be set in the past',[1] the description fits classic American musicals like *Show Boat* (1927) or *Carousel* (1945) far better than *Starlight Express* (1984), *Time* (1986) or *Chess* (1986), all three supposedly prime examples of the form. The same problem arises with another allegedly 'defining characteristic [...] of the megamusical' – its '[i]mpressive, complicated, expensive sets'[2]: were not *Pacific Overtures* (1976) and *Sweeney Todd* (1979) rightly praised for their astounding set design? While it is correct to assert that the majority of British musicals that transferred to New York in the 1980s and 1990s 'were generally not loved by critics',[3] Sternfeld does not problematize the reviewers' *caveat* that the 'crowd-pleasing, enjoyable shows [...] did little to educate or challenge'.[4] After all, the same critics never had any qualms about praising purely entertaining American musicals without a socio-political agenda from *Anything Goes* (1934), *Damn Yankees* (1955), *Hello, Dolly* (1964) to *Thoroughly Modern Millie* (2002) and *Something Rotten* (2015). Finally, one could also ask why the American press felt the need to come up with a new term for productions that British journalists simply categorized as musicals.

Therefore the very concept of the 'megamusical' needs to be thoroughly examined in respect of its viability as an appropriate generic category. The question needs to be asked: why and how did these particular shows emerge in Britain at the time, and what may the presumed 'subgenre' mean in the context of *British* culture and society? This chapter (like the book as a whole) is meant as a first step in this direction.

Introduction

Jesus Christ Superstar (*JCS*), initially released as a double album in 1970, found a novel way for British theatre to present new musicals to the public. The approach of using the music industry to promote a new show via sales of a recording rather than by mounting a theatre production also changed the way British musicals told their stories: the rock opera by lyricist Tim Rice and composer Andrew Lloyd Webber introduced the sung-through format, which would dominate the West End for decades to come. This new style of musical later diversified with regard to its source materials and was complemented by other forms such as shows built around the back catalogue of a famous recording artist.

Ever since their first big success, Rice and Lloyd Webber have remained leading creative forces within the theatre industry. By examining the careers of these two artists as well as additional examples, this chapter aims to point out the distinctive features of the various approaches to narrative and story-telling that have prevailed in the West End since the beginning of the 1970s. The key subgenres of British musical theatre in the last five decades consist of:

- concept recordings (i.e. *Jesus Christ Superstar*, 1970; *Evita*, 1976)
- sung-through shows (i.e. *Cats*, 1981; *Starlight Express*, 1984; *Martin Guerre*, 1995)

- stage adaptations of novels and other literary works (i.e. *Matilda*, 2011; *Jeeves*, 1975; *Les Misérables*, 1985; *The Phantom of the Opera*, 1986; *Aspects of Love*, 1989; *The Woman in White*, 2004; *From Here to Eternity*, 2013)

- original stories (i.e. *Blondel*, 1983; *Chess*, 1984; *The Beautiful Game*, 2000; *Love Never Dies*, 2010; *Stephen Ward*, 2013)

- jukebox musicals (i.e. *Mamma Mia!*, 1999; *Tonight's the Night*, 2003; *Viva Forever!*, 2012)

- stage adaptations of films (i.e. *Mary Poppins*, 2004; *Billy Elliot*, 2005; *Sunset Boulevard*, 1993; *Whistle Down the Wind*, 1997; *Made in Dagenham*, 2014)

These six formats, which sometimes overlap or are combined, will be investigated in roughly chronological order from 1970 to the present day.

3.1 CONCEPT RECORDINGS: WHEN WHAT YOU SEE IS WHAT YOU HAVE HEARD

While there had been rock operas or concept recordings released prior to *Jesus Christ Superstar*, it was the musical retelling of the last seven days of the Son of God that had the most immediate and lasting effect on the English-language musical. Moving in less than two years from chart-topping album to concert tour and then fully staged Broadway and West End productions, Andrew Lloyd Webber and Tim Rice's first big hit has now become a staple of the musical theatre.

The decision to present *Jesus Christ Superstar* to the public initially in the form of a concept recording rather than a theatrical presentation was not deliberate but dictated by circumstance. Lloyd Webber later explained: '[T]he whole idea of doing anything on record first, instead of as a stage musical, was a total accident. It was forced on us by the fact that nobody would touch the piece.'[5] Today, Rice insists that the enthusiastic response to the 1970 musical is a consequence of the concise story-telling required and the sound quality afforded by the recording process: 'I am certain that if we had written *Jesus Christ Superstar* for the theatre in the first instance, it would never have been a hit. It would have been long-winded, with dialogue continually interrupting the flow of the music, and would never have the dynamic bang-up-to-date arrangements that we knew were vital for record success.'[6] The innovative format of narrating events solely through musical numbers changed their function, since it placed additional weight on the lyrics and relied heavily on recitative; it also modified the dramaturgy. As John Snelson explains, *Jesus Christ Superstar* is not plot-driven in the vein of earlier musicals; instead its 'series of musical scenes presented a drama of attitudes and responses rather than action.'[7]

If a musical is first introduced to the public on an LP, the acquaintance a theatre audience has with the material leads to certain expectations: it surmises that it will hear the songs exactly like they sounded on the recording, which has implications for the sound design; it also affects the possibility of making later changes to the piece. Due to its instant popularity, it was more or less impossible to replace certain lyrics of *Jesus Christ Superstar* that Tim Rice was unhappy with, for instance because they featured unclean rhymes; those lyrics had been written under enormous time pressure to get the recording done, on the assumption that they could be fixed before the show went to the stage. But once the recording topped the charts, major alterations in the lyrics would only have irritated and alienated audiences.[8] Moreover, people enjoyed the recording as it was; that is, with all its imperfections. Therefore, it was more than 25 years before Rice altered some of the lines he felt he could improve upon for the 1996 London revival, only to be attacked by the show's fans who still didn't want any changes.[9]

Musicals that premiere as concept recordings are customarily not written with staging in mind, which can be both a blessing and a curse. On the one hand, they allow a director complete artistic freedom as s/he is not restricted in her/his approach to the piece; but, on the other hand, the musical numbers may not coalesce into an organic whole if there is no strong creative vision to provide a framework through which to link the album tracks both visually and dramatically. There are instances in which *Jesus Christ Superstar* clearly betrays its origin as a concept recording. The scene of Mary Magdalene's big solo 'I Don't Know How to Love Him' is one of them: the compelling ballad follows immediately after Jesus has been overwhelmed by the demands of the crowds to ameliorate their plight. He breaks down after realizing 'There's too many of you – / [. . .] / There's too little of me'. Upon this line Mary enters and soothes him with a reprise of 'Everything's Alright'; immediately afterwards she goes into her next song. But there is no time for an actress to move from one emotional state – calm assurance and altruistic concern – to the mood of increasing despair expressed in 'I Don't Know How to Love Him', without any help from the director. On the album, these are two

144

separate tracks, clearly set apart by the brief pause between numbers on an LP, but in a theatrical production, it falls to the director (and the actress) to figure out how to make this rather abrupt change work.

When reflecting upon the importance of the director for successfully transferring a concept album to the stage, it is also illuminating to contemplate how Gale Edwards staged 'I Don't Know How to Love Him' itself for the first major London revival in 1996.[10] Attempting to devise a dramatic arc throughout the song, the director has actress Renée Castle register a vast array of emotions: Castle goes from surprise to annoyance, contempt, determination, doubt, desperation, sarcasm, grief, tenderness and finally desolation, all in the course of less than three minutes. The problem with this presentation of the song is that the many changes in Mary's feelings are not borne out by the music of the song. 'I Don't Know How to Love Him' is a folk-style ballad with a simple AABA structure that includes several climactic moments, but does not feature any abrupt modulations or continuous alterations of mood. But in Edwards and Castle's take on the song, the acting and with it the whole scene turns over-dramatic, thus negating what made the number so affecting to begin with.

The next joint project of Rice and Lloyd Webber benefitted enormously from having a director with a precise vision for how to best present the material in the theatre; consequently the original staging of *Evita* (1976) has become one of the most iconic productions in the history of musical theatre. As the procedure had proved so effective with *Jesus Christ Superstar*, the two songwriters decided to release their follow-up project as a concept recording as well: *Evita* told of the meteoric rise and untimely death of Eva Perón, the wife of fascist Argentinian dictator Juan Perón, who died of ovarian cancer when she was just 33. Like the musical about Jesus of Nazareth, the new work was conceived without a traditional libretto, but instead presented a carefully thought-out and clearly structured sequence of musical scenes.

When Harold Prince brought the musical to the stage in 1978, he found a directorial style and developed a thematic concept that gave the numbers on the album unity and additional weight. Although he saw *Evita* first and foremost as a political play, Prince was also intrigued by another aspect of the show: 'Media manipulation, that's what's it about.'[11] Eva Perón uses politics as a perilous form of mass entertainment and that is what links her with the musical as a genre, as this theatrical form also plays a high-risk game of literally seeking to be applauded by as many different people as possible. In Prince's production, Evita's manipulation of her admirers finds

Figure 11 Media manipulation as theatrical topic and theatrical means – Elaine Paige (Eva Perón) and Joss Ackland (Juan Perón) in *Evita*, Prince Edward Theatre 1978. Photograph by Chris Davies. Courtesy of ArenaPAL.

its equivalent on the levels of staging and design, which in turn manipulate the audience – the whole evening is an illustration of and a lesson in politics as show.

The London production of *Evita* stayed fairly close to the concept album, with Prince's subtle tweaks to the show's narrative and structure showing off the original to best advantage. More than any other musical in British theatre history, *Evita* proves that not every concept album needs to be completely reconceived or rewritten when it is transferred to the theatre – sometimes all it takes is a visionary artist who perceives and then realizes its full potential.

Case Study 9: *Jesus Christ Superstar*

Every adaptation of a religious text is bound to cause controversy. When Andrew Lloyd Webber and Tim Rice decided to re-tell the last seven days of

Jesus Christ in song, they knew that their choice of subject would inevitably be closely scrutinized, and not just by official representatives of Christianity. As Rice later put it: 'We had no wish to offend or to be controversial, although we were well aware that we were entering sensitive territory.'[12]

There were initial protests when *Jesus Christ Superstar* premiered on Broadway in 1971 by both Catholics and Protestants, who organized demonstrations and pickets in front of the theatre, as well as by the 'American Jewish Committee' and the 'Anti-Defamation League of B'nai B'rith', who complained about what they perceived to be anti-Semitic tendencies.[13] As John Snelson expounds: 'The use of rock was thought by some to debase the story of the last days of Christ, the show's focus on Judas and its conclusion with the Crucifixion rather than the Resurrection also aroused misgivings.'[14] Over the last 45 years, though, those protests have completely died down; the show is no longer regarded as blasphemous, but has become part of the established canon of musical theatre works.

The musical's genesis and story-telling

To turn to the New Testament for inspiration, on the one hand, seemed like a logical progression since the two songwriters had had their first taste of public recognition with *Joseph and the Amazing Technicolor Dreamcoat*, another religious story, albeit from the Old Testament. On the other hand, the various social upheavals of the late 1960s, from the student unrest and protests against the Vietnam War to the hippie movement, Jesus people and other representatives of the counterculture, had ushered in a new interest in all sorts of concepts and practices of spirituality, especially if they were pacifist and challenged the established order. Within that framework, an exploration of the Gospels was both timely and canny.

Nonetheless, the record companies in London were wary when the project was offered to them. The British company Decca rejected the idea as 'too controversial',[15] and even though MCA UK was interested, it insisted on testing the market first to see whether there was an audience for this kind of show or whether it would merely cause an uproar that didn't translate into record sales. On 21 November 1969, the title song interpreted by Murray Head was released as a single on the British market, but it was called simply 'Superstar' so as to avoid unnecessary provocation. It is ironic that the track was propelled to success in a way that nobody could have predicted: 'Although the "Superstar" single failed to sustain its initial impact, through unexpected popularity in a Dutch gay bar it became a top-selling single in the Netherlands.'[16] Once the recording turned into a hit in various countries, MCA committed to financing a whole (double) album, and the rest of the musical came together between October 1969 and March 1970, with roughly 95 per cent of the material being written in the first three months of 1970.[17]

Within a couple of weeks of its release, the 'rock opera', as it was called on the cover of the double album, turned into a (sales) phenomenon, especially in the United States, where it reached the top of the album charts. It proved so popular in North America that several unlicensed productions with people lip-synching to the recording were staged, which were quickly shut down by the legal team of Robert Stigwood, manager of Lloyd Webber and Rice. Yet those unlicensed stagings also made evident that audiences appreciated the work in its original form without waiting for/needing revisions and additions. As *JCS* achieved cult status in only a few short months, the originally planned far-reaching rewrites not only proved unnecessary, but to a certain degree impossible, as audiences expected to see and hear exactly what they had listened to on and memorized from the double album.

In its re-telling of the last days of Jesus Christ, the musical basically follows the structure of the Gospel of Luke; various elements have been taken from the other three Gospels, such as the temple scene from Matthew and Mark, while Pilate's question concerning the 'truth' is a detail found in the Gospel of John. The words Jesus utters on the cross, on the other hand, are a combination of all four Gospels. Finally, the opening monologue is an invention by Rice.[18]

The musical's plot thus already mapped out by the source material, Lloyd Webber and Rice were left with very few choices of their own when it came to their work's narrative shape: as in the Bible, Mary Magdalene remains a supporting character, who in the show gets lost along the way, which no doubt later led to the addition of 'Could We Start Again Please?' (for the Broadway production) – an attempt to boost the presence of the only major female role/voice in the score. The songwriters decided to introduce the main players as well as the 'villains' of the piece, the High Priests, early on and to limit the appearances (and thus reduce the importance) of both the Apostles and the crowd to carefully selected key moments. Compared to the New Testament, the musical shifts the focus towards Judas, who has more songs (and tellingly more solos) to sing, while representing Jesus of Nazareth predominantly as human, as a man with weaknesses and needs who seems, faced with an overwhelming task, to despair.

Using the maximum time afforded by a double album, *JCS* runs 87 minutes and 16 seconds and covers the last seven days in the life of the eponymous character. Like most traditional musicals (or operas for that matter), *Jesus Christ Superstar* starts with an 'Overture', before Judas enters to express his disappointment with the leader of the movement he has joined in 'Heaven on Their Minds', accusing Jesus of falling for his own propaganda and of losing track of their important goals: 'Jesus! You've started to believe / The things they say of you / You really do believe / This talk of God is true / [...] / You've begun to matter more / Than the things you say'.[19] Although Judas dresses up his misgivings as concern for the man he has followed ('And they'll hurt you if they think you've lied'), the change of subject from first person singular to first person plural halfway through the song ('Don't you see *we* must keep in *our* place? / [...] / And they'll crush *us* if *we* go too far') implies that he is also very much worried for his own safety and that his constant criticism is grounded in self-preservation.

Jesus counters Judas' objections with the advice to focus on the here and now instead of on eventualities that may never arise, partly because he already knows what will happen to him, even if he doesn't fully grasp the reasons behind it: 'If you knew the path we're riding you'd understand it less than I.' (This lack of clarity when it comes to God's motives will continue to disquiet Jesus and will finally erupt in full in 'Gethsemane'.) The number 'What's the Buzz / Strange Thing Mystifying' furthermore reveals another disagreement between the two main characters: whereas Judas with his rigorous demands that all money should go to the destitute instead of to comforting one individual seems completely dogmatic, Jesus is no longer quite so preoccupied with following his own teachings. His defence of Mary and his own inconsistent behaviour ('There will be poor always, pathetically struggling') already hints at his exhaustion caused by attempting the impossible, that is, saving the whole world by himself.

'This Jesus Must Die' introduces the villains of the piece, the High Priests, who exhibit a Machiavellian obsession with power as they fear the ongoing 'Jesusmania' is undermining their own position. The flippant, arrogant stance from which the religious leaders dismiss Jesus and his achievements reveals not only a total lack of understanding, but also a shocking disregard for the common people. Still, they also pinpoint why Jesus has so many followers, with Caiaphas, the leader of the High Priests, acknowledging, 'One thing I'll say for him – Jesus is cool,' and another priest observing, His glamour increases / [...] / He's top of the poll.

The number is the first to identify the crowd as 'mob' in the lyrics booklet, and Jesus' triumphant arrival in Jerusalem continues the musical's perpetual theme of the people as fickle, as a mass that can easily be swayed, partly because their actions are too often dictated by self-interest; in 'Hosanna', the groups who cheer Jesus when he enters the Holy City do not even bother to hide their assumption that supporting Jesus will get them a (heavenly) reward: 'Christ you know I love you / Did you see I waved? / I believe in you and God / So tell me that I'm saved'. While Judas urges Jesus to make the movement less incendiary by de-emphasizing politics, Simon Zealotes, encouraged by their reception in Jerusalem,[20] wants Jesus to seize the moment and to start the revolution by inciting the crowd against Rome. Jesus refuses and utters a line that puzzles his Apostles but which makes perfect sense to anyone familiar with the Gospels: 'To conquer death you only have to die'. The Temple scene underlines once more the musical's focus on Jesus as human, although given a super-human task; faced with a misery that even he cannot alleviate, he breaks down shouting: 'There's too many of you – don't push me / There's too little of me – don't crowd me / Heal yourselves'.

Judas' secret visit to the High Priests shows him torn between loyalty and the desire to save all their hides. He is finally swayed to betray his leader by the suggestion that his 30 pieces of silver can buy a lot of charitable work. Caiaphas reminds him: 'Think of the things you can do with that money / Choose any charity – give to the poor', thus offering him a solution to his conundrum by providing him with a less objectionable motive.

Two days later, Jesus celebrates 'The Last Supper' with his followers; the Apostles, who all throughout the piece leave an unfavourable impression, are revealed as self-obsessed and unconcerned with the horrible fate awaiting their religious leader. Their self-satisfied statement, 'Always hoped that I'd be an apostle / Knew that I would make it if I tried / Then when we retire we can write the gospels / So they'll still talk about us when we've died', enrages Jesus, who then attacks Judas for his impending betrayal. With emotions already running high, Jesus moves into his one big solo, 'Gethsemane', giving in to his despair and fear and trying to get explanations – he repeatedly insists, 'I'd wanna know'/'I'd have to know'/'I'd have to see' – that never come as God remains silent. Finally his rebellion collapses into resignation ('Alright I'll die').

After 'The Arrest', the crowd reveal their ugly side, taunting the man they previously showered with adoration with anachronistic jibes à la, 'You'll escape in the final reel', before relishing his fall: 'Hey JC, JC please explain to me / You had everything where is it now?' The mockery reaches its height with 'The King Herod's Song', a number that is different from everything else in the score, both in musical style (it's a traditional ragtime song) and mood, as it is the only comic song in the show, with the Jewish king demanding, among other things, 'Prove to me that you're no fool walk across my swimming pool.' Although one could argue that Herod's turn stands out to such a degree that it undermines the coherence of the show as a whole, it also offers some much-needed comic relief before the final harrowing scenes of Judas' suicide, the 39 lashes and the crucifixion.

First, the musical presents us with 'Judas' Death'; utterly distraught at what he has unleashed to the point where even his speech breaks down completely, Judas sings a reprise of 'I Don't Know How to Love Him', which links him to Mary Magdalene (another sinner, but one who already has been forgiven) and her obsession with Jesus. He quarrels with God and accuses him of ruthlessly making him a means to an end: 'My God I am sick and I've been used / And you knew all the time / God!'

Meanwhile, Jesus stands 'Trial Before Pilate', still in doubt about his exact fate ('There may be a kingdom for me somewhere – if I only knew'). Before he is whipped and crucified, the musical makes a daring detour that takes the audience out of the story via the title song, which – like a Greek chorus – interrupts the action, albeit in the form of a big production number, to question the motives of the eponymous character: Judas demands of Jesus to explain his rationale, but like the Son of God himself in 'Gethsemane' he does not get any answers. He asks questions that any youth reading about the Passion of Christ in the early 1970s might have asked: 'Why'd you choose such a backward time and such a strange land? / If you'd come today you would have reached a whole nation / Israel in 4 BC had no mass communication.' Because Judas here acts as a stand-in for the audience, his previous actions appear in a new light, daring the viewer/listener to imagine her/himself in Judas' place and indirectly implying that anybody would have behaved similarly. The song also expands the religious connotations by including Buddhism and Islam in its list of spiritual movements whose teachings need to be (re)examined.

The musical ends with Jesus' death on the cross and a final instrumental number whose title 'John 19:41' references the Bible verse 'Now in the place where He was crucified there was a garden and in the garden a new tomb in which no one had yet been laid.'[21] The score thereby omits any reference to the resurrection, which, depending on one's reading of the Gospels, could be considered their most important part. Yet it is exactly this omission as well as the focus on Judas' dilemma that according to John Snelson secured the recording's unique and widespread appeal: '[T]he work moved from religious morality play to a play about morals, thus also open to a secular reading.'[22]

Jesus Christ Superstar is entirely characteristic for both of its creators, Lloyd Webber and Rice. Perhaps no other score incorporates so many of the composer's musical influences while growing up: his parents' love of classical and church music, his admiration of American musicals of the Golden Age and the rock and pop music of his youth filtered through Lloyd Webber's own sensibility, all form the basis for this ambitious musical. These influences combine to constitute, for Snelson, an attention-grabbing 'inventive musical style'[23].

For Rice, on the other hand, the story offered a great opportunity to explore the plight of people who stand out from the crowd and are subject to their admirers' tiring demands and fickleness, with adulation quickly turning into resentment and even hate.[24] It was the lyricist who came up with the catchy title for the show, no doubt inspired by 1960s icon Andy Warhol and his entourage who freely bandied around the term 'superstar' to distinguish themselves from other celebrities. Many people noticed the parallels in the portrayal of Jesus to the career of certain musicians, with Jack Kroll explaining in *Newsweek*: 'He is a Jesus who cannot help reflecting all the self-immolating, scapegoat rock superstars – Jim Morrison, Brian Jones, Jimi Hendrix, even Janis Joplin – who buckled before the monstrous demanding energy of a call beyond their powers to sustain.'[25]

Categorizing the show's leading characters and genre

It could be pointed out that the show's title *Jesus Christ Superstar* is actually a misnomer, as it is Judas Iscariot who dominates the proceedings since he has more songs and especially more solos to perform. In many ways, Judas with his anger and desperation, which find expression in his sarcastic taunting and hostile attacks on the man he professes to love as well as in the rock star stylings – some may call them histrionics – in the score, is the meatier (because showier) role. Jesus on the other side is the more difficult part to master; the actor incarnating Jesus has to achieve and maintain a very difficult balance. He has to show the audience the man who has inspired one of the most influential religions in history, but then the musical presents a spiritual leader who is decidedly human and now – with the painful end of his life very close – is both physically and mentally exhausted as well as full of doubt. If the actor is too forceful and dynamic, he will be at odds with the show's plot, as Jesus up until his main solo 'Gethsemane' mainly re-acts. Yet if the performer over-emphasizes the character's anguish and prickliness, Jesus may come across as self-pitying and unlikely to have inspired literally billions of people to follow his teachings.

The musical draws subtle parallels between protagonist and antagonist; both Judas and Jesus use the same words and phrases when talking to the person/entity they argue with – Judas' 'Listen Jesus' is mirrored later in 'Gethsemane' by Jesus' 'Listen, surely I exceeded', and they also both broach the topic they want to discuss with 'I only want to say'. What also twins them is the subject of free will: the musical asks (but doesn't answer) the question of how far Judas' reputation as the most famous betrayer in all of history and his subsequent categorizing as a villain is really justified. If God sent his son Jesus down to earth to die for our collective sins, the end – that is, the crucifixion and the resurrection – was pre-ordained; that means Judas was a mere tool in God's plan, unable to prevent what had to happen as a higher power had it all mapped out without consulting him. But if Judas only carried out what God wanted him to carry out, can we really hold him responsible?

When Judas first arrives at the High Priests', he claims, 'I really didn't come here of my own accord', and once he has decided to turn Jesus in, a (heavenly?) choir sings: 'Well done Judas / Good old Judas' – who are these voices if not God's angels? Judas accuses Jesus repeatedly of wanting his disciple to betray him ('You want me to do it!') and even threatens to spoil the plan: 'What if I stayed here / And ruined your ambition?' Later, in the scene ending with his suicide, he accuses God of cruelly using him as a means to an end: 'But I did what you wanted me to / [...] / God! I'll never know why you chose me for your crime / [...] / You have murdered me!'

How free in his actions, on the other hand, is Jesus? In 'Gethsemane' he asks his father a lot of questions without receiving any answers; his attempts to renegotiate his fate fall on deaf ears, and in the end he is resigned to his own cruel destiny to be crucified for the salvation of humankind, a death he hasn't chosen himself.

The main characters of the musical have all been delineated through a particular style of popular music:[26] Judas' songs can be characterized as rock, while Jesus, who oscillates between emotional outbursts and resignation, alternates between soul and soft rock. Female protagonist Mary Magdalene sings folk; and for King Herod, Pilate, the Apostles and the public, Lloyd Webber uses forms such as Ragtime and the Charleston, as well as a melodic and harmonic language that can be found in musical theatre and other forms of traditional Broadway entertainment.

Right from the beginning, the fact that *JCS* crosses generic borders made it both a stand out and led to criticism; the score's recourse to classic, rock and musical theatre elements proved that those various musical styles could be combined and that such combination could find a large and appreciative audience, but for adherents of each of those genres the inclusion of the other two irked them as an unwanted distraction. Because the 'rock opera' could not accurately be categorized as 'rock' and did not sound like a traditional musical or opera either, purists of all three genres regarded the piece with a certain fascination, but more often than not with utter disdain.[27] What caused further irritation and consternation and would lead to repeated criticism in the decades to follow is Lloyd Webber's use of melodies and musical motifs in a way that renders symbolic connections between the various appearances in the form of classical leitmotifs questionable if not downright illogical.[28] Hansgeorg Mühe tried in vain to explain why Lloyd Webber in 'Trial before Pilate' re-uses the ostinato motif first heard when Judas makes his stage entrance, and even Jessica Sternfeld, who otherwise often offers insistent and ingenious explications of how the various musical sections in this and later musicals by the British composer and others (like Claude-Michel Schönberg) may be thematically linked, admits: 'The guitar ostinato that accompanies the 39 lashes Jesus receives is played in the overture 27 times (for no obvious reason).'[29]

Michael Walsh uses the term 'thematic recollection' to describe Lloyd Webber's *modus operandi* and points out that this practice was quite common in nineteenth-century opera;[30] Joseph P. Swain on the other hand categorizes this compositional technique of reprising a piece of music with completely new lyrics as 'contrafactum'.[31] While Lloyd Webber may use the passages of songs which have already been introduced or are still to come as a means to lend his score more coherence and continuity,[32] in later years, especially with *The Phantom of the Opera* (1986) and *Aspects of Love* (1989), the constant reappearance of the same melodies also triggered accusations of a lack of inspiration and musical monotony.

Staging/interpreting Jesus Christ Superstar: *Broadway 1971 and beyond*

Because the double album was so much more popular in the United States, it seemed sensible to strike while the iron was hot and to premiere the stage version on Broadway. It was manager Stigwood who decided on the director, and he chose Tom O'Horgan, famous for his provocative, sensationalistic productions, as the New Yorker had just caused a stir with another rock-based show, *Hair*. O'Horgan's extravagant and visually excessive staging not only displeased many reviewers, it was also not at all what the show's composer wanted, but because he had no power to change it, Lloyd Webber later lamented that the opening night of *JCS* on 12 October 1971 was one of the most depressing nights of his entire life.[33] It was back then that Lloyd Webber vowed never again to forego artistic control over his compositions,[34] which later would result in contractual obligations to re-produce any of his shows in a way that copies every detail of the original production, from set and costume design to choreography, a much-criticized demand that became notorious as one of the assumed 'characteristics' of the megamusical.

JSC lasted for 711 performances on Broadway, less than could have been expected considering that the show opened with record advance ticket sales, although it did turn a profit.[35] The less-than-stellar reviews may have been at least partially responsible for its early closure, with critics either expressing bafflement at the attention the work had received[36] or refusing to be impressed at all, like Clive Barnes of the all-important *New York Times*, who came to the scathing conclusion: 'It all rather resembled one's first sight of the Empire State Building. Not at all uninteresting, but somewhat unsurprising and of minimal artistic value.'[37] The show fared much better with both reviewers and audiences in London, where it set a new record for musicals in the West End when it ran at the Palace Theatre for eight years and 3,358 performances.

Tom O'Horgan's flamboyant production was made possible by the fact that the score wasn't written with a specific staging in mind. The comparative vagueness of an overriding concept allows every director to come up with her/his own encompassing interpretation of the events depicted in the musical. As all three of them are readily available on DVD,[38] it is instructive to compare the varying approaches of Norman Jewison for his 1973 film adaptation, of Gale Edwards for her 1996 London revival, as well as of Lawrence Connor's 2012 arena staging.

Director Jewison and co-screenwriter Melvin Bragg wanted a purist approach to their screen adaptation, which is why they hired a mostly unknown cast and shot the film in remote locations in the Israeli desert.[39] It is difficult to gauge the commercial success of the movie, with claims that the film flopped[40] being contradicted by other sources;[41] nonetheless, it deserves careful evaluation, and not just because it has become a cult item.[42] The film is more carefully thought out than it is customarily given credit for, taking advantage of the intimacy afforded by a pre-recorded soundtrack and offering many striking images (courtesy of cameraman extraordinaire Douglas Slocombe) which support and complement the score, such as Judas being chased by tanks or running in front of a flock of sheep as well as (in the second half of the film) introducing the High Priests with shots of circling vultures. While not all of the veteran director's choices may be successful – the freeze-frames following the line 'Hey JC, would you die for me?' are jarring in their self-consciousness – at least they are always intelligent and provocative like the montage of famous paintings depicting the crucifixion after Jesus demands 'See how I die' during the song 'Gethsemane'.

Similar to the other two productions under consideration, Jewison's movie already sets up its general reading in the opening sequence. It begins with establishing shots of mountains and ruins in the Israeli desert. Then a group of young people arrive in a bus, bringing with them props and costumes. They get dressed, put on make-up and then proceed to enact the last seven days of Christ. What Jewison and Bragg present here is a modern variation of the medieval passion play, which traditionally saw Christians investigate the meaning of the Passion of Christ by re-staging it in found locations and with their own costumes and props. The latter two elements were not necessarily historically correct, as the historicizing approach to both theatre and religious rituals developed later, which helps explain the machine guns and tanks in the movie. From an early 1970s perspective, it made sense to show men and women in their late teens and early twenties trying to figure out how they can relate to the stories of the Gospels and what truth they hold for them.

When Gale Edwards was asked to direct the first major London revival of *JCS*, she set out to prove that the musical was not a relic from the 1970s without any contemporary relevance, but instead a timeless classic. Therefore, her production combines elements of the past with a set resembling an old Greek or Roman temple, the (then-) present – Jesus and the Apostles wear modern apparel (such as tank tops, combat boots or leather jackets), carry machine guns and practice martial arts – and the future, as the Roman soldiers resemble Darth Vader. The poster for the production, showing Jesus among regular people on the street, left no doubt that Edwards aimed to base her staging on the assumption that 'Jesus walks among us' or at least to ponder what would happen *if* Jesus walked among us today.

The 2012 tour of *Jesus Christ Superstar* was conceived and designed for the biggest concert venues in Britain and Australia. By hiring Australian cult comedian Tim Minchin and former Spice Girl Mel C. to play Judas and Mary, and then casting the eponymous character via a reality-TV show, Andrew Lloyd Webber made sure that the new staging had both the publicity and the star power to fill the huge arenas it was booked into. The show's director Lawrence Connor was inspired by current global socio-political events. He referenced recent anti-war demonstrations, the 2011 London riots as well as the 'Occupy' movement, filling the stage with protesters/revolutionaries with dreadlocks, tattoos or tattoo sleeves, hoodies and Che Guevara T-shirts and the forces of law and order in riot gear. The crowd carries banners or posters that read 'Rome Lies', 'People over Profits' as well as 'The 12', and later on – once Jesus has been arrested and sentenced – 'Faith Healer', 'Lord of Lies' and 'Threat to Rome'. The prison that Jesus is taken to suggests Guantanamo Bay, and during 'Could We Start Again Please?' Jesus' followers collect signatures.

While Connor's interpretation clearly aims for social significance, it isn't entirely logical: not only does it seem highly unlikely that members of the 'Occupy' protests would turn against their leaders and demand their death, one of the main disadvantages of that protest was that it didn't have one person who for the general population and the mass media came to signify the movement and what it stood and fought for. Also problematic in its backward stereotypical thinking are Connor's representation of the Jewish priests as arch capitalists and the use of sex and sexuality as signs of decadence in the Temple scene. All of these inconsistencies and questionable details go to show one thing: *JSC* is a musical that needs detailed reinterpretation if any staging is supposed to be persuasive and turn the plot into a coherent whole.

3.2 SUNG-THROUGH SHOWS: WHEN THE SPOKEN WORD IS SHUNNED

Upon opening in the West End in 1972, *Jesus Christ Superstar* was celebrated for its groundbreaking technique of telling its story: 'The most important and welcome innovation is that the authors have entirely dispensed with a book – notoriously the weakest element in modern musicals.'[43] A few years later, Andrew Lloyd Webber publicly expressed his discomfort with the traditional libretto in musical theatre, its alternation of spoken words and musical numbers:

> I find a snag with the musical. Even in the very finest shows I find worrying that awkward moment when you see the conductor raising his baton and the orchestra lurching into life during the dialogue which indicates the impending approach of music. [...] I like to write something where the music and words can get uninterrupted attention without jolts from one style to another.[44]

As David Chandler interprets this statement, the composer evidently 'considered the elimination of spoken dialogue to be his major departure from, and refinement of, the American musical',[45] regarding the all-sung format as his main contribution to the catalogue of musical theatre styles.

Yet while sung-through shows avoid the supposedly 'awkward' moment when dialogue changes into song, they have other potential drawbacks: on the one hand, they usually rely on recitative to impart some of their information, which puts the composer on the spot as these passages need to be more than filler material if they are not to be perceived as second-rate or tedious. On the other hand, when every word is set to music it alters the purpose of the lyrics, as they now have to carry such traditional dramaturgical functions as exposition as well as rising-and-falling action on their own.

Not every story lends itself to being treated this way; whereas musicals with simple plots (like *Starlight Express*) or familiar storylines (like *Joseph and the Amazing Technicolor Dreamcoat*, 1968; *Jesus Christ Superstar*, or *Spend, Spend, Spend*, 1999) can use the format to their advantage as it encourages brevity and avoids superfluous digressions, the adaptation of more complicated or subtle narratives is trickier as it requires a sure hand in story-telling, as can be seen by the respective success and failure of such musicals as *Les Misérables* and *Aspects of Love*.

Lloyd Webber's first musical without a traditional lyricist premiered in 1981; it was the composer's idea to set T. S. Eliot's 1939 collection of children's poems, *Old Possum's Book of Practical Cats*, to music. The troubled genesis of what later became *Cats* has been well documented; suffice it to say, that practically nobody believed in the project, partly because it had no storyline: each of the poems describes either the world the Jellicle Cats inhabit or deals with a different feline. Musicalized, they resemble numbers in a song cycle, which is why the final version was often categorized as a 'thematic revue'[46] or as a 'suite'[47] as opposed to a more traditional musical. Whatever (weak) link there is between the various vignettes was developed by Trevor Nunn in collaboration with the cast and the rest of the creative team during rehearsals, and concerns the question of which cat will ascend to the Heavyside Layer and will thus get the chance to have a new life.

From a dramaturgical point of view, it is perfectly legitimate to call *Cats* a revue; in this context, it should not be forgotten that the West End has relied on and tolerated revue elements in shows that were advertised as musicals far more often than Broadway: for instance, the scene at the beauty parlour and the nightclub acts in *Salad Days* (1954), one of the biggest smashes in London before Lloyd Webber came along, are basically revue sketches. (Revues were also a staple of the London theatre from the 1910s to the mid-1950s.)

Considering the totally unexpected and record-breaking success of *Cats*, it is not surprising that the composer continued in the same vein with *Starlight Express* (1984), which tellingly doesn't even credit a librettist. The musical details the rivalry between steam, diesel and electric locomotives and the races those (male) engines carry out together with their (female) carriages to become the fastest train in the world. In the end it is the underdog, the steam locomotive Rusty, who comes off as the winner of both the climactic competition and of the affections of beautiful observation car Pearl after getting encouragement from the mythical title train. Because the musical's cast portrays the trains while circling the auditorium on roller skates, similar to the actors dressed as cats prowling through the theatre in the earlier show, it was immediately dubbed *Cats II*.[48] Critics on both sides of the Atlantic chastised the roller skate derby for having even less of a plot than the 1981 musical.[49]

Depending on one's temperament, it is possible to see *Starlight Express* as either endearingly childlike or frustratingly childish, with most critics opting for the latter. For Michael Ratcliffe from *The Observer*, the dearth of three-dimensional characters and narrative finesse resulted in a show that amounted to much ado about nothing: 'The mountain labours marvellously for more than two hours and brings forth a mouse.'[50] Audiences were undeterred, though, and *Starlight Express* turned into one of the biggest hits in British theatre history, lasting for 17 years and 7,406 performances at the vast Apollo Victoria Theatre, but the New York transfer became the first major flop Lloyd Webber had on Broadway, where the musical closed after a mere 761 performances.

After *Jesus Christ Superstar*, *Evita*, *Cats* and *Starlight Express*, Andrew Lloyd Webber had established sung-through musicals as the norm in British musical theatre, and the form proved equally capable of unfolding complicated epic stories (e.g. *Les Misérables* – see Case Study 10) as it was at achieving powerful effects through the suggestiveness of musical and theatrical means (e.g. *The Phantom of the Opera* – see Case Study 11). The two musicals had been produced by Cameron Mackintosh, who went on to bring three musicals by Alain Boublil and Claude-Michel Schönberg to the London stage. The last of these was the lavish *Martin Guerre*, loosely based on the real-life sixteenth-century French impostor of the same name. The story of Arnaud du Thil, who returns to his Catholic village from fighting the Huguenots, pretends to be the eponymous character and then falls in love with Guerre's wife Bertrande, was certainly the kind of epic, emotionally charged subject that according to co-lyricist Stephen Clark[51] lends itself to be presented in the consistently heightened way of the sung-through musical.

Yet the show was not the global triumph everybody expected it to be: after receiving mixed reviews upon its première on 19 July 1996, *Martin Guerre* was extensively retooled by its creative team and reopened on 11 November of the same year. That version went on to win the 1997 Laurence Oliver Award for 'Best New Musical'; nonetheless, the show closed after a disappointing 675 performances. Still not content with the way the story had been told, in 1998 the writers took the opportunity to revise the musical once again for the West Yorkshire Playhouse in Leeds; this third variant featured a completely rewritten libretto and several new songs. The 1999–2000 US tour then offered yet another rendering of the tale; at the time, Mackintosh estimated: 'Forty percent of the current material was not in the original.'[52] The fourth attempt to get it right also did not result in a definitive rendition, and in May 2014 Boublil and Schönberg announced that they were again reworking the show.

Looking back at the complicated gestation of the musical, Mackintosh later concluded: 'With *Martin Guerre* I don't think either Alain or Claude-Michel realized how big a problem it is to write a dramatic musical not based on an existing source.'[53] Indeed, the show's tepid reception in all its existing versions can be mainly attributed to a lack of narrative congruity and thematic unity; in spite of its several rewrites, the show did not manage to relate the developments of the plot convincingly to its subject of religious intolerance. As Clark later admitted: 'One of the biggest problems with *Martin Guerre* has always been to get the Protestant and Catholic backdrop to tie in with the love story.'[54] The checkered history of the show demonstrates that sometimes even 'musical dramatists with a mastery of the sung-through form'[55] like the two Frenchmen may encounter difficulties when trying to shape their material to their satisfaction.

3.3 STAGE ADAPTATIONS OF NOVELS: WHEN THE WRITTEN WORD BECOMES THEATRICAL ACTION

The reasons why so many artists engaged in musical theatre are attracted to the work of novelists are obvious: great books already supply carefully developed storylines, usually with copious forward momentum, and well-rounded protagonists; they also deal with universal questions. Considering the sheer length of most books, a certain simplification of both its plot and characters is in most cases unavoidable during the adaptation process for the stage. Yet even the bare bones of the original may be sufficient in helping to bring structure to an evening of song and dance, while the book's narrative drive can still propel the musical towards its final scene in a thoroughly engaging and entertaining way. In certain cases, on the other hand, not that many alterations are necessary.

For instance, when playwright Dennis Kelly and songwriter Tim Minchin musicalized Roald Dahl's 1988 children's book classic *Matilda* for the Royal Shakespeare Company in 2011, they reordered the events described in the novel, but otherwise made just a few crucial changes in order to strengthen the narrative coherence of the musical version. Matilda's mother, Mrs Wormwood, got a new hobby: instead of constantly playing bingo, she is wildly obsessed with ballroom dancing, which lends itself more naturally to being explored on stage in a musical. Kelly also added the ongoing fable Matilda spins for the librarian Mrs Phelps about a world-famous acrobat and his love, an escapologist. This not only later in the show provides an unexpected link to Matilda's future foster mother, Miss Honey, but also illustrates the little girl's love of story-telling. Furthermore, it will prove that good fiction can magically spring to life – just like *Matilda* did in front of the audience's eyes.

Although some novels may need updating to remain relevant for contemporary audiences, others work best as period pieces, because this is what constitutes their charm. P. G. Wodehouse's stories about disorganized idle gentleman Bertie Wooster and his unflappable butler Jeeves belong to the latter category, and formed the foundation of Andrew Lloyd Webber's first attempt to adapt a novel – or, in this case, several stories. It was also his first and, for nearly two decades, only attempt to write a traditional book musical. After Tim Rice dropped out because he felt he couldn't do justice to the source material,[56] Lloyd Webber proceeded to adapt the Wodehouse stories together with Alan Ayckbourn, already a revered playwright, but a novice at both lyric and libretto writing. When the show premiered on 22 April 1975 in the West End, *Jeeves* emerged as an enormous flop, with Sheridan Morley calling it 'a disaster of Titanic proportions'.[57] The production closed after 38 performances, and it is very likely that Lloyd Webber's humiliating experience with *Jeeves* reinforced his opinion that musicals work better without dialogue scenes.

Unbeknownst to him, Lloyd Webber's *Jesus Christ Superstar* had inspired two Frenchmen to try their hand at writing in the sung-through format.

After first tackling one of the most important historical events of their country in this style with *La Révolution Française* (1973), Alain Boublil and Claude-Michel Schönberg turned their attention to one of the most revered novels ever to come out of France, Victor Hugo's rousing tale of social injustice, political struggle and personal redemption, *Les Misérables*, and the result was one of the biggest hits in theatre history (and the subject of Case Study 10 below).

In the years that followed, there were many who tried their hands at musicalizing 'serious subjects of epic dimensions'[58] adapted from beloved literary works. By far the best received of these was Boublil and Schönberg's next musical, *Miss Saigon*, a paraphrase of Giacomo Puccini's *Madama Butterfly* set during the Vietnam War. The 1904 opera was partially based on Pierre Loti's autobiographical novel *Madame Chrysanthème* (1887), itself another inspiration for the musical.[59] The tragic love story between American GI Chris and Vietnamese bar-girl Kim, who meet just before the fall of Saigon in 1975, ran for ten years and 4,264 performances in London and lasted nearly as long in New York, where it closed after 4,092 performances. Most of the time, though, attempts to follow in the footprints of *Les Miz* resulted in disaster: several notorious West End flops, such as *Tess of the D'Urbervilles* (1999) or *The Far Pavilions* (2005), illustrated what a formidable achievement the Victor Hugo retelling was.

In 1986, Andrew Lloyd Webber also presented a musical based on a French novel: *The Phantom of the Opera* was loosely adapted from Gaston Leroux's 1910 romantic mystery. The show, together with its successor *Aspects of Love*, 'mark[ed] a return to strong storyline and a new exploration of characterization through music'[60] for the composer. The suspenseful tale of the ghost haunting the Parisian Opéra Populaire is the first musical for which the composer was credited with the book,[61] and although the libretto is far from perfect, it wisely retains the key elements that made the source material so attractive: its near-mythical constellation of menace and innocence, embodied in the potentially lethal, abhorrent-looking creature hiding in the dark, and the beautiful girl who could set it free; its three archetypical main characters (the tortured, disfigured musical genius; the ravishing ingénue and the dependable young aristocrat), as well as its majestic backdrop. Both Harold Prince's staging and the score imbue *The Phantom of the Opera* (which will be discussed in detail at the end of this section) with perpetual forward momentum; in this respect, as Jessica Sternfeld explains, the sung-through format facilitates the unravelling of the enigmatic events at a steady, measured pace: 'Many numbers feature only vague beginnings or ends and run without pause into the next number, with the result that much of the score cannot be divided into set pieces at all. A continuous string of material moves the story from event to event.'[62]

Like Leroux's novel, the source material for Lloyd Webber's next musical had been more or less forgotten by the British public when the composer announced that he would musicalize David Garnett's 1955 novella *Aspects of Love* – in many ways just as crucial a show for the composer's career as *The Phantom of the Opera*. On the one hand, it is the first of his musicals to deal with ordinary human beings (as opposed to biblical figures, animals, mechanical objects or larger-than-life characters like Eva Perón or Jeeves). On the other hand, it showcased for many reviewers the limitations of the sung-through format, and they were very vocal in their objections.

Aspects of Love is the rare musical where most of the book trouble lies in the first act and not in the second. The show has five major characters: English soldier Alex, his uncle, *bon vivant* and artistic *éminence grise*, George, French actress Rose, Italian sculptress Guilietta and teenager Jenny, the daughter of George and Rose. The love roundelay between them gets off to such a flying start in the first half of the evening, with Rose shifting her affections back and forth several times between Alex and his uncle and then having a quick lesbian affair with Guilietta, that it is impossible to take any of the protagonists' feelings seriously. The plot becomes more believable in Act Two, when most of the characters approach middle age and Alex feels tempted to bed his young cousin Jenny, an urge that he seems more and more unable to resist. With George afraid of losing his daughter and Rose fearing old age and loneliness, the show finally portrays sentiments of mortality and loss that ground the proceedings in a recognizable reality.

One of the drawbacks of a sung-through show, according to director Nicholas Hytner, is 'that banalities have to be sung because it's impossible to tell a story on stage without at some point having to have banal exchanges of information or mundane conversation'.[63] This was certainly the case with *Aspects of Love*, and for many theatregoers Andrew Lloyd Webber and his lyricists – once again no librettist was credited – pushed the concept of the dialogue-free musical to its absolute limits by having the actors intone even the most prosaic of remarks. Reviewers remained unconvinced of the result and complained that having every single utterance set to music did not suit the subject matter; for many, the convention simply seemed silly. Kenneth Hurren demurred: 'When such lines as "Shall I make some coffee?" or "Have a pleasant journey" are *sung*, I hardly feel that we are touching matters that only music can express. It just strikes me as foolish and diminishing.'[64] The Garnett adaption did not do as well as hoped for, especially when compared to Lloyd Webber's previous works; on Broadway *Aspects of Love* turned into one of the biggest flops in history.[65] It would be another 15 years before Andrew Lloyd Webber set out to adapt a novel again.

Wilkie Collins' *The Woman in White* is regarded as the first 'sensation novel' and caused a sales mania upon publication.[66] With its convoluted mystery, the intricately plotted voluminous book poses several major challenges to any adaptor, especially if it is to be turned into a sung-through musical of less than three hours. Yet it is not just the inevitable and difficult task of whittling down the plot to a manageable length that may give one pause; there are two other potential stumbling blocks. On the one hand, the events of the novel are told by numerous different narrators via diary entries, letters, official documents and other means, so that the protagonist (with her/his point of view on the events) and thus the focus of the story changes constantly. On the other hand, the whole mystery revolves around the family background of the antagonist, Sir Percival Glyde, who tries to prevent anyone from discovering that he is illegitimate, a fact that would rob him of his title and social position.

From a modern perspective, the secret of being born out of wedlock hardly seems to justify the elaborate machinations set in motion to conceal it, which is why the creative team behind the musical version, comprising Lloyd Webber, lyricist David Zippel, librettist Charlotte Jones and director Trevor Nunn, struggled to come up with a suitable replacement, in the end settling for the story that Glyde had raped Anne Cathericke, the titular 'woman in white', and later drowned their child. In addition, although the story has a great villain in Count Foscoe, and in Marian Halcombe features one of the first active heroines in a mystery novel, it has a lot of plot, yet often rather scant characterization, especially when it comes to the central pair of lovers, Laura Fairlie and Walter Hartright.[67] The musical deals with these potential shortcomings by opting for a retelling that is 'freely adapted'[68] from its source material; it dispenses with several major characters and provides more depth for those who remain by clarifying their motifs: in the stage version, Marian is also in love with Walter and therefore first acts out of jealousy and later out of contrition, Walter struggles with alcoholism and Laura grows throughout in determination, demonstrating considerable moral strength at the end of the musical when she forces Glyde to confess to his crimes.

The musical starts its story right away, moving swiftly from beginning to end; there is neither an overture nor an entr'acte. It benefits enormously from a carefully delineated structure, which subtly foreshadows and thus prepares for later plot developments,[69] as well as from narrative clarity. The first of these merits comes most likely courtesy of librettist Jones, while the latter is a trademark of the directorial style of Nunn. Praise should also go to Zippel's deft handling of lyrics, which here function as characterization, but at the same time also serve as exposition, rising action and climax. The nefarious criminal activities of the villains, and the protagonists' desperate attempts to thwart them, required rapid changes of scenes and locations, which was only made possible by one of the show's most controversial elements: set designer William Dudley employed full-scale, complex projections in place of traditional scenery. They not only changed constantly, but so often shifted perspective that some theatregoers felt nauseous. In spite of its achievements *The Woman in White* struggled to find an audience, mainly because its producers did not know how to market it – the show changed its poster and advertising campaign four times in order to impart a proper impression of what the musical was about and what it was like. Later revisions did not help and the musical closed early;[70] it still awaits rediscovery.

While Tim Rice seemingly lost his way in the 1980s, with two commercial disappointments in a row, his star began to ascend again in the 1990s, with the help of Disney. The two shows he wrote for the corporation – *Beauty and the Beast* (1994) and *Aida* (1999) – both had traditional books by Linda Woolverton, and their successful runs in New York must have eased his decision to agree to work on a musical that also would feature dialogue scenes: a stage adaptation of James Jones' novel *From Here to Eternity*. Rice and his collaborators Stuart Brayson (music) and Bill Oakes (book) were nothing if not ambitious – to translate Jones' magnum opus in its original, uncensored form of 842 pages into a musical of less than three hours was a formidable challenge. The bestseller covers military life on Hawaii in the months leading up to the attack on Pearl Harbor on 7 December 1941 and depicts two love affairs, the one between Sergeant Warden and Karen Holmes, the wife of his superior officer, and that of private Prewitt and prostitute Lorene. For the most part, the musical unfolded its complicated storyline remarkably well, even if it lacked clarity and transparency at key moments, which slightly undermined its emotional impact.

The show got off to a shaky start with a confusing opening: the first person to appear on stage is Angelo Maggio, a peculiar choice as he is an important, yet ultimately secondary character. The next scene introduces the two female protagonists Karen and Lorene as they meet when both of them leave Hawaii; since this happens at the end of the novel, it turns the rest of the show into one long flashback – a dramaturgical ruse which fails to add meaning or suspense. Crucial bits of information were either never introduced (for instance, why Prewitt refuses to bugle any more) or were easy to miss so that the suicide of a minor character could be misconstrued as happening without any real motivation. The show also left the audience guessing about the fate of its second male protagonist, Sergeant Warden, as it never became clear whether he had survived the attack of the Japanese. In addition, director Tamara Harvey occasionally blundered in her task to focus audience attention where it was needed, undermining Angelo's big number in Act Two 'I Love the Army' through distracting scenery and excessive movement in the background; there was also too much going on during Prewitt's last song ('Almost Perfect Lie') for it to register with full force.

At a time when most West End and Broadway musicals are content to adapt well-known movies, hoping that their popularity with all age groups translates into ticket sales, in addition to hiring pop stars as composers as well as TV stars as actors to attract publicity, *From Here to Eternity – the Musical* went a refreshingly different route: this was a musical for grown-ups

Figure 12 A musical for adults dealing with war, death, military life and sexual desire – Robert Lonsdale (Prewitt, standing on the right), Marc Antolin (Angelo, sitting on the right) among the male chorus in *From Here to Eternity*, Shaftesbury Theatre 2013. Photograph by John Persson. Courtesy of ArenaPAL.

that tackled adult themes. With Rice himself the only 'name' in the creative team and a cast made up of unknowns and West End veterans, the show may have flopped,[71] but at least it flopped with artistic integrity.

Case Study 10: *Les Misérables*

'Where are they going to put the guillotine?'

(Overheard at a performance of *Les Misérables* at
London's Queens Theatre[72])

It is a common misperception that *Les Misérables*, or *Les Miz* (as it has been affectionately dubbed by its fans), the longest-running musical in London history, plays out its epic story with the French Revolution as its backdrop. But instead of covering the events of 1789, it is built around an otherwise little-known student uprising and riots, which are deemed to be 'very minor happenings'.[73] That did not seem to matter to the initial readers of Victor Hugo's epic tale: the original publication in 1862, accompanied by a mass-marketing machine, was a media event[74] and created such excitement that the 'original Paris print run of 7,000 copies sold out within 24 hours'.[75] The public may have taken *Les Misérables* to its heart immediately, but the critical establishment, judging the epic tale as overly sentimental, at first did not, and this reception history would be repeated when, more than 120 years later, a musical based on Hugo's (by now universally admired) tome opened at London's Barbican Centre in 1985.[76] But that show, co-produced by the Royal Shakespeare Company (RSC) and Cameron Mackintosh, was not the first version of the adaptation: the French songwriting team of Alain Boublil and Claude-Michel Schönberg had started work on the show in 1978, and released a French-language recording of their material in 1980, which sold 260,000 copies and quickly led to a highly popular stage production in Paris.[77]

Excursus: the French variant of musical theatre

Though it may not be widely known in the UK, the French have their very own form of musical theatre, which is usually performed in huge venues and consists of works that are mostly based on popular novels, plays or films. Since the audience shares at least a basic acquaintance with the story of the source material, the writers of these musical adaptations can forego a detailed retelling of the plot, including expository scenes which set up the characters. Basically, the songwriters musicalize highlights of the story, key moments of the drama that even people who haven't read the book or seen the movie the musical is based on can recall, so that it might be fitting to categorize them as 'loosely based' on their sources. Boublil has pointed out that in the case of *Les Misérables* most people in France are so familiar with the novel's plot that 'they would grow impatient if they were taken through the whole story.'[78] It should be emphasized, though, that this impatience with an overly detailed and faithful narrative covering the whole story is a specific feature of French musical theatre only; it does not extend to TV or movie adaptations.

Because these musical productions are housed in sports palaces or rock arenas, they are usually cast with popular singers, rather than actors – performers who have the experience in playing to a huge crowd and can attract enough fans to fill the space. The choice of venue is dictated partly by the fact that neither the subsidized French theatres nor the private theatre companies ever put on musicals with open-end runs, which means those established venues are unavailable. Yet if a much larger stage is the only alternative, it affects every detail of the production, not just the casting: the set, the choreography, the costume and lighting design need to go for bold artistic statements instead of subtle indications. In order for the creative decisions and ideas to be picked up by an audience of up to 5,000 people, they have to be big and spectacular, which explains the term *spectacle musical*.

Boublil and Schönberg's *La Révolution Française* (1973), the very first of these musical dramas, was inspired by *Jesus Christ Superstar*, and practically all of the *spectacle musicals* that followed took their cue for how to handle their dramaturgy from the 1970 British rock opera: not only did they dispense with dialogue, but they progressively relied on the audience to fill in any gaps in the story-telling, which at times was reduced to the absolute minimum. Among these French works, which inevitably premiered in Paris either at the Palais des Sports (4,500 seats) or the Congrès de Paris (3,723 seats), are (in chronological order): *Starmania* (1979) by Michel Berger and Luc Plamondon,[79] *Les Misérables* (1980), *Notre-Dame de Paris* (1998), a musicalization of Victor Hugo's 1831 masterpiece *The Hunchback of Notre Dame* by Richard Cocciante and Luc Plamondon, and *Roméo et Juliette* (2001) – adapted from Shakespeare's tragedy – by Gérard Presgurvic.

Because a *spectacle musical* has a completely different approach to narrative than a West End or Broadway show, it is misleading to label it a 'musical' for an English-language audience. That financiers and creatives have insisted on doing so has more than once been their undoing, since the terminology they employed raised expectations, which their productions simply could not fulfil. In this context it is very telling how London critics responded to two other French 'musicals' that crossed the Channel in the early 2000s. *Notre-Dame de Paris* managed to survive for 17 months in spite of devastating notices, with most reviewers decrying a disastrous lack of dramaturgical know-how. In the opinion of the *Independent on Sunday*, '*Notre Dame de Paris* makes no effort to dramatise the story or waste any time on characters or scenes. [...] there's no pause, no reflection, no dramatic insight.'[80]

Gérard Presgurvic's adaptation of Shakespeare's *Romeo and Juliet* got similarly harsh reviews in November 2002 and closed after less than four months. Once again, the way the famous tale of the 'star-crossed lovers' was set to music provoked the ire of the London critics, with Matt Wolf blasting the 'musical' for being 'of such mind-numbing ineptitude that one only wishes it were that little bit worse so it could qualify as a camp classic.'[81] His colleague Lyn Gardner shared his disdain: 'It is truly tragic – but not in the way that Shakespeare intended, and surely not in the way that the producers had in mind. [...] The plot remains largely as imagined by Shakespeare. Regrettably though, all passion and poetry have been carefully excised.'[82]

Mainly because the 1985 London version of *Les Misérables* was significantly shaped by its British producer, British writers and British directors, its commercial fate was different. But then, Alain Boublil has underlined that the main inspiration for the Hugo adaptation was two British musicals, so there was already a link to the West End. First, he and his writing partner Claude-Michel Schönberg wanted to follow the path forged by Andrew Lloyd Webber and Tim Rice's *Jesus Christ Superstar* (1970). The two Frenchmen not only modelled their dramaturgical format on that concept album with its innovative approach of telling its story entirely through song,[83] but also encouraged Schönberg to construct his score in a similar fashion to the earlier musical by using reprises and contrafacta exactly like the British composer had done.[84] Lionel Bart's *Oliver!* (1960) provided the second impetus: while seeing a London revival of the Charles Dickens adaptation, the Artful Dodger, one of its most colourful characters, reminded Boublil of street urchin Gavroche in Hugo's novel, and that was the starting point for the whole project.[85] Ironically, one of the few territories where *Les Miz* failed to find an audience is France; when the rewritten musical returned to its place of origin, it only lasted seven months and lost

$3.7 million[86] – it seems that, just like the British, the French prefer the kind of musical theatre they are accustomed to and reject alternative approaches.

From Dickens to Hugo: the influence of The Life and Adventures of Nicholas Nickleby

Although impresario Cameron Mackintosh was very taken with the musical material of the 1980 *Les Misérables* when he first encountered it in form of the French recording, he realized that in order to present it to a British audience not that familiar with Hugo's novel, it would need to be extensively rewritten. The producer approached Trevor Nunn and John Caird, who had proven a few years prior to *Les Miz* that they knew how to handle such a demanding assignment when their epic stage production of Charles Dickens' *The Life and Adventures of Nicholas Nickleby* (1979) turned into an artistic triumph for the RSC. There was also the additional link that both Hugo and Dickens incorporated elements of melodrama with its abundance of accidental encounters and sentimental episodes into their respective novels to transport profound and harsh criticism of the ills and injustices of their society, in order to make their socio-political agenda palatable to their readers.

The nine-hour retelling of *Nicholas Nickleby* shares several important elements with the Hugo musical, especially in its approach to stage design and comedy. (The latter will be discussed in greater detail below.) The designer of both shows, John Napier, would devise a set for *Les Miz* that for the most part was just as pivotal and similarly spare,[87] but featured one truly spectacular element, the barricade. Napier came up with a stage design for nineteenth-century France that restricted itself to a colour palette of 'down-to-earth', as *New York Times* critic Frank Rich put it.[88] Depicting a world of 'grey cobblestones [and] grey-granite Haussmann buildings', the scenery is complemented by a costume design (courtesy of Andreane Neofitou) that is also dominated by the colour grey, yet adds subtle accents to emphasize the specific nature of a group of characters – the clothes of the farmers have an orange tinge, while the factory workers are dressed in a shade of bluish grey.[89]

Reviewers were quick to pick up on the artistic connections between the two RSC productions, highlighting that *Les Miz* was '[v]ery much in the style'[90] of *Nicholas Nickleby* and that is was akin to the latter 'gone gloriously show biz – [...] with conviction, inspiration and taste',[91] indicating that in this case the collaboration between subsidized and privately funded theatre, at first regarded with suspicion by the British theatre industry and the British press, had actually brought out the best in each other.

How to turn a spectacle musical into British stage entertainment

Any theatre production that goes beyond a certain length will have to find ways to keep the audience intrigued. Since the novel *Les Misérables* is truly epic in that it combines attention to historic detail with multilayered story-telling, its sheer volume[92] and narrative complexity require careful adaptation in order to maintain its pace and entertainment value throughout what most likely will be a rather long evening in the theatre. Because the musical as a genre can encompass so many various forms of performance, musical theatre writers usually endeavour to offer constant diversity by alternating and mixing its presentational modes to vary both the rhythm and the atmosphere of the piece. As lyricist Richard Maltby Jr. expounds: 'Generally, it's a case of ballad followed by action, followed by dance movement; comedy at regular intervals, a flow from solos and duets to chorus numbers.'[93] *Les Misérables* only emulates this template to a certain degree: first of all, as it is sung-through, the musical eschews the alternation of dialogue scenes and musical numbers and thus one of the most commonplace variations in performance modes. Moreover, in Act Two it presents three ballads in a row ('A Little Fall of Rain', 'Drink with Me' and 'Bring Him Home'). Finally, it has no choreography or even stylized movement, a decision that the two co-directors made right at the beginning of their work on the musical.[94]

This means that on the one hand *Les Miz* foregoes many features that make up a 'traditional' West End or Broadway show. On the other hand, it employs certain elements that define the best of all musicals. To begin with, the Hugo adaptation is a perfect example of collaboration, the most important prerequisite for creating a successful show. The seven members of the creative team – producer Cameron Mackintosh, composer Claude-Michel Schönberg, French lyricist Alain Boublil, original English lyricist James Fenton, his replacement Herbert Kretzmer, as well as co-directors Trevor Nunn and John Caird – challenged and complemented each other to the point where it was difficult to identify who exactly came up with what idea. John Caird emphasized: 'As to which of the creators is responsible for what, it is always impossible to disentangle the complexities of a true collaboration. You lose your contribution in everybody else's, which is one of the most exciting things about the musical theatre.'[95]

The show also has a rousing Act One finale, 'One Day More', which sets up high expectations for the second half of the show. In form and impact resembling an oratorio,[96] this number brings together all the various plot strands of the musical by assembling the whole cast on stage with each of the characters expressing their fears and hopes regarding the impending uprising. Lyricist Kretzmer proudly remarked that, for him, 'it's a scene of huge musical ingenuity, and it is undoubtedly one of the high water marks of twentieth century musical theatre'.[97] Moreover, as Kathryn Grossman and Bradley Stephens demonstrate, 'the unification and interaction of the different melodies perfectly exhibit Boublil and Schönberg's dedication to channeling how Hugo understood individual experience as part of a sublime collective'.[98]

Another staple of musical theatre is to finish on a high note (in this case, literally), and the final moments of *Les Miz* follow this blueprint in two different ways: first, we see Jean Valjean reunited in death with Fantine and Eponine, which is 'reassuring'[99] to the audience. This scene leads to a reprise of the rousing 'Do You Hear the People Sing', a song that its composer Schönberg describes as 'uplifting'[100], although not everybody agreed: for William A. Henry III, commenting in *Time*, the show 'denies itself the indulgence of even a muted happy ending. Its last image is of struggles to come.'[101] Irrespective of whether the individual theatregoer interprets that last number as heartening or defiant, it never fails to get the audience to its feet and roar its approval.

Although Boublil insists that it already comprised 70 per cent of the final show,[102] Trevor Nunn, who co-directed the 1985 London production, has emphasized that the French original would be more accurately described as 'Scenes from *Les Misérables*' or 'A Musical Impression of *Les Misérables*'.[103] It took more than three years before the reconceived musical had a form that adhered to 'traditions of English story-telling'.[104] What has rightfully been praised as the 'seamlessness'[105] of the show's plotline and its 'emotional clarity'[106] is the result of a painstaking process, which included the co-directors drawing up 'a very detailed, scene-by-scene synopsis'[107] of how they wanted to adapt the narrative, which served as a guide to the rest of the creative team. The French original had a running time of less than two hours and omitted the whole backstory of the main protagonist. There were no solos for such major characters as Javert, Marius or Eponine; also missing were 'Dog Eat Dog', 'Turning' and the ballroom scene.[108] While Valjean had one big number ('Who Am I?') at the beginning of the show, he had no song during the whole section of the riots,[109] which led to the addition of 'Bring Him Home'.

When it turned out that the original English lyricist James Fenton, a journalist and literary critic, could not write the kind of lyrics needed for the production since they were 'too poetic, too intellectual, and in parts just not singable',[110] he was replaced by Herbert Kretzmer, whose lyrics have their share of clunkers with several lines neither in period nor in character (like Fantine's decidedly modern 'And her father abandoned us, leaving us flat'[111]) but were later praised by critics as 'succinct, well-pointed and economically dramatic'.[112] Yet Fenton made one crucial contribution to the show: he suggested adding a prologue that showed Jean Valjean's release from prison and his conversion to a devout Christian after the kindness of a clergyman brings on a spiritual crisis.[113]

The Bishop of Digne is a true representative of the Christian faith who practises what he preaches; he helps out his fellow man with food and shelter, even though he himself is far from affluent. Even more importantly, he is willing to forgive: by confirming Valjean's lie that the silver he stole was a gift and then shaming him by forcing him to also accept the silver candlesticks, he illustrates to Valjean the altruism demanded by the New Testament. He trusts that his act of kindness will not only make the thief repent, but will win him over to a Christian life of sacrifice. Leading by example, he practises the most persuasive of religious recruitment strategies, since he shows that behaving kindly will change your own life and the lives of those around you for the better.

With the addition of the prologue and the other numbers listed above, the musical gained both narrative clarity and complexity, but threatened to become far too long for one evening.[114] In order to compress the source material as much as possible, fascinating facts that enriched the original, like the revelation that Gavroche and Eponine are siblings, were jettisoned, 'because they overcomplicated the story'.[115] As a result, the musical 'chooses sweeping and hurtling motion over the savoring of minute details'.[116] In the end, the show settled for a running time of less than three hours, which 'equals the time it takes most people to read less than 5 per cent of Hugo's text'.[117] Edward Behr insists that 'surprisingly little' of the novel was left out of the musical version, since it merely 'condenses the action, [thus] speeding up the plot'. But it does substitute bold and courageous deeds for interior struggles, which is not surprising for a stage adaption as it has to externalize what a novel can impart via narration, so that the musical theatre Valjean gains 'the status of an action hero'.[118] Moreover, the omissions and compressions alter the pace with which the story is told: 'Whereas the novel enjoys an expansive rhythm, with long descriptive periods alternating with (sometimes equally long) periods of action and high drama, the musical moves quickly from one major episode to another.'[119] Still, the musical retained the tome's vitality,[120] even if it 'is more overwhelming than subtle.'[121]

The creative team of *Les Miz* achieved its objective of narrative clarity, which is so important for attracting theatregoers who are unfamiliar with the novel, partly through the musical's staging and stage design. Both were developed based on considerations of how best to present the show's rapidly evolving story: because right from the prologue, the musical's setting changes constantly and because Trevor Nunn saw Javert's unremitting pursuit of Valjean as a never-ending chase, he and designer John Napier decided to employ a revolving stage.[122] This allowed for perpetual motion when telling the narrative but also gave the production cinematic flair – as did another of the musical's most famous directorial flourishes, the use of slow motion in key moments (like the accident with Fauchelevent's cart and the Act One finale). The more or less continuous flow of music, including ceaseless underscoring during scene changes, serves a comparable purpose of creating a fast-moving production that only catches its breath at carefully chosen instances. A fine example for the latter is 'Bring Him Home': after avoiding interruptions by applause for most of the evening, this stirring ballad builds up such a surge of emotion in the audience that it needs the cathartic opportunity to express its feelings (and its admiration for the performer who delivers the song), and so Nunn and Caird wisely left a tiny window for the inevitable cheering and bravos.

The metaphysical elements in the novel and in the musical

The creators struggled not only with cutting the plot down to a manageable size, but also found it difficult to render the novel's religious dimension. In the end, the former proved easier to achieve than the latter. John Caird explained: '*Les Misérables* is actually a very simple story, not like a Dickens story, which has got incredible detail and hundreds of different interrelating characters.'[123] Not everybody would agree with that statement – the plot summary of the musical given in the original Broadway cast recording is in the tiniest of fonts, but still fills a whole page[124] – but it is definitely true that the religious philosophy underlying Hugo's novel is very carefully conceptualized, with three major characters representing three contrasting principles of faith: through his experience with the Bishop, Jean Valjean comes to believe in the forgiving God of the New Testament who allows you to makes mistakes, thus accepting human fallibility, and loves you nonetheless, whereas Inspector Javert is a staunch believer[125] in the God depicted in the Old Testament who demands strict obedience of the (religious) law and severely punishes those who defy him.[126] The third side of the triangle is represented by the nihilism of Thénardier, who 'not only believes that God is dead but that he died a long time ago and that we are fair game to him'.[127]

Each of the three characters was given a song that epitomized their stance on life and that according to Caird did not serve any 'dramatic function whatsoever',[128] but were a dramaturgical requisite: 'What you need the songs for is to deepen the emotional experience and understanding of these three characters and to appreciate their positions more clearly.'[129] In chronological order these three solos are 'Stars', 'Bring Him Home' and 'Dog Eats Dog'. As Valjean's conversion to Christianity has already been described in detail above, and the prayer-like 'Bring Him Home' merely serves as a confirmation of his altruistic, self-sacrificing principles, it is the other two numbers that shall be focused on here.

In 'Stars', the first of these three added songs, Javert reveals to the audience why he is so obsessed with recapturing Jean Valjean: for the inspector, the former prisoner is 'a fugitive running, / Fallen from grace' (p. 177), and as representative of both the state and the church ('Mine is the way of the Lord', p. 177), it is Javert's task to bring the criminal to justice, and this task must be fulfilled without compassion or mercy, because once you have broken the law you can never be redeemed.[130] Only by acting out what he perceives to be the Lord's demands, does Javert preserve his own chance to enter Paradise after his death: 'Those who do follow the path of the righteous / Shall have their reward' (p. 177).

Thénardier gets an opportunity to disclose his philosophy of life in Act Two when he robs the men who have fallen during the uprising, a scene fittingly located in the Parisian sewers. The innkeeper-turned-thief has no second thoughts about stealing from the dead: 'And God in his Heaven / He don't interfere / 'Cos he's dead as the stiff at my feet' (p. 187). Without a higher authority to judge (and penalize) your actions, there is no incentive to behave anything but selfishly: it's survival of the fittest, and the meek only serve as fodder to those who are stronger and less scrupulous.

Since Hugo was a devout Christian, it comes as no surprise that it is Valjean's faith that persists. The altruistic, humane attitude of Hugo's epic tale finds its most succinct expression in a lyric sung at Valjean's deathbed, where the dying protagonist as well as Fantine and Eponine sing in perfect harmony, thus giving three-voice support to the statement: 'And remember / The truth

that once was spoken, / To love another person / Is to see the face of God'
(p. 191). Trevor Nunn relates that 'when that line came from Herbie
[Kretzmer] we knew that we'd got absolutely to the center of the work and
had said something that Hugo would be moved by and acknowledged the
truth of.'[131]

In contrast to Valjean, both Javert and the Thénardiers fail to remodel
French society according to their principles: the inspector cannot live with
the fact that his life was spared by a former criminal and starts to doubt his
whole outlook on life; unable (and unwilling) to accept that his worldview
may have been wrong, he commits suicide. In the novel, Madame Thénardier
dies and her husband leaves France, finding a new occupation as a slave
trader.

Although the musical stays very close to the philosophical underpinnings
of its source material, there are aspects of the show that divert from the
novelist's religious worldview. For Hugo, the 'plight of the *misérables* is that
of the world entire, in which an individual descent into wretchedness can
still find deliverance through altruism and humanity.'[132] Thus the French
writer, who by the time he concluded *Les Misérables* in the early 1860s had
become a 'genuine radical',[133] was convinced that to live according to
Christian principles as he understood them would ultimately make the
world a better place. Edward Behr underlines that Hugo's concern for
humanity 'stemmed from a profoundly romantic belief in the existence of
an all-high Divine Providence rewarding the good and punishing the
evil.'[134] With that in mind, the song 'Turning' as well as the survival of the
Thénardiers who, in a striking departure from the novel, in the musical do
not get their comeuppance, but escape justice and most likely will continue
to thrive ('We're the ones who make it in the end! / [...] / Clear away the
barricades / And we're still there!', p. 190) clearly go against the novelist's
outlook on life.

One element that Nunn and Caird did not want to do without, as it had
been essential for the success of *Nicholas Nickleby*, was humour. While
Hugo's epic offers an embarrassment of riches including multitudes of deftly
sketched characters, narrative sweep, set pieces both thrilling and moving as
well as 'book-length digressions [...] on religion, Napoleon, Waterloo,
French politics in the first half of the nineteenth century and French slang',[135]
what it does not resort to is comedy, probably because the iconic French
writer 'was first and foremost, by nature as well as by conviction, a romantic'.[136]
His treatment of the melodramatic incidents which form a large part of the
book's plot is entirely earnest, thereby ensuring their full impact.

176

When the creators of *Les Miz* turned the Thénardiers into comic relief – they have the only funny numbers in both the first and the second act ('Master of the House' and 'Beggars at the Feast')[137] – they became the villains the audience loves to hate, instead of the despicable criminals of the novel. Notwithstanding the way in which the two characters have been reconceived in both the writing and acting renders them more Dickensian than Hugo-esque, there is no denying that the depiction of Madame and Monsieur Thénardier as comic scoundrels is an important factor of the show's continuing popularity.

'Turning' (sometimes referred to as 'Carousel'), the women's fatalistic reaction to and wistful reflection on the failed student uprising, came about because Caird and Nunn wanted to give the female members of the chorus something to do in Act Two.[138] The number was the idea of Herbert Kretzmer, but its defeatism ('Nothing changes, nothing ever will', p. 188) contradicts Hugo's belief that no good deed done for your fellow man is ever in vain, because it is a necessary stepping stone to a better future. The inclusion of this song is particularly puzzling as Caird has correctly identified that *Les Misérables*, both the novel and the musical, 'is ultimately a piece about sacrifice. Fantine sacrifices herself for Cosette, Eponine sacrifices herself for Marius, Valjean sacrifices himself for Fantine and Cosette and finally for Marius, Enjolras and the students sacrifice themselves for what they believe',[139] so for the stage version to suggest that the latter action was pointless is illogical.

Here, the musical wonders whether altruism always changes the world for the better; it also questions the chances of bringing to justice those people who, like the Thénardiers, exploit others, and that skepsis could be seen as a response to the political climate in the UK during the 1980s. When the musical premiered six years into Margaret Thatcher's reign as Prime Minister, the drastic overhaul of Britain's social services (and its arts funding) was already widely felt, especially by the less privileged members of the population. With the miners' strike about to collapse, Hugo's passionate diatribe against selfishness and a society where the powerful and the ruthless build their name and fortune by trampling over the weak must have seemed both fascinating in its radicalism and quaint in its optimism.

Conclusion: do you hear the people cheer?

The musicalization of *Les Misérables* transforms the powerful narrative of the novel into an equally exciting stage presentation. Hugo's appeal to kindness has not been diluted by its move from page to stage; as Edward Behr has pointed out: 'No other play, in the history of the theatre, has generated such social concern, or raised so much money for charity.'[140] In addition, one could argue that 'no single adaptation has perhaps done more to popularize Hugo's bestseller than the work that is today universally known as Les Miz'.[141] Producer Cameron Mackintosh is honest enough to give much of the credit for the undimmed popularity of the show to Victor Hugo: 'I don't think any other musical is likely to be blessed with such a strong foundation.'[142]

Although the initial reviews in the London press were hardly encouraging, with only a handful of critics praising the show and most of the others criticizing the musical for its bleakness and tragedy-filled plot or calling it a bowdlerization of a literary masterpiece,[143] it managed to survive that critical mauling to become an international sensation: in the 30 years since its opening, it has been seen by more than 70 million people in 42 countries.[144] Les Misérables stands as a lesson that in the end it is the audience that determines the fate of a production, and in this case the audience loved what it saw. In the words of critic Jack Kroll: 'If ever a show was made by that evanescent power, word of mouth, this one is it.'[145]

Case Study 11: The Phantom of the Opera

Gaston Leroux' novel Le Fantôme de l'Opéra (1910) was mostly known and mainly remembered for its several film adaptations, before Andrew Lloyd Webber decided to musicalize the story of the ingenious artist hiding in the vaults of the Parisian opera house who falls in love with a beautiful soprano. After turning her into a star, the Phantom loses her to her childhood sweetheart, a rich and handsome aristocrat. Lloyd Webber was first and foremost interested in using the material as a showcase for his second wife, the actress Sarah Brightman, for whom the role of young singer Christine Daaé seemed perfect: 'I just thought it was a very good idea for Sarah. I thought it was a wonderful vehicle. I wrote it for her and round her voice.'[146]

Lloyd Webber's first choice of lyricist was Richard Stilgoe, who had just worked with him on Starlight Express (1984), already a smash hit in London; it soon turned out, however, that Stilgoe's style of writing was sorely lacking in romance,[147] and so the composer turned to Alan Jay Lerner, the man behind My Fair Lady (1956). Lerner would have been a perfect fit, but unfortunately had to bow out shortly after agreeing to work on the project because he was severely ill.[148] It was producer Cameron Mackintosh who then recommended 25-year-old Charles Hart; the Cambridge graduate penned three lyrics on spec and was subsequently hired,[149] continuing where Stilgoe left off.[150]

The 'strange affair' of the haunted Paris opera house

The Phantom of the Opera (POTO) begins in 1905,[151] when an auction is held at the former Opéra Populaire, which has fallen into disrepair. When finally a refurbished chandelier is put on sale, the auctioneer refers to the 'strange affair of the Phantom of the Opera', because the lighting device 'figured in the famous disaster'.[152] After these words the chandelier is switched on, it starts to flicker and is raised from the stage to its place above the theatre audience while the opera house is restored to its former glory as we move more than 40 years into the past, to the year 1861.

From then on the main story unfolds as one continuous flashback; curiously, we never return to the auction or 1905, meaning that the introductory scene does not constitute a conventional framing device and seems more like a red herring. Its main raison d'être seems to be to proffer the first of several astounding theatrical set pieces. One could argue, though, that the raising of the chandelier is one of director Harold Prince's few miscalculations: because everything that goes up can surely come down again, it isn't really surprising when the chandelier falls to the stage at the end of Act One.

In 1861 at the Opéra Populaire a rehearsal is underway, a scene that imparts several important pieces of exposition; the performance is interrupted by a crashing backdrop, an incident that the theatre ensemble attributes to a mysterious 'opera ghost'. When diva Carlotta, upset by this latest in a whole series of accidents, refuses to go on, her place is taken by young chorus girl Christine who has been taught by a 'great teacher', although the girl herself doesn't know who he is and has never seen him, a striking fact that everybody seems too preoccupied to investigate further at that particular moment. Because of its position in the score, 'Think of Me' seems to resemble a typical 'I Am' song,[153] yet it doesn't quite fit into this category: while one could argue that the number hints at the return of Christine's former childhood sweetheart Raoul in the next scene, its lyrics are both too general and too inconsistent[154] to characterize the singer and her former love.

Raoul has recognized his ex-girlfriend on stage and visits her in her dressing room to renew the acquaintance, an unexpected arrival that enrages the Phantom because he wants Christine for himself. Now that he has engineered Christine's first public triumph, her teacher decides it is time for them to meet face-to-mask; after appearing on the other side of her dressing room mirror, he takes her through hidden pathways to his lair underneath the opera house, which is reached by crossing an underground lake – a journey that brings on a boat trip across the misty waters lit by hundreds of candles, one of the most iconic scenes not just of this musical but of all of musical theatre. Throughout this first close encounter between the composer and his protégé, he insists that Christine is not only his mirror image,[155] mainly because she and her style of singing reflect his musical tastes, but also that she is his means of communicating with the outside world/the world above ground – Christine realizes: 'I am / The mask you wear', and the Phantom confirms: 'It's me / they hear', with the latter comment also implying that the girl, like a ventriloquist's dummy, has no will and no thoughts of her own.

Harold Prince stated that for him the production fell into place when he saw a documentary about the sexuality of People with Disabilities (PWDs),[156] and the next scene brings a song of seduction whose suggestive image clusters leave no doubt that the Phantom craves more from Christine than merely her pure voice, metonymically standing in for her virginity. It is not surprising that 'The Music of the Night' has become a musical theatre standard, considering the opportunities it offers to a performer: the music and the lyrics operate as a thinly veiled metaphor for sexual fantasies, for giving in to yearnings that can only be succumbed to when no one can see (i.e. alone at night in the dark), as these desires are officially forbidden or at least strictly regimented by society. The song thus denotes the physical sensations of sexual discovery, arousal and climax, and those references need to be explicated in the performer's voice and body language. The final lines ('You alone / Can make my song take flight – / Help me make the music of the night') not only constitute the most direct invitation to join the Phantom in his quest to 'create beautiful music together', but also emphasize that he needs Christine to achieve his own artistic and sexual gratification.

The next number ('Notes / Primadonna') brings together most of the major characters in what over the course of the scene turns into a carefully constructed septet, which features not only some of Lloyd Webber's most ambitious writing, but also reveals Charles Hart to be a clever, efficient and elegant lyricist. The over-elaborate playfulness of his lyrics with their predilection for run-on lines to construct dazzling rhymes link him closely with Lorenz Hart, even if at times they give off a hint of a young writer keen to show off his prowess. The stubbornness of the two opera directors to replace Carlotta with Christine leads straight to the big coup de théâtre at the end of the first half. Carlotta is publicly humiliated on stage when the Phantom makes her croak like a frog. The pandemonium seemingly finds its climax when stage manager Buquet's garrotted body is thrown onto the stage, another person who receives his punishment at the hands of the opera ghost. Christine and Raoul escape to the roof of the opera house, where they declare their love for one another in 'All I Ask of You'. This song with its repeated references to times and places where nothing is hidden and all is in plain sight ('daylight', 'every waking moment', 'light', 'no more night' and 'each morning') is set up in direct contrast to the nocturnal images of 'The Music of the Night', without being either as elegant or evocative. Yet the Phantom has observed the two lovers and feels betrayed to a degree that not even the fact of Christine finally being allowed to star as he requested can mollify him, and so at the end of the performance he cuts loose the chandelier, which crashes to the stage, landing at Christine's feet and providing a spectacular finale to Act One.

The second half of the show begins with its biggest production number ('Masquerade'), depicting the annual masked ball at the opera house. Six months have passed without any signs from the Phantom, and in the meantime Christine and Raoul have become secretly engaged. But the Phantom hasn't actually disappeared – he was merely busy finishing his own opera, *Don Juan Triumphant*, which he demands will be put on next with Christine in the female lead. Rehearsals for *Don Juan Triumphant* prove taxing for the whole ensemble, with especially star tenor Piangi finding it difficult to master the unusual intervals in the Phantom's compositions; then the piano starts playing on its own, putting everyone under its spell, which in Christine's case leads her to her father's mausoleum and her big Act Two solo 'Wishing You Were Somehow Here Again'. The song allows the girl to express her longing for the father who died while she was still very young and prepares the audience for her decision to move on, to marry Raoul and thus to turn a new page. The Phantom makes one of his surprise appearances, and tries to lure Christine towards him, only to be thwarted in his plans by Raoul, who finally manages to break the spell his fiancée is under by exclaiming: 'Christine! [...] Whatever you may believe, this man ... this thing, is *not* your father!' This line is highly disturbing as it gives the erotic tension between the man in the mask and the young soprano an incestuous tinge. It is the young girl who prevents a violent confrontation between her two suitors when she pulls Raoul away from the graveyard, which leaves the stage free for the inevitable showdown later in the musical.

On the evening of the première of *Don Juan Triumphant*, a trap is set for its composer, but once more the Phantom outwits his opponents by turning up where they don't expect it – on stage. At first unbeknownst to the audience, he kills Piangi when the tenor is briefly out of sight. He takes over in the role as the notorious womanizer, which allows the Phantom not only to make sure that the leading singer does justice to his score but also to share the stage with Christine. The parallels between the characters the opera ghost has designed for them both to play in his opera – the devious seducer and the innocent maiden – and their relationship behind the scenes (which he hopes to conduct in a similar vein) are driven home in their duet 'The Point of No Return'. The very title of the number also signals to the audience that the musical is nearing its climax as the Phantom is unmasked for everyone to see. The attempt to arrest him fails and he once again disappears with Christine as his hostage into the basement of the opera house.

With both the mob and Raoul in pursuit, the Phantom brings Christine back to his lair. The young woman finally stands up to the man who has tried to control her every move, accusing him of both outrageous violence and of intending to rape her ('Am I now to be / Prey to your / Lust for flesh?'). The Phantom denies the latter charge with a rather unexpected explanation: 'The fate, which / Condemns me / To wallow in blood / Has also / Denied me / The joys of the flesh'. This is puzzling because it can only mean that he is physically incapable of making love – in other words, he is impotent – which in turn renders non-existent all the sexual tension that up to this moment has driven most of the plot.

Raoul is the first to reach the lair where he is immediately captured by the Phantom. Christine now has to choose between her teacher and her fiancé who will die should she refuse to start a new life with the Phantom. Yet Christine by this time has reached an understanding of her captor that allows her to find an alternative; she approaches the Phantom and kisses him 'long and full on the lips', a very touching moment that represents the emotional high point of the musical, for who cannot identify with somebody who hopes to be loved in spite of his flaws and shortcomings? As a result of her unexpected demonstration of affection, the Phantom resents his ways; he releases Raoul and sends the lovers on their way to safety, seemingly to face the encroaching mob. Mournfully reflecting that 'You alone / Can make my song take flight – / It's over now, the music of the night', he sits down on his throne and then vanishes in his final magic trick, only leaving his mask behind, which suggests that he no longer needs it. The final tableau has Meg holding up the mask to the audience as the light fades.

In trance and in command: the mesmerized soprano and the not-always-present ghost

It has been pointed out that the Phantom's infatuation with Christine has many famous predecessors, from the fairy tale *Beauty and the Beast* and Victor Hugo's *The Hunchback of Notre Dame*, to George Du Maurier's melodrama *Trilby* (both the novel and his later theatrical adaption).[157] There are especially close parallels to the sway Svengali holds over Trilby as Christine spends most of her time on stage mesmerized in a state that bears traces of both hypnosis and somnambulism; that trance also has sexual overtones. She is introduced in Act One, Scene 1 as a member of the corps de ballet who 'always has her head in the clouds' and after the gala the Phantom's praise ('Bravi, Bravi, Bravissimi') renders her 'bewildered' (Scene 2), even though she should be familiar with his voice from her singing lessons. That bewilderment increases to her being 'spellbound' as soon as the 'Angel of Music' addresses her from behind her dressing-room mirror (Scene 3), and her words and 'extravagant' vocalizing during the following title song (Scene 4), ending on a 'desperate, strangely spellbound high E',[158] suggest that she remains in that state. In Scene 6, coming back to her senses in the Phantom's lair, the music of the musical box 'keeps her in half-trance'. In Scene 10, the final scene before the interval, Christine confesses to Raoul: 'But his voice / filled my spirit / With a strange, sweet sound / [...] / And through music / My soul began to soar! / And I heard / as I'd never heard before'. These words are uttered 'trancelike', with Christine 'becoming more and more ecstatic'. Six months later, the hold the Phantom has over the young singer hasn't diminished; when he appears at the opera ball, she approaches him 'mesmerized'. Then, like everyone else, she falls into a trance during the rehearsals for *Don Juan Triumphant*, but it is only Christine that this trance somehow induces to visit her father's grave where the Phantom with a 'more and more hypnotic' voice beckons the '[b]ewildered' singer to return to him. That the young soprano thus rarely seems to be in possession of her full faculties limits her for long stretches to being merely reactive, as John Snelson observes: '[O]nly late in the story does [Christine] make herself an active part of [a] process of self-definition.'[159]

That the show was written as a showcase for Sarah Brightman in the role of Christine is borne out by close scrutiny of the score; the composer's focus not only 'brought renewed lyricism to Lloyd Webber's style',[160] but resulted in a musical that gives the female lead three times as much material to sing as the Phantom, although he is the title character.[161] The disfigured 'genius' isn't

Figure 13 A young girl constantly spellbound – Sarah Brightman, the original Christine, in *The Phantom of the Opera*, Her Majesty's Theatre 1986. Photograph by Clive Barda. Courtesy of ArenaPAL.

actually on stage that much, but as Michael Walsh rightfully points out, his presence is '[s]o pervasive'[162] – thanks to no small degree to the suggestive staging and décor, which will be analyzed shortly – that he seems to be around even when he isn't.

In many ways this could be described – for lack of a better term – as the 'Hannibal Lector' effect, which can be observed in Jonathan Demme's multiple-Oscar-winning horror film *The Silence of the Lambs* (1991), another *Beauty and the Beast* retelling (albeit one in which the Beast decidedly remains a monster). Although nobody questioned the brilliance of Anthony Hopkins' now iconic portrayal of serial killer Lector, the fact that he is only on screen for 16 minutes of the 118-minute-long thriller made the decision by the Academy of Motion Picture Arts and Sciences to nominate him in the 'Leading Actor' category and not as 'Best Supporting Actor' highly controversial. Yet nobody who has seen the film would deny the fact that

Hopkins' diabolical character dominates the film and that his sinister and mysterious presence colours whatever happens once he has been introduced. The same thing occurs in *POTO*.

Ingredients for a world-wide smash

When asked, people usually give the same two answers in their attempt to explain the musical's unprecedented global popularity: the love story and its lush score. Right from the very first London preview, audiences reacted enthusiastically to the story of the disfigured composer who lives in the catacombs beneath the Parisian opera house. As the famous logo of the show suggests, the musical combines romance (symbolized by the rose) and mystery (the mask), and it is this combination of passionate love story and suspenseful intrigue that turned the musical into one of the most successful entertainments ever devised.

The uninhibited emotionality of the score has drawn comparisons to classical Italian Opera;[163] in addition, the show's setting allowed for several parodies of classical composers (like Giacomo Meyerbeer), although on the whole the music does not stray too far – or, at least not for very long – from the mode of a traditional musical.[164] When discussing the merits of Lloyd Webber's compositions for *POTO*, critical opinion fell into one of two extremes: either reviewers, especially those from the classical field, panned the score, including its parodic elements, as a failure, or they praised it as the creator's masterpiece. Problematic for many observers was once again the composer's conscious decision to limit the number of songs/melodies/melodic motifs per show: convinced that the limited capacity of an audience's short-term memory works against too much musical innovation,[165] Lloyd Webber restricts his new musical material so as not to overtax theatregoers. While the show has decidedly fewer numbers than for instance *Porgy and Bess* (1935) or *Kristina från Duvemåla* (1995), which each has nearly 40 different songs, what songs there are in *POTO*, even those that didn't enter the British charts – from the simple 'Think of Me' to the complex ensemble 'Prima Donna' and the elaborate Act Two opener 'Masquerade' to the plaintive 'Wishing You Were Somehow Here again' and the forceful 'The Point of No Return' – all have 'earworm' quality.

But there are two other major contributors whose responsibility for turning the show into a pop culture phenomenon cannot be valued highly enough: director Harold Prince and designer Maria Björnson. By working closely together, these creatives ensured through their staging and scenography that 'the Phantom's search for sexual fulfilment helped not only to shape the show and the performances, but the sets as well; rich fabrics drape the stage, candles and shadows abound'.[166] For her stage sets, Björnson was inspired by the actual Paris Opera house,[167] while her costumes drew from Edgar Degas, the circus and *commedia dell'arte*,[168] to realize Prince's original concept.

As Harold Prince's strongest suit as a director is his ability to create evocative stage images,[169] he made the conscious decision not to follow then-current Broadway trends: 'I was tired of what spectacle had become: high-tech, multi-media. If our *Phantom* was spectacular it would be through the use of Victorian stage techniques, signaling a return to an earlier sense of theatrical occasion.'[170] Prince's recourse to more traditional forms of theatrical enchantment did not go unnoticed by the critics; Sheridan Morley raved: 'The whole of this *Phantom* is in fact a tribute to the old Victorian theatrical values.'[171] His colleague Michael Billington praised the show in similar ways: 'In the end *The Phantom* works [...] because it delights in the possibilities of theatre.'[172]

Prince concluded that the grand emotions expressed in Lloyd Webber's soaring melodies were best served by a fast-moving, vigorous staging. Therefore he decided to encourage a similarly unembellished approach from the actors in their portrayal of the characters: 'I didn't want something subtle or psychologically buried; instead I wanted to stress the rudimentary psychology that is at the core of the material.'[173] As a result, the depiction of the characters is psychologically astute without being naturalistic, and considering that certain details of the plot seem rather far-fetched, if not to say implausible, this was a very wise decision.

The plot and its improbabilities

Take for instance the basic set-up of the protégé-teacher/mentor relationship between Christine and the Phantom, which is already in place when the musical begins and which seems utterly preposterous when spelled out in its details: at a very young age, the future singer is approached when on her own somewhere on the vast premises of the opera house by the disfigured genius. The Phantom offers her singing lessons in exchange for, on the one hand, following his instructions without any questions and, on the other hand, for being taught without actually ever *seeing* him. Christine accepts these conditions, partly because she assumes that the lessons by voice only are delivered by the 'angel of music' her father promised to send her after his death to protect her. That Christine never expresses suspicion or trepidation at this arrangement makes her seem either frightfully naive or exceptionally gullible.

While it makes sense for the disfigured genius to kill stage manager Buquet, as the man is foolish enough to poke fun at the 'opera ghost', the murder of tenor Piangi is less easy to understand. The Italian has difficulty coping with the Phantom's atonal score for *Don Juan Triumphant* and therefore may be guilty of 'murdering' the Phantom's music, but to kill Piangi for that seems rather excessive as it would have been just as effective to knock him unconscious if all the opera ghost wanted was to step into the tenor's role as Don Juan. That the Phantom afterwards goes on to replace Piangi on stage causes another problem of plausibility as they not only look totally different in every production of the show I have ever seen, they also customarily don't *sound* alike either, which makes it illogical that no one in the audience notices the change until Christine removes the Phantom's mask.

Finally, although her compassionate recounting of the Phantom's miserable earlier life explains why ballet mistress Mme Giry helped him to hide from his tormentors after his escape, her later actions are less convincingly motivated, as there isn't any real logic behind her continuous protection of the Phantom once he starts taking people's lives. Her decisions concerning when to impart important pieces of information about the opera ghost and his hideaway (in Act Two, Scenes 2 and 7) to Raoul of all people, a character with whom she otherwise has no dealings whatsoever, seem dictated more by mechanical plot requirements than by plot developments or her own character.

On the whole, though, the musical's story-telling is often very efficient, with the action moving swiftly from one major event to the next; in contrast to this, what little dialogue there is, more often than not, is handled clumsily, with the protagonists declaring war against each other not once, but three times throughout the show, in Act One, Scene 8, as well as in Scenes 3 and 5 in Act Two.

That the show works as well as it does despite its narrative shortcomings can be attributed to both its powerful score and brilliant staging, which provide thrills and romance in equal measure amid an atmosphere of mystery and seduction. In the early 2000s, when the stage musical was brought into cinemas, it became obvious that the former element isn't really as effective without the latter. The 2004 movie adaptation, financed by Lloyd Webber himself after the project remained stuck for more than a decade in what Hollywood refers to as 'development hell', was directed by Joel Schumacher, who was chosen by the composer himself because he admired the director's 1987 film *Lost Boys*. Often unfairly singled out as one of the 'worst directors in movie history',[174] Schumacher turned out to be unable to repeat the stage musical's success on the big screen. The film became a hit in the UK, South Korea and Japan, but flopped badly everywhere else[175] and got widely panned by reviewers. Maybe because film as a medium carries with it the imprimatur of 'realism' – justified or not – the movie adaptation seems to emphasize and thus expose the many plot holes and plot contrivances of the material, whereas the stage version manages to ride right over them without stumbling. It doesn't help that Schumacher's directorial approach is full of inconsistencies, like the anachronistic moment of vogue-ing during 'Masquerade', or the fact that among a cast of French characters only Miranda Richardson's Mme Giry employs a French accent. The movie's eclecticism includes shots stolen from Jean Cocteau's classic *La Belle et la Bête* (1946), but there the image of a wall full of human arms serving as candelabras is part of an over-riding artistic conception; here, it is simply one isolated surrealistic element that doesn't tie in with anything else in the film. The movie also botched the big revelation at the end – the Phantom without the mask – as the image isn't particularly shocking.[176]

The consequences of the show's astounding success

When *The Phantom of the Opera* opened on Broadway in January 1988, Jack Kroll speculated that the show 'may well turn out to be the biggest smash of all time',[177] and his prophecy turned out to be correct – the Broadway production recouped its investment in about a year and since then has been hugely profitable.[178] At the time of writing, nearly three decades after its world première, the musical is still playing in both London and New York.[179]

With *POTO*, Lloyd Webber reached the pinnacle of his financial success; the importance of the show for his public image and the reception of the musicals he has written since then cannot be stressed highly enough. It is with the Leroux adaption that the estimation of both critics and the general public undergoes a change; after 1986, the tide begins to turn, and even the British press, which up to that time had often praised Lloyd Webber as the 'local boy made good', started to report sneeringly on his professional and private activities.[180] As Michael Walsh underlined in 1990: 'In less than 20 years, he has gone in critical estimation from being the exciting, and penniless, young firebrand who was bringing a fresh new voice to a tired genre to the millionaire hack whose overwrought works are emblematic of what ails Broadway.'[181]

The unprecedented profit generated by *POTO* and its 'semieternal run'[182] was evidence for many that Lloyd Webber conceived his shows for the broad masses by aiming straight for the lowest common denominator. What could be observed here is a rather astonishing reinterpretation of the meaning of commercial success in a theatre system that after all is geared entirely towards turning a profit: before Lloyd Webber had hit after hit, creating a musical that ran for years was regarded as an indicator of artistic ability, but the career of the British composer was now seen as a demonstration that mass popularity equalled lack of artistic integrity and originality.[183] In particular, American journalists and critics were very harsh in their evaluation of Lloyd Webber's oeuvre; Steven Suskin's summary of what made the composer the star that he is, as evidenced by his name above the title of his shows, is symptomatic in this regard: 'Innovative staging, spectacular scenery, and innocuous song after song often derivative and set to inexpert lyrics: this would come to be the pattern for many [...] of Andrew Lloyd Webber's musical entertainments. Curious, in that Lloyd Webber's music itself is far less memorable than the overall effect.'[184]

It could be argued that the disdain many members of the public and the artistic community held for Lloyd Webber and his work has only started to decrease in the last decade, since the composer appeared on British television in casting shows such as *How Do You Solve a Problem like Maria* (2006), where he exhibited an unexpected sense of humour as well as an endearing inability to hide his discomfort and displeasure at some of the less accomplished performances. His frank admission of his ongoing fight against prostate cancer has also won him many supporters. Whatever his public reputation, though, Lloyd Webber is most likely to be remembered for *The Phantom of the Opera* – the last and the biggest in his unprecedented series of global hit musicals.

3.4 ORIGINAL STORIES: WHEN THE CONTENT IS UNKNOWN

There is a reason why so many composers, lyricists and librettists resort to musicalizing previously published or screened material: an adaptation may have its own inherent demands and problems, but at least the novel, play or movie that is to be turned into a musical already prescribes a narrative with its own inner logic, focus and arc of suspense. All of these elements need to be invented for original stories, and the fact that many of the shows under discussion in this section were extensively rewritten or reconceived after their première proves that musicals which succeed straight away by telling a new story are indeed rare.

Since the 1950s, British musical theatre has had its share of hit musicals that could be categorized as genuinely 'new', even if some of these original shows have recourse to specific genres to provide at least an underlying structure: *The Rocky Horror Show* (1975) playfully references science fiction and horror films from the 1930s and 1950s, while *Blood Brothers* (1983) incorporates standard elements of both nineteenth-century melodrama (like the constant chance encounter of the protagonists) and classic tragedy (the narrator as the voice of doom; the mythical set up of the brothers separated at birth). *Bombay Dreams* (2002), on the other hand, has as its starting point the often-told rise of an unknown actor to stardom. Of course, all three musicals then add their very own narrative ingredients, which set them apart from their inspirations and forebears, such as the glam rock and gender-bending of the 1970s (*The Rocky Horror Show*), the very specific background of the Catholic working class in Liverpool (*Blood Brothers*) and the antagonistic forces of progress and tradition in modern Mumbai as evidenced in the Indian film industry (*Bombay Dreams*).

Figure 14 The old and the new – the antagonistic forces of progress and tradition in *Bombay Dreams* at the Apollo Victoria Theatre 2002. Photograph by Colin Willoughby. Courtesy of ArenaPAL.

Attempts to tell original stories that did not derive from previously published material proved to be especially challenging for Tim Rice and Andrew Lloyd Webber, both of whom have been far less successful with those of their works that feature original storylines than with musicals that were adaptations. The lyricist failed twice when trying to come up with completely new storylines (*Blondel* and *Chess*), and his former writing partner had three flops in this subgenre (*The Beautiful Game*, *Love Never Dies* and *Stephen Ward*).

Rice had his first experience of how difficult it can be to write original musicals with the satirical *Blondel*. In spite of featuring some of the lyricist's best work, the show failed to accommodate the fact that audiences by the early 1980s had developed a taste for more serious musicals, and so the irreverent comic romp about minstrel Blondel and his hapless endeavour to locate and free King Richard I became the lyricist's 'first important stage flop'.[185] It was later rewritten and occasionally re-titled *Lute!*, without ever finding an audience. Yet those changes were minimal compared to the alterations made over the decades to Rice's next show, *Chess*. Co-written with the Swedish composers Benny Andersson and Björn Ulvaeus, the musical is about the battle for the title of Chess World Champion between Anatoly Sergievsky, a Russian, and Freddie Trumper, an American player, and the woman – Florence Vassy – who is caught between them. Set during the Cold War, the work was first released as a double album that resulted in several international chart hits (like 'One Night in Bangkok' and 'I Know Him So Well'). All subsequent attempts to bring the concept recording to the stage, though, underlined the fact that *Chess* remains a marvellous score in search of a coherent book. Although the show ran in London for three years and turned a tiny profit, it was completely overhauled for its 1988 Broadway premiere. Against Rice's wishes, Nunn brought in a book writer, Richard Nelson, who changed large sections of the story and turned the original sung-through work into a more traditional book musical with extended dialogue scenes; all those highly disputed changes were in vain, however, and the New York *Chess* flopped badly, closing after less than two months.

In the years that followed, there have been so many different versions of the show, resetting the story in different places and at different times and redistributing the songs between the various protagonists, that Rice later admitted that even he had lost count.[186] The lyricist himself financed a 2008 concert staging at the Royal Albert Hall that largely went back to the 1984 concept recording and is testament to his belief that all later changes were mistakes which only detracted from the initial impulse behind the musical and his original artistic vision. But the concert presentation merely confirmed that the original vision is severely flawed as Rice evidently thinks in songs, not in consistent characterization. The presentation once more exposed the various plot holes and illogical story elements that were less problematic on the double album as one assumed they would be addressed when the work was staged. To list just a few of the contrivances and unanswered questions that undermine the plot:

- Why is Freddy such a staunch anti-Communist when it should be Florence who has deep-seated resentments against Russia? After all, it is she who has lost both her father and her home country when the 1956 Hungarian uprising was defeated.

- Why doesn't Florence know that Anatoli is married?

- Anatoli leaves not only his wife but his children when he defects to the West – a selfish act that is hard for any audience to accept.

- The musical never gives us any insight into the marriage between Anatoli and his wife Svetlana, which means the audience does not understand what is at stake when she later tries to win him back.

- If Freddy is so obsessed with money, why does he quit being a professional chess player and become a chess expert for television, most likely not a job that is well-paid? Surely it would be a revenge match between East and West that would earn him a fortune?

So far, all efforts to address these shortcomings have proved insufficient, but the search for a workable version of *Chess* continues, as there will always be directors and performers who will want to salvage what remains one of the greatest of all musical theatre scores.

Andrew Lloyd Webber didn't fare any better when he tried to combine fictional characters with a long-standing political conflict based on history. *The Beautiful Game*, with book and lyrics by stand-up comedian Ben Elton, tells of a group of football-playing friends in the 1960s whose lives are tragically affected by the 'Troubles' in Northern Ireland. The composer's attempt to change direction both on the level of content – an original story about Britain's recent past – and in terms of his collaborators – he hadn't worked with any of the creative team before – found neither critical support nor an appreciative audience, and it closed after 11 months. Just as had been the case with *Sunset Boulevard* seven years earlier, several critics praised the 'return of the book'.[187] Yet although the reversion to a more traditional form of musical theatre story-telling counted as a plus for many observers, in this particular case the resulting plot and characters were judged to be severely lacking. Ben Elton's contributions as both librettist and lyricist were deemed 'didactic and simplistic'[188] and the storyline that he had invented with Lloyd Webber was attacked for 'its predictability'.[189] Meanwhile, the political sentiments expressed throughout the show were singled out for their naive paternalism; for Kate Chopstick in *The Scotsman*, the musical amounted to 'an insult of unbelievable arrogance. It puts the "pat" into patronizing.'[190]

Love Never Dies, the 'continuation' of *The Phantom of the Opera*, had the twin burden of being both a sequel and an original story, meaning that it not only had to present a plot that rivalled the mystique and drama of the earlier show, but also had to convincingly bring back all the beloved characters of the Leroux adaptation. This leads us directly to the major problem of the 2010 musical: none of the people on stage have much in common with those of the 1986 smash hit. By the time this belated follow-up finally opened in the West End, millions of theatregoers around the world had already imagined their own versions of what happens to their favourite characters after the final curtain comes down in *Phantom*. It is doubtful whether the plot of *Love Never Dies* even remotely resembles any of these scenarios.

The story, set on Coney Island ten years after the events in the Parisian opera house, was concocted by a profusion of librettists – the official credit reads: 'Book by Andrew Lloyd Webber and Ben Elton, with Glenn Slater and Frederick Forsyth.' It grows more and more bewildering as it unravels, mainly because none of the characters is recognizable. The Phantom, the former avant-garde opera composer and aesthete, presents vaudeville ditties such as 'Bathing Beauty' in his fairground attraction. Even worse, whereas before he drove the plot with his elaborate schemes, here he mostly *re*-acts. Instead of the archetypal young ingénue enthralled and frightened by the masked creature who controls her life and career, we get a Christine who is reduced to doting mother and devoted wife. Raoul has become an alcoholic and a gambler who has squandered the family fortune; because he is thus clearly no longer suitable for Christine, the love triangle falls flat. Mme Giry has turned into Mrs Danvers out of Alfred Hitchcock's *Rebecca (1940)*, and her daughter Meg not only is a fully-fledged neurotic, but has also inexplicably fallen for the Phantom. None of this is explained in any of the lengthy songs that fill the audience in about what happened in the intervening years.

The musical begins with a superfluous prologue, which reveals everything that follows as a flashback, just like the opening auction scene in *Phantom*, except that the auction scene is followed by a stunning *coup de théâtre* (the restoration of the Paris Opera to its former glory), whereas the first scene in *Love Never Dies*, which is set on the shores of Coney Island, is merely confusing. The irritation of the audience reaches its peak with the really poor ending, as Meg accidentally kills Christine and the Phantom disappears once again, this time with the young son he had with the singer.

The plot lacks both surprise – that the boy will turn out to be the Phantom's offspring is obvious the minute he appears – and drama: on Coney Island, where there are countless 'freaks', the former opera ghost does not really have to hide. It is no wonder that the show could not find an audience, notwithstanding its later (better received) Australian production.[191]

Lloyd Webber's last musical to open in the West End, *Stephen Ward*, was based on a political scandal that shook England to the core in the early 1960s. It was the eponymous osteopath and socialite who introduced 19-year-old model Christine Keeler to John Profumo, the Secretary of State for War, thereby initiating their later affair. When it became known that Keeler may also have had a relationship with Captain Yevgeny Ivanov, a Soviet naval attaché, the chance of a potential security risk exploded in the press into the notorious Profumo affair, which led to Profumo's as well as Prime Minister Harold Macmillan's resignation and Ward's suicide.

What could have been an intriguing revisiting of one of Britain's most infamous cases of public outrage faltered because the show's creative team (Lloyd Webber, lyricists/librettists Christopher Hampton and Don Black as well as director Richard Eyre) seemingly never agreed what kind of show they were aiming for. A sharp satire on the English establishment? A romantic musical about the tragic fall of a well-meaning playboy? A sweeping kaleidoscope of the early 1960s and people's desperate attempts at (sexual) liberation? A passionate indictment of the hypocrisy of the political system?

Stephen Ward coheres neither thematically nor musically; several songs – like 'I'm Hopeless When It Comes to You' – serve no real purpose, and extended musical scenes like 'The Police Interview' and 'The Trial' go on long after the audience gets their fairly obvious point that the police forced small-time criminals to give false testimony and that the court was biased. As a result, the drama pulls in various directions, none of them particularly original or interesting. It's not that 50 years after Profumo's resignation the public might no longer be engrossed by the affair or its aftermath; the problem with its musicalization is rather that the show fails to make a convincing case for why it *should*.

3.5 JUKEBOX MUSICALS: WHEN YOU KNOW
ALL THE SONGS

The next major development in story-telling techniques was ushered in during the late 1990s. Even though the idea of creating a musical based on a collection of well-known pop hits wasn't in any way new in 1999, *Mamma Mia!* took the theatre industry by surprise by demonstrating how vast the audience for this type of subgenre could be.

To a certain degree, shows that build their story around a collection of pre-existing songs (usually the back catalogue of a famous rock or pop artist) are the natural progression from concept recordings that find their way to the stage, since in both cases the theatregoers come in already knowing the musical material. Productions that tailor a narrative to suit an already composed score have become known as 'jukebox musicals', which is a slightly misleading term: once you have paid for it, a jukebox not only allows you to choose from a limited number of recordings, but also permits you to decide in which order they will be played; but in the case of jukebox musicals, that privilege only extends to the librettist of the show, not to the audience.

It is in the last 20 years that jukebox musicals have become increasingly popular among producers and audiences, although celebrated examples of the subgenre can already be found in the 1970s and 1980s: for instance, the 1978 Tony Award Winner for 'Best New Musical', *Ain't Misbehavin'*, had a score comprised of Fats Waller hits; and *Buddy – the Buddy Holly Story* (1989), which recounted the life of the eponymous rock'n'roll star through his songs, lasted for more than 5,000 performances in the West End.

Notwithstanding the odd earlier break-out hit musical, it was arguably the totally unexpected success of *Mamma Mia!*, based on the back catalogue of Swedish pop sensation ABBA, that changed the theatrical landscape all around the world. With ticket sales through the roof everywhere it was produced, the show was followed by a never-ending plethora of musicals that attempted to dip into similar wells of nostalgia and idol-worshipping. Yet it quickly became evident that *Mamma Mia!* was a singular phenomenon, in that its astounding popularity was not brought about by a formula that was easy to replicate. Neither could all jukebox shows count on a built-in audience: for every musical that succeeded – like *We Will Rock You* (2000), which survived a critical drubbing and lasted for 12 years at one of London's biggest theatres, the Dominion – there are literally dozens of shows that flopped miserably. In Britain alone, these include: *Our House* (2002; using the songs of Madness), *Tonight's the Night* (2003; Rod Stewart), *Daddy Cool* (2006; Boney M), *Desperately Seeking Susan* (2007; Blondie), *Never Forget* (2007; Take That) and *Viva Forever!* (2012; The Spice Girls).

Some of the box-office disappointments listed above were quite ambitious in their story-telling: *Our House* explored the parallel plotlines scenario set up by the hypothetical 'what would happen if', which was also used in the 1998 movie *Sliding Doors* and the 2013 Broadway musical *If/Then*. *Desperately Seeking Susan*, on the other hand, tried to match the hits of New Wave band Blondie to Susan Seidelman's 1985 cult film of the same title. These were special cases, though; as George Rodosthenous asserts, most of the other shows were 'a mere puzzle of unsophisticated interlocking narratives in order for the songs to be presented within a forced dramaturgical framework'.[192]

Among those writers who were content to forego narrative ingenuity or complexity and settled for the merest pretence of a storyline as long as it allowed them to incorporate as many of a performer's hits as possible, was Ben Elton. What follows is a plot summary of his Rod Stewart musical, *Tonight's the Night*, taken from the website of the show's touring production:

> *Tonight's the Night* tells the story of a shy young man, so tongue-tied that he cannot find the courage to declare his love to the girl of his dreams. One night out he strikes a deal with the Devil, trading his soul for Rod's. It seems like a good idea at the time but this guy is about to find out the hard way that you can't find true love using another man's moves and that devil or no devil, there's only one Rod Stewart![193]

While Elton got away with a similarly risible storyline one year earlier in *We Will Rock You*, his 2003 musical did not find such a forgiving audience and closed after one year. That lightning doesn't necessarily strike twice was also a lesson to be learned by the producer who started it all, Judy Craymer, the woman who had the idea for *Mamma Mia!* and shepherded her brainchild to become a global sensation. When Craymer hired comedienne Jennifer Saunders to write a musical based on the music of the Spice Girls, the result was a financial and critical catastrophe that closed after a mere seven months, lost at least £5 million[194] and received the kind of reviews that every producer dreads.

Tim Walker called it 'a show that's so bad, it ought, if there were any justice, to be accorded a minus-star rating'. Not content with this devastating verdict, he then added, 'it is definitively, monumentally and historically bad'.[195] As so often happens with musicals, the show's libretto received most of the blame. David Benedict underlined that '[Saunders'] lack of experience in long-form writing is painfully clear' and that the musical's 'satire is as lazy as it is seriously second-hand'.[196]

So what exactly is it that sets *Mamma Mia!* apart from all the shows that tried to emulate it and failed? The answer to this involves the show's songs, song placement, storyline and themes, all of which will be considered at due length in the following case study.

Case Study 12: *Mamma Mia!*

ABBA is without a doubt one of the most famous acronyms of the twentieth century: as is common knowledge, it was made up of the first names of the four artists who formed the Swedish pop quartet – Agnetha Fältskog, Björn Ulvaeus, Benny Andersson and Anni-Frid Lyngstad. The band stayed together for merely ten years, and has the unusual distinction that it, in the words of Andersson, 'never started, never ended',[197] meaning that neither the musicians' collaboration nor their break-up was ever officially announced.[198] Yet while the group's beginnings may have been 'indefinite'[199] and their final albums may not have registered as such at the time, what happened in between recording their first song in 1972 ('People Need Love') and the release of their last single in 1982 ('Under Attack') definitely did not go unnoticed: the band winning the 1974 Eurovision Song Contest in Brighton, recording eight studio albums and dominating the charts throughout most of the 1970s and early 1980s.

By 1982, though, ABBA's worldwide popularity had started to wane. The album 'The Visitors' didn't do as well as previous releases. For the band itself, it 'represented a new step and a new direction, [but] it seemed that a fair portion of their audience wasn't prepared to follow them along that path'.[200] The band's repute declined further throughout the rest of the 1980s, a downward trajectory that was to reverse direction in 1992, a year that saw the release of two important recordings: Erasure's UK No. 1 hit 'ABBA-esque', an EP homage with covers of four of the band's hits; and the compilation album 'ABBA Gold'. In the UK, the latter topped the charts and with more than 5.1 million copies sold, is the second-best-selling record ever to be released in Britain.[201] Further proof of ABBA's longevity was provided when in 1994 not one, but two films from Australia, both of which went on to become cult hits, featured the band and its music as important plot elements: *The Adventures of Priscilla, Queen of the Desert* and *Muriel's Wedding*.

The renewed interest in ABBA's musical legacy and what it meant to people was the first sign that the public view of the group was undergoing a change. In the words of Karl French, author of *ABBA Unplugged*, over the last 30 years there has been 'a dramatic shift in perception, journeying through various levels of appreciation – pre-ironic, ironic, post-ironic' to nowadays, 'simply beloved'.[202] Oscar winner Colin Firth put it like this: 'Everybody has to come out sooner or later – let's face it, you either love ABBA or you're lying.'[203]

It is in this climate of restored appreciation that in January 1997 producer Judy Craymer met with playwright Catherine Johnson and – together with Ulvaeus – began to discuss potential ways of creating a stage musical featuring the songs of ABBA, on the condition that it wouldn't be a biographical musical – that is, that it would not tell the story of the group.[204] Without doubt ABBA was widely popular; after all, the band has sold nearly 400 million records worldwide,[205] and their back catalogue of songs is exceeded in financial value only by that of the Beatles.[206] Obviously, there had been plenty of interest in using the band's back catalogue in the theatre over the years, as evidenced by five earlier shows in London that used ABBA songs,[207] including *Abbacadabra* (1983), the English stage adaptation of a French children's musical conceived by Alain Boublil that fitted out hits of the Swedish band with new lyrics. But it would take *Mamma Mia!* to rival the success of the recordings on the stage. The challenge faced by the artistic team was to extend interest in the musical beyond the traditional devotees of the Swedish quartet. Craymer expounds: 'The fans will give you an instant audience [...], but getting beyond those first few months is the real test.'[208]

As in all jukebox musicals, the intimate knowledge of the musical material 'works to create a backdrop of familiarity for viewers, enabling connections to be made with their own experiences of relationships, history, friendship and moments of celebrations.'[209] Consequently, the target audience for the show seemed first and foremost ABBA fans, those who enjoyed the band's music in the 1970s and 1980s when the group was still together, as well as those who had discovered their hits after the Swedish quartet disbanded. Among those fans has always been a large number of gays – ABBA has its own entry in the *Routledge International Encyclopedia of Queer Culture*[210] – and it certainly helped to attract that specific segment of the public when the show moved into the Prince Edward Theatre, which is situated in the centre of Soho, or, as the show's production designer Mark Thompson termed it, 'the heart of Gayworld'.[211] Moreover, the poster – with its deliriously happy bride – expands that audience to include women of all age groups, who would turn out to be the show's staunchest supporters. Finally, the fact that the show features a lot of attractive men in various stages of undress appeals to both gay men and straight women.

How to situate twenty-two hits around a wedding

In the end, the artistic team, also including celebrated director Phyllida Lloyd from November 1997, settled for a humorous story set in Greece. The plot seems at first to tell of a 20-year-old girl about to get married who is trying to find her father, but then takes some rather surprising turns: Sophie lives with her mother Donna on the island of Kalokairi, where Donna owns a tavern. The girl is engaged to Sky, a young man who has made a fortune on Wall Street and then decided to leave the world of high finance behind him. Never knowing who her father was, she has discovered in her mother's diary the names of three men who may be the parent she never met. Without telling Donna, she invites them to her wedding. A day before Sophie walks down the aisle, her mother's two best friends, Rosie and Tanya, with whom she used to perform in a band called 'Donna and the Dynamos', arrive on the island as, to Donna's dismay, do the potential fathers, Bill, Harry and Sam. During the ensuing comic complications, Donna and Sam realize they still have feelings for each other and marry, Rosie and Bill discover their mutual attraction, and Sophie decides that she'd rather first explore the world with Sky than become his wife straight away.

With its constellation of three female best friends from both the mother's and the daughter's generation, of three prospective fathers and a groom who is not only strikingly handsome, but so fabulously wealthy that he doesn't have to work, *Mamma Mia!* takes recourse, on the one hand, to fairy tale themes.[212] But, on the other hand, the show has pointed references to the financial struggle of single mothers, the importance of female friendships that last while romantic relationships or marriages may break up, and the life choices women face at a time when the feminist fight for equality no longer makes headline news that especially women of all ages can relate to. It is probably this clever mixture of escapism and realism that accounts for the musical's enduring popularity.

All in all, Johnson's libretto uses 22 ABBA songs – 23 if one includes 'Waterloo', which is performed as the final number during the megamix curtain call. The latter was added 'due to popular demand, and after an incredible amount of debate'.[213] The inclusion of 'Waterloo' leaves only one of the group's chart toppers out of the show, 'Fernando', resulting in a musical that apart from that one exception features every single song included on the best-selling compilation album 'ABBA Gold', as well as four tracks – 'I Do, I Do, I Do, I Do, I Do', 'Honey, Honey', 'Our Last Summer' and 'Under Attack' – that were part of the follow-up CD 'More ABBA Gold' (which was released in 1993 as a means to cash in on the enormous success of the first compilation).[214]

The 22 songs in the stage show are employed in four different ways:

1. **as classic book numbers**

   This works perfectly well for 'Does Your Mother Know?', 'Slipping through My Fingers' and 'The Winner Takes It All', but is less persuasively handled with 'Money, Money, Money' and 'Knowing Me, Knowing You'. Two other songs – 'Chiquitita' and 'Take a Chance on Me' – that at first sight seem to belong to this category, actually operate on a different level and will be discussed in more detail below.

2. **as performances**

   'Donna and the Dynamoes' regroup for a one-night-only appearance at Sophie's hen party and sing 'Super Trouper'.

3. **as background music**

   ABBA hits like 'Voulez-Vous' and 'Gimme! Gimme! Gimme! (A Man after Midnight)' play during both the hen night and the stag party; 'I Do, I Do, I Do, I Do, I Do' serves a similar function in the church during the wedding ceremony.

4. **as a fun part of daily life**

   Using hairbrushes, blow dryers and other props as impromptu microphones, the characters sing/sing along to pop hits such as 'Dancing Queen', as people have been doing in the privacy of their own homes ever since records became available.

It is the fourth category that is the most interesting here as it acknowledges the way popular music forms part of the fabric of all of our lives. This is especially relevant for a jukebox musical because it reminds audiences of their own use of the music they listen to and have listened to over the years, thus inviting both recognition and nostalgia for the presumably more careless times when all of us would mime to our favourite chart hit.

Figure 15 Singing along to the pop hits that form part of the fabric of everyday life – Louise Plowright (Tanya), Siobhan McCarthy (Donna) and Jenny Galloway (Rosie), the original 'Donna and the Dynamoes' in *Mamma Mia!*, Prince Edward Theatre 1999. Photograph by Richard Mildenhall. Courtesy of ArenaPAL.

Another key factor is song placement: what has often been brushed aside as a 'seemingly random insertion of ABBA songs into an already illogical set-up, heedless of their narrative or emotional relevance',[215] is in fact only arbitrary when judged by the standards of the classic book musical. *Mamma Mia!*, however, has chosen an alternative approach to story-telling, and consequently, the rendition of its musical numbers diverges from that of a traditional West End or Broadway show. By employing a variety of different means to tie the pre-existing songs into the musical's tale, Charlotte Jones' libretto puts a post-modern spin on the tradition of the integrated book musical. On the one hand, the show's programme does not give the exact order in which the musical numbers will be performed, but instead merely lists the songs alphabetically so that the evening involves a guessing game for the audience as to when and how the songs will turn up.

On the other hand, the musical does not try to hide the fact that several of ABBA's hits are shoehorned into the plot; rather than pretending all songs fit naturally into their slots, the musical plays off the audience's knowledge that certain hits simply *have* to be featured. Because we as spectators want the hits to be included, we understand the authors' predicament and thus can appreciate their problems of accommodating our desire to see our favourite songs performed. Therefore, the sheer inappropriateness of 'Chiquitita' and – to a lesser degree – of 'Take a Chance on Me' for the situation in which they are presented never fails to elicit sympathetic laughter from an audience who is in on the meta-theatrical joke. Because the movement from dialogue into the rendition of an ABBA song in these two scenes is neither smooth nor well prepared, they 'are comic, create distance from identification with the story, and create a new camp context for the songs'.[216] The musical seems to wink at the theatregoers and to admit its apparent failure at finding a more ingenious way of incorporating the number during such moments; it revels in the absurdity of its own song placement as well as delivering an ironic comment on the song placement in other, more traditional, musicals.

In this context, it is telling that the song that has the biggest emotional impact on the audience[217] is the single track not to be included on either 'ABBA Gold' or 'More ABBA Gold'. 'Slipping Through My Fingers', the least widely known number of the score, is a wistful reflection on how despite the best of intentions, parents are 'not grabbing every moment'[218] and thus are inevitably missing important steps of their son or daughter growing up. The ballad is perfectly placed in a scene where Donna helps her daughter prepare for the wedding and strikes a powerful chord with many audience members, especially those who have children. The song's full potential as a moment of intense, heightened emotion – a perfect example of a traditional number in a classic book musical – is realized, when at the end of this intimate scene between mother and daughter, Sophie asks Donna to give her away at the altar because, as she says, 'I'm so proud of you, Mommy!' This sincere appreciation of her parent's efforts demonstrates the loving bond between the two generations. Moreover, it complements the inherent sadness of 'Slipping Through My Fingers' with a stoic acknowledgement of the vagaries of life as well as with an element of wishful thinking, for who does not want to hear the people they are closest to express admiration for what they have tried to achieve?

On the whole, *Mamma Mia!* oscillates between a straightforward, conventional and a post-modern, self-reflexive use of musical numbers, both of which can be savoured by the audience. For the show's director, Phyllida Lloyd, it is precisely these moments of complicity between creative team and playgoers, when the song placement is either handled with ingenuity or affectionately ridiculed, that the audience enjoys the most: '[O]n the whole, I think it works best where the choice of song raises a smile, because you're thinking, "Oh, how ridiculous, they're using that song", or "Ah, that's clever"".[219]

A feminist statement in the form of a musical comedy

The musical takes a feminist stance in its re-gendering of the ABBA hits by assigning lyrics that were originally sung by a woman to a male character and the other way round. Because Johnson gives 'Knowing Me, Knowing You' – a song about the harrowing effects of a divorce – to Sam, the librettist allows him an unexpected vulnerability,[220] tying in with the complete lack of macho posturing throughout the whole show: 'Donna's middle-aged male contemporaries practice absolute gender equality, are non-judgemental about female sexuality and non-competitive about their own.'[221]

On the other hand, when Tanya takes on flirtatious Pepper in 'Does Your Mother Know?', the switch from male singer (Björn Ulvaeus on the original recording) to female performer completely transforms the song: whereas the ABBA version presents an older man patronizingly rejecting the advances of a much younger girl, the musical reconceives the number as a sarcastic dismissal of a young man's sexual bragging by a woman, secure in both her feelings and her own sexuality, who is neither in thrall of his virility nor dumbfounded by his attention and advances.[222]

The mother-and-daughter duo at the heart of the musical makes conscious decisions to avoid 'traditional heteronormative narratives'[223]: Donna's earlier resolution to remain single and to be a single parent as well as her daughter's choice not to marry at the age of 20, the final outcome of Sophie's journey 'from post-feminist to feminist',[224] are both presented by *Mamma Mia!* as intelligent and appropriate. The audience is left in no doubt that the bond between these two women will not be weakened by the men in their lives.[225]

The musical also refrains from judging or criticizing Donna for having had several affairs when she was younger. The fact that Sophie's mother slept with three different men within a couple of days is dismissed as insubstantial by the jukebox show and most of its audience, yet its forward-thinking stance on female sexuality did not please everyone. This 'laissez-faire approach to Donna's youthful sexual immodesty'[226] led to the musical being attacked for its 'loose morals' in Canadian magazine *Maclean's*, which asked the question: 'How did the sleazy plot of *Mamma Mia!* wind up as wholesome family entertainment?' and then went on to condemn the production as a 'salacious, sex-obsessed show'.[227]

The poster of the show features a young girl in a wedding dress laughing in a moment of pure bliss, but it is just as misleading as the initial set-up of the narrative.[228] Not only does the girl decide not to get married at the last minute, but the happy bride turns out to be her mother; furthermore, the question that triggers the events of the plot, namely who out of three prospective candidates is the biological father, is ultimately brushed aside as unimportant. These unexpected twists have led to accusations by I. Q. Hunter that the plotting of *Mamma Mia!* 'is loose to the point of capricious misdirection: we never find out who the father is [and] the marriage at the end is not the one the story arc requires'.[229] What Hunter fails to realize is that it is exactly those apparent plot holes that constitute the show's anarchic quality and widespread appeal, particularly to women of 40 and over.

Perhaps the most radical aspect of *Mamma Mia!* is its refusal to reveal who Sophie's real father is. When both mother and daughter as well as the three potential progenitors come to the conclusion that biological paternity is immaterial, the musical breaks away dramatically from one of the oldest tropes in high and popular culture: for centuries what Sarah Godfrey fittingly identifies as 'the widespread cultural fixation on father hunger',[230] the exploration of who fathered a child and what it means to be the 'real' dad, has driven the plot of countless plays, novels, movies and TV series. Its manifestations range from stage classics (like August Strindberg's *The Father*, 1887) and arthouse movies (Hirokazu Kore-eda's *Like Father, Like Son*; 2013) to soap operas (like *Dallas* and *Empire*), daytime talk shows (like *The Jeremy Kyle Show*) and science fiction films (Irvin Kershner's *The Empire Strikes Back*; 1980).

When Bill, Harry and Sam agree to 'share' Sophie, that is, to practise joint fatherhood, the musical implies that 'it takes more than one man to provide a fully rounded paternal role in Sophie's life, and that Donna has been, and remains, the singularly most reliable and nurturing agent in her daughter's world'.[231] *Mamma Mia!* thus not only deliberately avoids relating Sophie's well-being and happiness to the knowledge of who her father is, it also stands up for the achievements of single mothers, so often reviled as responsible for most of society's ills, since there can be no doubt that Donna has brought up her daughter to be sensible and level-headed – bright and un-neurotic, she validates her mother's decision to raise her on her own.[232]

The show's feminist stance – its heroine spends most of her time on stage dressed in dungarees, that most stereotypical of adornments of a fighter for women's rights – and its progressive politics, both sexual and otherwise, have often been explained by the fact that the creative team of the show was made up of three women[233] who were all born in 1957[234] and who thus were each in their early forties when they started to work on *Mamma Mia!*. With its trio of friends who don't necessarily look for but find romantic love and/or sexual satisfaction later in life, the musical highlights the topics of female bonding and female sexuality in women of a certain age. Thereby it speaks directly of and to a segment of the public that is often marginalized, precisely because it is desexualized: mature women.

By putting front and centre three single women who are old enough to have adult children, the musical offers strong roles for mature actresses. The men meanwhile remain strictly secondary characters: when interviewed, Stellan Skarsgård (who played Bill in the movie) underlined that in *Mamma Mia!* for once it is the male protagonists who are 'the bimbos'.[235] As the objects of desire, they remain 'mere stereotypes'[236] and their main function is to give the audience someone to fantasize about.

Irrelevant, imperfect and inviting: a show unlike any other

The musical carefully avoids the impression that it takes itself too seriously; it has 'not a whiff of self-importance'[237] about it. The self-deprecating tone is set at the very start of the evening by a pre-show announcement: 'Ladies and gentlemen: people of a nervous disposition should be aware that silver platform shoes and white spandex are featured in this performance.'[238] But there are several more features that set Phyllida Lloyd's production apart; the director was determined to avoid (stereo-)typical elements of theatrical entertainment, by insisting that '[i]t must not look like a musical'.[239] That approach was not limited to the design; it also infused other aspects of the staging – for instance, the choreography by Anthony Van Laast, who opted for simple moves over complicated dance routines that could only be executed by professionals with years of training. In the words of associate choreographer Nicola Treherne, the director's brief was: 'An audience should come to watch *Mamma Mia!* and say, "That could be me, or my sister, or my mother."'[240]

The result is musical staging that on the one hand ostensibly confirms the clichéd saying that British audiences love amateurism, but on the other hand is a key factor in the show's enduring popularity. By foregoing choreographic movement that inspires awe and admiration and replacing it with stage activity that seems easy to emulate, the show encourages its audience to do in public what they have been doing all their lives in private, namely dancing along to ABBA songs: *Mamma Mia!* may have been the very first musical that had its viewers dancing in the aisles – a reaction that is unlikely to occur during *West Side Story* (1957) or *Chicago* (1975), because neither show leaves the theatregoers under the illusion that they, too, could execute Jerome Robbins or Bob Fosse's demanding choreography.

Phyllida Lloyd has described the *modus operandi* of *Mamma Mia!* as 'a sort of chaotic roughness. A state of imperfection where anything can happen: you might fall on your arse, or you might jump in the air and do the splits.'[241] Her refusal to let someone's competence and expertise dictate her artistic choices found its most controversial expression in her casting of the male leads in the screen adaptation of *Mamma Mia!*. Critics were quick to denote that none of the three actors playing Donna's love interests could carry a tune, with Pierce Brosnan (who had the most singing to do) being repeatedly ridiculed for his inability to hit the right notes.[242] Yet complaints like this are only relevant if a movie aims to cast the best singer and then fails to do so; in the case of *Mamma Mia! The Movie*, they simply are beside the point, because Brosnan's mediocre crooning serves a completely different purpose: it encourages the viewer to sing the ABBA songs her/himself.

Sing-a-long screenings of film musicals have become very popular in the last decade, but they normally involve movies for the whole family, like *The Sound of Music* (1965) or *Frozen* (2013). These screenings usually work because children have a lower inhibition threshold to sing in public than adults, since they are less afraid of being off-key or making fools of themselves. But when screen idol Brosnan – after all, a former James Bond – doesn't mind exposing his limited vocal skills for all to hear, then why should we?[243] Kate Egan and Kerstin Leder Mackley researched the appeal the screen version had especially for older cinemagoers and found that watching the actors sing and dance imperfectly in the film 'made them feel that they wanted to be (or could imagine being) in the film dancing with the actors.'[244] As a result, *Mamma Mia! The Movie* had people singing along with the characters on screen, even in cinema showings that weren't explicitly designated as sing-a-longs.[245]

While some credit for the extraordinary public response to *Mamma Mia!* must go to the witty libretto and Phyllida Lloyd's fluent direction, another major factor are the songs themselves. Producer Judy Craymer has called the songwriting of Benny Andersson and Björn Ulvaeus 'innately theatrical', and throughout their ten years of composing for ABBA, the two Swedes moved continuously closer towards musical theatre. The collection of songs chosen for the musical – which include hits like 'Honey, Honey' from 1974, the early phase of Björn's writing in English – is somewhat misleading in that it implies that the lyrics are all qualitatively on the same level. Yet even cursory listening to the band's later albums reveals that by the early 1980s ABBA employed both music and words in a far more sophisticated manner to conceive self-contained little stories, often written in character. This is most evident on their last album 'The Visitors', where tracks like the ominous title song, the contemplative 'Slipping Through My Fingers' or the elegiac 'Like an Angel Passing through My Room' create evocative scenarios, each with a distinctive atmosphere, that are a long way from the joyful pop ditties that first put ABBA on the map. Getting back to composing after the release of the 1982 album, Andersson and Ulvaeus realized that they 'kept drifting into musical-type tunes all the time'[246] instead of writing traditional pop music. The two artists credit the 1970 concept album of *Jesus Christ Superstar* with raising their interest in exploring songwriting that would take them beyond individual songs to more complex musical and story-telling structures.[247] Their first foray into this area was a 25-minute mini-musical 'The Girl with the Golden Hair', which premiered as part of ABBA's 1977 European tour. Later, this 'significant first step towards writing complete musicals [...] and to creating musical dramas on stage'[248] would lead to the full-length musicals *Chess* (1984), co-written with Tim Rice, and *Kristina från Duvemåla* (1995), based on four novels by Vilhelm Moberg.

Conclusion: in praise of (older) women

The stage musical *Mamma Mia!* so far has grossed in excess of £2 billion[249] and has been seen worldwide by more than 54 million people.[250] The show has been credited with giving the songs of ABBA 'a whole new lease on life'[251]; it has renewed interest in the band's music, leading to a surge in CD sales and increased airplay. On Broadway, *Mamma Mia!* closed in September 2015 after running for 14 years, an impressive achievement considering that ABBA never was as popular a music act in the United States as it was in Europe, Australia and parts of Asia. In London, more than 16 years after its premiere, the show remains a beloved theatre experience. Maybe the main reason why *Mamma Mia!* has found such an enthusiastic audience both on stage and in cinemas is because it offers female theatre- and cinemagoers a rare opportunity 'to experience sisterhood and female empowerment'.[252] Moreover, both in its plot and through its production history, the musical confirms that women, especially mature woman, 'can do' – it stands as testament to how much the supposedly 'weaker sex' can achieve in the theatre industry as well as other areas of life, and for that alone it deserves to be celebrated.

3.6 STAGE ADAPTATION OF FILMS: WHEN THE CINEMATIC BECOMES THE THEATRICAL

If a movie is chosen as the source material for a stage musical, the adaptors have to maintain what made the film so popular and unique to begin with, in order not to disappoint the ticket buyers, most of whom are likely to attend because they enjoyed the previous version. As most films tend to be shorter than a regular West End show of 150 minutes, the material usually needs to be expanded, which offers the opportunity to make the stage adaptation special in its own right. But whatever additions are decided upon, they need to match the original in tone. They should also use the tools of musical theatre (i.e. tell the story through the songs instead of simply adding singing and dancing to the script), and replace cinematic means of expression with theatrical ones.

For instance, when Disney and Cameron Mackintosh joined forces to bring the 1964 classic *Mary Poppins* to the stage, they realized that they needed to alter both the story and the score, because certain iconic scenes from the movie – like the dancing penguins – could not be reproduced in the theatre, and because certain narrative elements, like Mrs Banks' secret support for the suffragettes, had lost their appeal 50 years after the movie had come out. By including several new songs and an adjusted storyline,[253] the stage *Mary Poppins* demonstrated that with sensitive modifications it is possible to retain what made the original such an audience favourite, while still devising a theatrical experience that has its very own merits.

Billy Elliot (2005) is another good example of an outstanding screen-to-stage transfer as it rethinks and re-conceives the well-loved film released in 2000 and creates a work that actually improves on its source. It was composer Elton John who suggested to the movie's director (Stephen Daldry) and screenwriter (Lee Hall) that they should consider turning the story of the miner's son who desperately wants to become a ballet dancer into a musical. When shaping the material for the stage, the creative triumvirate took great care to get the balance right between the personal and the political, since both the movie and the stage show are set during the miners' strike of 1984–5, one of the key events in modern British history.

Daldry, Hall and John also addressed what could be regarded as one of the few missed opportunities of the movie – the fact that there is not enough dancing – by giving the title character several solos and duets throughout the evening, from the joyful 'Expressing Yourself' and the powerful Act One

208

finale, the 'Angry Dance', to the magical *pas de deux* between Billy and his future self, set to Tchaikovsky's *Swan Lake*, and the final demonstration of all he has learned in 'Electricity'. Yet the individual blossoming of Billy is always set in relief against the struggles of the mining community he grows up in, and every single scene contributes to the portrayal of the Northern working-class environment, its history, traditions, strengths and weaknesses. In what must be one of the most efficient libretti ever created for a musical, each song or dance either helps to propel the narrative forward or to paint another facet of the environment that shapes Billy, both by inspiring him and by holding him back.

One of the first creatives of the West End to enter the territory which is nowadays all the rage – screen-to-stage transfers – was Lloyd Webber in 1993. To musicalize a movie was exceedingly rare when the composer's choice for his next project fell on one of the most iconic movies about Hollywood, Billy Wilder's 1950 *Sunset Boulevard*. The classic black-and-white feature centres around aging silent movie diva Norma Desmond, who lives forgotten by the outside world in a spooky old villa on the eponymous street in Los Angeles. After a chance encounter with young screenwriter Joe Gillis, she hires him to work with her on a script about Salome, which is supposed to be her comeback. The relationship ends tragically: when Joe wants to leave her, Norma shoots him. Having gone insane, she delivers one of the most famous exit lines in movie history: 'And now, Mr De Mille, I'm ready for my close-up.'

Once Lloyd Webber and his collaborators, Don Black and Christopher Hampton, began to deliberate on how to turn Wilder's acerbic masterpiece into a stage musical, they realized that the material would lose impact if all of the movie's masterful dialogue was rendered in recitative, necessary for a sung-through musical. As the film's director proudly (and ironically) pointed out: 'The writers hit on a staggeringly good idea – they decided not to change [the movie].'[254] As a consequence, *Sunset Boulevard* is the first musical by the British composer since *Jeeves*, nearly two decades earlier, with a traditional libretto. Mark Steyn registered with satisfaction: '[I]n *Sunset* we have a Lloyd Webber show in which people walk around talking – not just the odd line, but whole scenes, no underscoring, no music at all and even, occasionally, an old-fashioned cue for a song. It could be a Broadway musical.'[255]

Still, although the stage version sticks closely to the screen play, what was less easy to achieve was a fidelity to its tone; after several reviewers complained that the mordant and bitingly cynical atmosphere of the Oscar-winning Hollywood exposé had been jettisoned for an overly sentimental rendering of the story,[256] the creative team took the unprecedented step of making changes after the show had already had its world premiere, later admitting that they themselves felt they had not achieved the right equilibrium between tragedy and black comedy.[257] This was not the first Lloyd Webber musical to be altered a few months into the run – *Aspects of Love* was similarly re-tooled, albeit to a less drastic degree – but *Sunset Boulevard*'s successful re-launch set an important precedent: practically all subsequent shows of the composer were more or less extensively reworked *after* their official opening, which gives a new meaning to the clichéd saying that musicals are not written, but rewritten. The widely publicized revisions led to a second round of reviews in all major British newspapers, which confirmed that the overhaul had achieved what was intended: 'The revamped version [...] represents an improvement in almost every respect. [...] Individual scenes have been tightened up: the storyline is clearer and sharper, the whole show has acquired fresh momentum.'[258] Other reviewers praised the musical's newly acquired 'narrative harshness',[259] taut story-telling and darkness.[260]

Whistle Down the Wind (1997), the composer's next musical, was based both on the 1959 novel by Mary Hayley Bell and its 1961 film version. It had an ill-received try-out in Washington, DC, before its American director Harold Prince was replaced by Australian Gale Edwards and its Broadway premiere was cancelled in favour of a London run. The musical tells the story of a group of children who discover an escaped convict in their barn and mistake him for the resurrected Jesus. It was duly and approvingly[261] noted by critics that Lloyd Webber had once again decided to abandon his customary sung-through approach for the project, even if he and his co-librettists Edwards and Patricia Knop did not receive high marks for their efforts: 'The script is a bit of a mess, with scrappy little scenes and often incoherent motivation and character development.'[262] That the adaptation moved the setting from the original Lancashire to Louisiana was another major point of contention, not least because Lloyd Webber's music does not employ the styles of music that have become associated with the American South, such as blues, jazz or ragtime, but instead settles for nondescript country-and-western sounds as well as 1950s rock'n'roll.[263]

While some observers contended that the switch of locations from the northwest of England to the American Bible belt in the 1950s could have worked, given the religious elements of the original, most of them lamented its unconvincing execution, and criticized the musical's portrayal of racism and race relations.[264] Matt Wolf castigated the show's concept as 'so inauthentic that it might as well take place on the moon'.[265] After the failure of *Whistle Down the Wind,* which ran for two and a half years in the West End, but failed to recoup,[266] Lloyd Webber would not adapt another movie to the stage for 18 years – his latest project is a musicalization of the 2003 comedy *School of Rock* – but in the new millennium instead focused mainly on musicals with original storylines.

A more recent West End casualty and one that should have run much longer than it did was *Made in Dagenham* (2014), which, like so many West End productions in the last ten years, was a musical based on a popular British movie released just a few years earlier, in this case the 2010 film about the 1968 strike of female workers at the Ford factory in Dagenham for equal pay. On the credit side, the show had a varied, melodious score by David Arnold, witty lyrics written both in character and period by Richard Thomas and an often laugh-out-loud book by Richard Bean. Yet the inexperience of the writers in how to structure a musical showed on several occasions. Officially opening at the Adelphi Theatre in November 2014, the musical had several imperfections that prevented it from achieving its full potential: Rita, the heroine, was not introduced via her own number, but only got a solo song near the end of Act Two. Instead the score included several – admittedly funny – solos for supporting characters that either didn't help tell the story (like 'Wossname') or went on too long (like 'This Is America' and 'Cortina'). A subplot about Rita's son being caned at school was abandoned half way through, and the death of her friend Connie did not make the intended impact on the audience because the trade union representative was diagnosed with cancer and died of it more or less in the same scene. Yet all of these book problems could have been fixed easily and none of them was grave enough to explain the show's early demise, which has to be accounted for by other factors.

Several other major screen-to-stage adaptations are already on the horizon – with musical versions of *Mrs Henderson Presents* (2005), *Calendar Girls* (2003), *Groundhog Day* (1993) and *Pride* (2014) either already in try-outs, in pre-production or publicly announced – so it seems that this last trend in British musical theatre is bound to continue into the foreseeable future; at least, that is, until a different type of musical theatre becomes the rage. To quote the title of yet another movie-turned-musical (this one American): Bring it on!

CONCLUSION

At the conclusion of a book such as this, a question inevitably arises about the future of the British musical. Given the paucity of critical texts on the subject, the question of the future of scholarship in the field of British musical theatre appears equally necessary. A transformation is under way to which this book acts as the precursor. Within British universities, music and theatre have long been regarded as separate disciplines with very different subjects and methodologies. In both music and drama departments, the study of popular and commercial forms of entertainment have traditionally been less valued than the study of high-art texts and practices. The ascendancy of the discipline of cultural studies in British universities since the late 1950s highlighted the importance of studying popular culture, eventually making the study of musical theatre acceptable in music and theatre departments. The growing trend towards interdisciplinary research has also supported the kind of thinking necessary to comprehend the complex form of a musical, with its combination of drama, song, music and dance. The enormous commercial success of British musicals internationally since the early 1980s gave rise to a great expansion in the number of theatre schools offering specialist professional training in musical theatre performance, while the increasing number of courses at universities reflects the high profile of musical theatre in both professional and academic contexts.

In response to these developments in the field, an international conference for the study of musical theatre, *Song, Stage and Screen*, was established in Britain in 2006. The first academic journal, *Studies in Musical Theatre*, began here in 2007. One consequence of the growing interest in the study of musical theatre generally was that scholars began to notice the lack of recognition given to British musical theatre, which led to the inauguration of the British Musical Theatre Research Institute in 2012. As a result, several projects have been initiated, including this book, the forthcoming publication of the *Oxford Handbook of the British Musical* (Oxford University Press, 2016) and the establishment of a book series, *Palgrave Studies in British Musical Theatre*. What all of these developments have in common is that they will offer future students and academic scholars the opportunity to research and teach British musical theatre in ways that have not hitherto been possible.

But what of the British musical itself? There are now a number of professional bodies designed to support the development of new musical theatre in Britain. Musical Theatre Network (MTN, established 2005) is a forum that, among other things, champions the development of new work. It hosts a biennial conference, offers a composer in residence scheme and in 2015 inaugurated a new award, the MTN Development Award, to support individuals or organizations demonstrating real potential in the creation of new musical theatre. MTN works in close partnership with Mercury Musical Developments (MMD) to jointly offer the schemes above with the support of Arts Council funding. MMD provides independent support for the authors (book writers, composers and lyricists) of musical theatre in the UK, offering workshops, seminars, master classes and writers groups, and in association with MTN, runs BEAM, an annual showcase event for new works. In 2007, Musical Theatre Matters established a series of awards to champion the next generation of musical theatre producers, writers and shows, though these awards are not focused only on British works.

In spite of the fact that producing musical theatre is comparatively expensive, fringe venues around the country, the Edinburgh Festival and some regional theatres are increasingly producing new musicals. It seems that the prospect for the development of new British musical theatre has never looked better. Only time will tell the directions in which British musical theatre will develop, but it does seem that the structures of support are currently in place for another burst of energy in the writing and production of British musicals, and that for the first time the attention of researchers and critics will be focused on documenting the history and analysing the musical dramaturgy manifest in the creation of modern British musical theatre.

TIMELINE

Year	Musical(s)	Political Event(s)
1945	Perchance to Dream	• End of Second World War • Labour Party wins a landslide victory in the general election
1946	Pacific 1860	
1947	Bless the Bride	• The British coal industry is nationalized • India gains independence from Britain
1948		• SS Empire Windrush arrives, carrying 500 Caribbean immigrants to Britain • The National Health Service is established
1949	King's Rhapsody	
1950	Ace of Clubs	
1951	Gay's the Word Zip Goes a Million	• The Festival of Britain • Conservative Party under Winston Churchill wins the general election
1952		• Elizabeth II succeeds her father, George VI
1953	The Boy Friend Cinderella	
1954	After the Ball Salad Days Wedding in Paris	
1955		• Conservative Party under Anthony Eden wins the general election. • Commercial television introduced in Britain
1956	Grab Me a Gondola	• John Osborne's Look Back in Anger opens at the Royal Court theatre, becoming the symbol of a revolution in British theatre and literature • President Nasser's nationalization of the Suez Canal prompts Britain and France to invade Egypt with the support of Israel

(Continued)

Timeline

Year	Musical(s)	Political Event(s)
1957		• Ghana becomes the first British colony in Africa to achieve independence
1958	*Expresso Bongo* *Valmouth*	
1959	*The Crooked Mile* *Fings Ain't Wot They Used T'Be* *Lock Up Your Daughters* *Make Me an Offer* *The World of Paul Slickey*	• Conservative Party under Harold Macmillan wins the general election
1960	*Johnny the Priest* *Oliver!*	
1961	*Stop the World – I Want to Get Off*	
1962	*Blitz!*	
1963	*Half a Sixpence* *Oh What a Lovely War!*	
1964	*Maggie Mae* *The Roar of the Greasepaint, the Smell of the Crowd*	• The Labour Party wins the general election under Harold Wilson
1965	*Twang!!* *Pickwick*	
1966	*The Match Girls*	• The Labour Party strengthens its position in the general election
1967		• Sexual Offences Act legalizes homosexual relations between men over 21 • The Abortion Act legalizes abortion under certain conditions
1968	*Joseph and the Amazing Technicolor Dreamcoat*	• Theatre censorship abolished
1969	*Ann Veronica*	• The beginning of the 'Troubles': British troops are sent to Northern Ireland to restore law and order

1970	*Jesus Christ Superstar*	• The Conservatives win the general election
	Scrooge	under Edward Heath
		• The Equal Pay Act makes it illegal to pay women less than men for the same work
1971		
1972	*The Good Old Bad Old Days*	• 'Bloody Sunday': the British army kills 14 people in Londonderry, Northern Ireland.
	Our Man Crichton	
	Trelawney	
1973	*The Card*	• Britain joins the European Economic Community (EEC)
	The Cheviot, the Stag and the Black, Black Oil	
	Jorrocks	
	The Rocky Horror Show	
1974	*Billy*	• Labour Party wins the general election under Harold Wilson with a very small majority
1975	*Jeeves*	• The Sex Discrimination Act makes it illegal for women to be discriminated against in work, education and training
1976	*Evita*	• Harold Wilson resigns to be replaced by James Callaghan
		• Britain forced to borrow money from the International Monetary Fund (IMF)
		• The Race Relations Act makes it illegal to discriminate on grounds of race in employment and education
1977		
1978		• A large number of simultaneous strikes characterize the 'winter of discontent'
1979		• Margaret Thatcher becomes Britain's first female Prime Minister
1980		
1981	*Cats*	• Racial riots in Brixton and other areas
1982	*Poppy*	• Economic recession leads to high unemployment
	Song & Dance	• Britain defeats Argentina in the Falklands War

(Continued)

Timeline

Year	Musical(s)	Political Event(s)
1983	The Black Mikado Blondel Our Day Out	• Margaret Thatcher wins a landslide victory for the Conservative Party
1984	Chess The Hired Man Starlight Express	• The Miners' Strike to prevent pit closures begins; it lasts 12 months before the miners capitulate
1985	Les Misérables/Les Miz	
1986	The Phantom of the Opera Time	• Major national industries are privatized
1987		• Margaret Thatcher wins a third term for the Conservative Party
1988		
1989	Aspects of Love Buddy – the Buddy Holly Story Return to the Forbidden Planet	
1990	Five Guys Named Moe	• Margaret Thatcher resigns to be replaced by John Major
1991		• Iraq War ('Operation Desert Storm') to liberate Kuwait won by Allies
1992		• The Conservative Party wins the general election by a small majority • Channel Tunnel opens, linking London and Paris by rail
1993	Abbacadabra Sunset Boulevard	
1994		
1995		
1996	Martin Guerre	
1997	Whistle Down the Wind	• Labour wins the general election under Tony Blair with a huge majority • Britain hands Hong Kong back to China • Scotland and Wales vote in favour of devolution

1998	*Shockheaded Peter*	• Devolved Northern Irish Assembly established by the 'Good Friday' agreement
		• Tuition fees of £1,000 introduced at British universities, ending the largely free system of higher education
1999	*Mamma Mia!* *Spend, Spend, Spend* *Tess of the D'Urbervilles*	• Britain decides against joining the single European currency (Euro)
2000	*The Beautiful Game*	
2001		• Labour wins the general election with a large majority
		• Islamist terrorists crash planes into the World Trade Center in New York and the Pentagon in Washington, DC (9/11), prompting George W. Bush to declare a worldwide 'war on terror'
2002	*Bombay Dreams* *Chitty Chitty Bang Bang* *Our House* *Taboo* *We Will Rock You*	
2003	*Jerry Springer – the Opera* *Tonight's the Night – the Rod Stewart Musical*	• Britain supports the United States in the invasion of Iraq to overthrow Saddam Hussein without a UN mandate
2004	*Mary Poppins* *The Woman in White* *The Big Life*	• Civil partnerships between same-sex couples became legal in the UK
		• Student fees raised to £3,000, with the introduction of a system of student loans
2005	*Acorn Antiques* *Billy Elliot* *The Far Pavilions*	• Labour Party under Tony Blair wins third consecutive general election
		• First civil partnership between same-sex couples
2006	*Daddy Cool* *The Harder They Come* *Into the Hoods*	
2007	*Desperately Seeking Susan* *Never Forget*	• Tony Blair resigns as Prime Minister and is succeeded by Gordon Brown
2008	*Soho Cinders*	

(Continued)

Timeline

Year	Musical(s)	Political Event(s)
2009		• Barack Obama becomes first African American President of the United States • Global financial crisis produces an economic recession
2010	*Love Never Dies* *Matilda – the Musical*	• General election fails to produce an overall majority, so the Conservative Party under David Cameron form a coalition government with the Liberals under Nick Clegg
2011	*Betty Blue Eyes* *London Road* *That Day We Sang*	• Osama Bin Laden killed in Pakistan
2012	*Some Like It Hip-Hop* *Viva Forever!* *Glasgow Girls* *The Wah Wah Girls*	• Fees of between £6,000 and £9,000 introduced by English and Welsh universities
2013	*Charlie and the Chocolate Factory* *The Commitments* *From Here to Eternity* *Stephen Ward*	
2014	*Made in Dagenham*	• The jihadist group ISIL (Islamic State of Iraq and the Levant) becomes de facto ruler of large parts of northern Iraq and Syria • Same-sex marriage legislation comes into force in England, Scotland and Wales
2015	*Bend It Like Beckham* *Calendar Girls*	• In May, the Conservative Party wins the general election, with David Cameron as Prime Minister • On 13 November, ISIL is responsible for co-ordinating terrorist attacks in various parts of Paris, which killed 130 people and injured 368 • On 3 December, the UK initiated airstrikes on selected targets in Syria, in support of French and American military strategy against ISIL

NOTES

Introduction

1. Gerald Mast: *Can't Help Singin'. The American Musical on Stage and Screen*, Woodstock/New York: The Overlook Press, 1987, p. 334.

1 Musicals and social change

1. For a discussion of the physical and emotional effects of the bombing during the Blitz, see Alan Sinfield, *Literature, Politics and Culture in Postwar Britain,* London: Continuum, 2004, pp. 7–11.

2. P. J. Marshall, cited in Dominic Sandbrook, *Never Had It So Good*, London: Abacus, 2013, p. 279.

3. See ibid., pp. 28–9.

4. Paul Gilroy, 'Why Harry's Disoriented about Empire', in *The Guardian*, 18 January 2005.

5. See Arthur Marwick, *British Society since 1945*, Harmondsworth: Penguin, 4th edition, 2003, pp. 3–4.

6. British men and women were actually physically smaller than their American counterparts, largely as a result of their more restricted diet.

7. In every decade since 1945, the longest-running musicals in the West End have been not American but British: *The Boy Friend* (1954) – 2,084 performances; *Salad Days* (1954) – 2,283 performances; *Oliver!* (1960) – 2,680 performances; *Charley Girl* (1965) – 2,202 performances; *Canterbury Tales* (1968) – 2,082 performances; *Jesus Christ Superstar* (1972) – 3,358 performances; *The Rocky Horror Show* (1973) – 2,960 performances,

8. See Sandbrook, *Never Had It So Good*, pp. 276–307.

9. For a detailed discussion on the psychological effects of the break-up of the British Empire, see Sinfield, *Literature, Politics and Culture*, pp. 132–67.

10. For consideration of the humiliating realization of Britain's powerlessness in the face of American intervention to stop the Suez war, see ibid., p. 265.

11. Sinfield compares the attitudes of different classes during and after the war in the light of the postwar notion of consensus (ibid., pp. 6–36).

Notes

12. For an account of the notion of 'consensus government' that dominated British politics between 1945 and 1979, see Marwick, *British Society since 1945*, pp. 73–84.

13. See ibid., pp. 27–39, for an analysis of the transformation of British governmental systems into the 'Welfare State'.

14. *Only Entertainment* is the title of a book by Richard Dyer.

15. The failure of the Spice Girls musical *Viva Forever!* and *I Can't Sing* based on the hit TV programme *X Factor* offer two recent cases in point, whereas the huge success of *We Will Rock You*, in spite of its universally poor reviews, only goes to prove that audience taste is not easily accounted for.

16. Raymond Williams, *Drama from Ibsen to Brecht*, Harmondsworth: Penguin, 1968.

17. *Thoroughly Modern Millie, Avenue Q, Urinetown, The Drowsy Chaperone, Legally Blonde, A Gentleman's Guide to Love and Murder* are a few of the productions that reveal this shift towards musical comedy.

18. The term 'megamusical', invented by a journalist to describe the blockbuster British musicals of the 1980s, is actually a misnomer, as most of these shows are much smaller than any pre-war show at Drury Lane or the London Coliseum; their only 'mega' aspect resides in the fact that they have been reproduced globally and made billions of pounds in profit.

19. See John Snelson, 'Ordinary People and British Musicals of the Post-War Decade', in Robert Gordon and Olaf Jubin (eds), *The Oxford Handbook of the British Musical*, New York: Oxford University Press, forthcoming 2016.

20. *Cavalcade* (1931), Coward's spectacular epic of modern British history, was one of the largest shows ever mounted at Drury Lane.

21. *The Boy Friend* (2,084 performances) and *Salad Days* (2,283 performances) far exceeded the length of run of every post-war musical until *My Fair Lady* and *Oliver!* But the two shows ran at the Wyndham's Theatre (759 seats) and the Vaudeville Theatre (690 seats), which are smaller West End theatres with approximately a third of the seating capacity of the Theatre Royal Drury Lane (2,196 seats), where *Oklahoma!* ran for 1,543 performances, or the Coliseum (2,558 seats), home to *Annie Get Your Gun* for 1,304 performances.

22. See Sinfield, *Literature, Politics and Culture*, pp. 84–9, for an illuminating analysis of the stereotyping of homosexuals as individuals most likely to betray their country.

23. See Frank Mort, *Capital Affairs*, New Haven: Yale University Press, 2010, pp. 42–5, for a detailed discussion of the perceptions of homosexual soliciting as endemic to street life in 1950s London.

24. For an illuminating analysis of the ways in which the police prosecuted campaigns to eradicate homosexual 'importuning' in London, see Matt Houlbrook, *Queer London*, Chicago: University of Chicago Press, 2005, pp. 21–37.

25. In Evesham in 1956, police enquiries resulted in one man gassing himself, one throwing himself under a train, leaving a widow and children, and an 81-year-old dying of a stroke before sentence could be passed. Fairly typical of press coverage of homosexuality was the infamous *Sunday Pictorial* feature 'How to spot a Homo' in 1963, featuring homophobic stereotypes of gays as mincing queens, child molesters or corrupters.

26. Richard Dyer presents a fascinating outline of the uses of camp by gay men before the partial decriminalization of homosexual relationships in 1968 in his chapter, 'It's Being So Camp as Keeps Us Going' (Richard Dyer, *The Culture of Queers*, London: Routledge, 2001, pp. 49–62).

27. 'Burlesque' is a term that in its original meaning denoted a sustained parody of a literary work or genre. In the nineteenth-century British theatre burlesque became a much more open-ended theatrical genre that used different types of comic parody mixed with elements of pantomime and dance; in America the British form was transformed to become by the end of the century a disreputable type of variety show that presented a series of risqué comic and striptease acts.

28. Wilson more-or-less disowned the production, which he felt was a distortion of the original that turned it into a grotesquely camp travesty.

29. For a parallel ambivalence between anti-Establishment attack and nostalgia for Edwardian values in the realm of 'high' culture, see Osborne's *The Entertainer* (1957).

30. The production, directed by Bill Bankes-Jones for Tête à Tête, garnered rave reviews.

31. The use of a mysterious tramp and a clown-like mime is tantalizingly redolent of the dramatis personae of Beckett's *Waiting for Godot*, which was first performed in English in 1954.

32. See Richard Dyer, *Only Entertainment*, London: Routledge, 1992, pp. 19–35; Jill Dolan, *Utopia in Performance,* Ann Arbor: University of Michigan Press, 2005.

33. Siân Adiseshiah, '"We Said We Wouldn't Look Back": Utopia and the Backward Glance in Dorothy Reynolds and Julian Slade's *Salad Days*', in *Studies in Musical Theatre*, Vol. 5 (2011), No. 2, p. 149.

34. Quotations from *Salad Days* refer to Dorothy Reynolds and Julian Slade, *Salad Days*, London: Samuel French, 1961.

35. Although a small wage, a young couple might just have been able to subsist on £28 per month in 1954.

36. This is one of the chief strategies of literary deconstruction.

37. For a detailed discussion of the impact of the 'Teddy Boy' and the rise of rock and roll in Britain, see Sandbrook, *Never Had It So Good*, pp. 443–84.

38. Richard Hoggart's *The Uses of Literacy* (London: Penguin 1969) reflects the prevailing British anxiety concerning the threatened colonization of British culture by American mass culture.

Notes

39. Harold Macmillan's most famous phrase is often misquoted as, 'You've never had it so good'; what he actually said was, 'Let's be frank about it, *most of our people have never had it so good.*' Cited in Sandbrook, *Never Had It So Good*, p. xxvi.

40. See ibid., pp. 86–102, for an analysis of the growth of Britain as an affluent society.

41. *Grab Me a Gondola* (1956) marked the start of a new generation of jazzy, Broadway-style musicals in the West End, which adopted American production values in staging and musical orchestration. The show ran for 673 performances.

42. Gambling joint.

43. George Wellwarth, 'John Osborne: "Angry Young Man"?' in *The Theater of Protest and Paradox: Developments in the Avant-Garde Drama*, New York: New York University Press, 1964, pp. 222–34.

44. Brecht is one of the few serious modern European playwrights to use songs in his plays, and the phenomenon is virtually unknown on or off-Broadway.

45. A Scottish and Irish social event involving folk singing and dancing.

46. See Part Two for a more detailed discussion of *The Cheviot, the Stag and the Black, Black Oil*.

47. See Vera Gottlieb, 'Thatcher's Theatre – or, After *Equus*' in *New Theatre Quarterly*, Vol. 4, No. 14, May 1988, pp. 99–104.

48. The term 'melodrama' derives from the late eighteenth-century French genre *melo-drame*, which literally meant 'music-drama'. As in the majority of popular films today, music in stage melodrama provided a kind of soundtrack evoking or anticipating the appropriate feelings and establishing the rhythm of a spectator's affective engagement with the events of the narrative.

49. Peter Coe, 'Introduction' to Wolf Mankowitz and Leslie Bricusse, *Pickwick*, London: Samuel French Ltd., 1991, p. viii.

50. These films include Calvalcanti's *Nicholas Nickleby* (1947), David Lean's *Great Expectations* (1946) and *Oliver Twist* (1948), and Noel Langley's *Pickwick Papers* (1952).

51. Its only rival is *Les Misérables*.

52. This was adapted into a film that was released in 2015.

53. The show was adapted for television and broadcast during Christmas 2014.

54. For obvious reasons Disney became in the 1990s Cameron Macintosh's biggest rival in the sphere of global musical theatre production.

55. Currently, the highest-rated New York tap dancer.

56. See Scott McMillin, *The Musical as Drama*, New Jersey: Princeton University Press, 2006.

57. Charles Spencer, Review of *Billy Elliot The Musical*, in *The Daily Telegraph*, 11 May 2005.

58. All quotations from the libretto of *Billy Elliot: the Musical* are taken directly from the *Billy Elliot Live* DVD 2014, Universal 830 064 6 11.

59. Pitmen are those mine-workers who actually go down underground in the mines.

60. The influence of Lloyd Newsom's *Enter Achilles* (1995) for DV8 is apparent in the movement vocabulary of this scene.

61. See Michael Gard, *Men Who Dance: Aesthetics, Athletics and the Art of Masculinity*, 2001.

62. For a detailed discussion of the representation of masculinity in *Billy Elliot*, see George Rodosthenous, '*Billy Elliot The Musical*: Visual Representations of Working Class Masculinity and the All-singing, All-dancing Bo[d]y', in *Studies in Musical Theatre*, Vol. 1 (2006), No. 3, pp. 275–92.

63. Peter Brown, *London Theatre Guide Online: West End Review*, 11 May, 2005, http://www.londontheatre.co.uk/londontheatre/reviews/billyelliot05.htm. Accessed 28 August 2015.

64. See Michael Billington's review in *The Guardian*, 11 May 2005. Both *Mary Poppins* and *Peter Pan* had recently been produced in London, featuring fairly spectacular moments of 'flying'.

65. See Jonathan Burston, 'Enter Stage Right: Neo-Conservatism, English Canada and the Megamusical', in *Soundings*, Issue 5, Spring 1997; and 'Spectacle, Synergy and Megamusicals: the Global-industrialization of the Live Entertainment industry', in James Curran (ed.), *Media Organisations and Society*, London: Arnold, 2000; also Dan Rebellato, *Theatre and Globalisation*, Basingstoke: Palgrave, 2009.

66. See ibid.

67. Robert McCrum, 'The Stories Children's Books Tell about the World They're Written in', *The Guardian*, 27 April 2009.

68. Rebecca Knuth, *Children's Literature and British Identity: Imagining a People and a Nation*, New York: Scarecrow, 2012, p. 111.

69. Ibid., p. 95.

70. Mariah Gubar, *Artful Dodgers*, Oxford: Oxford University Press, p. 6.

71. All lyrics quoted from *Matilda the Musical* are taken from *Matilda – The Musical*. Lyrics Booklet, Original Cast Recording, RSC Enterprises Ltd. 2011, RSCE 002.

72. The song refers to Guy Debord's idea of the 'society of the spectacle' expounded in Guy Debord, *The Society of the Spectacle*, trans. Donald Nicholson-Smith, London: Black and Red, 1970.

73. Debord, *The Society of the Spectacle*, Thesis 17, www.marxists.org/reference/archive/debord/society.htm. Accessed 20 September 2015.

74. Ibid., Thesis 42.

Notes

75. Jonathan Rose, *The Edwardian Temperament, 1895–1919*, Columbus: Ohio University Press, 1986.

76. Knuth, *Children's Literature*, p. 111.

77. Debord, *The Society of the Spectacle*, Thesis 4.

78. The election of a Conservative government in 2015 promises to keep alive the debate between liberal and reactionary attitudes to education.

2 British popular culture and musical theatre

1. Pantomime has incorporated specialty acts from variety, such as acrobats and magicians, right up to the present. More recently film, and even 3D film, has been incorporated into pantomime.

2. Although other countries recognize the term 'pantomime', outside the UK it is generally assumed to mean wordless mime. Many of the characters of commedia dell'arte have been adapted in pantomime: *Arlecchino* was a quick-witted and unscrupulous acrobatic comic who became Harlequin in England and later influenced pantomime's heroes and comics. His influence remains in working-class quick-witted rogues and heroes such as Bill Snibson in *Me and My Girl* (Noel Gay, Douglas Furber and L. Arthur Rose, 1937) the Artful Dodger in *Oliver!*, Kipps in *Half a Sixpence* (David Heneker and Beverley Cross, 1963) and Denry Machin in *The Card* (Keith Waterhouse, Willis Hall, Tony Hatch and Jackie Trent, 1973). Even Galileo and Scaramouche in *We Will Rock You* or Billy Elliot and Matilda fall into this category – poor working-class characters who succeed through their own wit, intelligence or talent against the odds and against powerful institutions. *Colombina* was the quick-witted maid who influenced the down-to-earth principal girls of pantomime and musical theatre – Sally in *Me and My Girl*, Ann in *Half a Sixpence* and even Mrs Johnstone in *Blood Brothers* (Russell, 1973).

3. See Millie Taylor, 'Continuity and Transformation in Twentieth-Century Pantomime', in Jim Davis (ed.), *Victorian Pantomime*, Basingstoke: Palgrave, 2010, pp. 185–200.

4. The role of Principal Boy is now often critiqued as being politically incorrect, though I have argued elsewhere that the presence of the Principal Boy is much more complex than this argument allows (Millie Taylor, *British Pantomime Performance*, Bristol: Intellect, 2007 pp. 105–22).

5. Peter Nichols, *Poppy,* London: Methuen 1982, Act One, Scene 2, 4.

6. Nichols, *Poppy*, Act One, Scene 6, 31

7. See Case Study 4.

8. Nichols, *Poppy*, Act One, Scene 2, 6.

9. This story is likely to be apocryphal since during my research on pantomime I haven't been able to establish that this ever occurred, and it may be that this

moment from *Poppy*, which critiques the incorporation of specialty acts into pantomime, is in fact the source of the myth.

10. Nichols, *Poppy*, Act One, Scene 9, 49.

11. Ibid., Act Two, Scene 3, 69.

12. Ibid., Act Two, Scene 6, 80.

13. Ibid., Act Two, Scene 8, 90.

14. Taylor, *British Pantomime*, pp. 38–9.

15. John McGrath, *The Cheviot, The Stag and the Black, Black Oil*, London: Methuen, 1981 [1974], p. x.

16. McGrath, *The Cheviot*, p. 59.

17. See Case Study 3 for more on this.

18. The programme of the 2014 production calls the production 'Joan Littlewood's Musical entertainment' and lists the authors in a different order as Theatre Workshop, Charles Chilton, Gerry Raffles and Members of the Original Cast.

19. Joan Littlewood, 'Introduction', in *Oh What a Lovely War!*, Revised and Restored to the original version by Joan Littlewood (Methuen Drama, 2000), p. ix.

20. Ibid.

21. These include The Imperial War Museum, Kaiser Wilhelm II, Generals Erich Ludendorff and Sir Henry Wilson, Field Marshals Graf von Schlieffen, Earl Haig and Sir John French, poets, writers, soldiers and newspaper reports. For personal help acknowledgements are given to, among others, 'Bert Sweet (ex-Gunner, 186 R.F.A., Deptford Gun Brigade) and many other ex-members of the armies of both sides in the 1914–18 war. And above all, to the unknown British soldier-composers of the Western Front' (Programme, 1963). A more detailed list is in the Appendix of the revised script (*Oh What a Lovely War!*, 2000) pp. 94–5.

22. One of the performers in the original production and the Theatre Royal, Stratford East's honorary archivist.

23. Littlewood, *Oh What a Lovely War!*, 2000, p. 86.

24. September 1964.

25. 1964, p. 11. Quoted in Nadine Holdsworth, *Joan Littlewood*, London and New York: Routledge, 2006, p. 111.

26. Littlewood, *Oh What a Lovely War!*, 2000, p. x.

27. Lez Brotherston, 'Designing the Show', in *Oh What a Lovely War!* (Programme, 2014).

28. Holdsworth, *Joan Littlewood*, p. 87.

29. Littlewood, *Oh What a Lovely War!*, 2000, p. 58.

30. Ibid., p. 78.

31. The pierrot is a white-faced clown who wears a loose-fitting white costume with a black ruff at the neck and black bobbles or pompoms down the front; the

pierrette is the female equivalent. Although the characters derive from French pantomime and commedia dell'arte – in which Pierrot pined for the love of Columbine – they had become much more diverse in character and had no fixed nationality by the first half of the twentieth century, and in fact pierrot costumes might be used, for example, for all the players in a play, variety or end-of-the-pier show.

32. Littlewood, *Oh What a Lovely War!*, 2000, p. x.

33. End-of-the-pier shows were variety shows performed in the summer months for visitors to seaside resorts in small theatres built on piers. There is one still operating in the UK in Cromer.

34. Leach, *Theatre Workshop*, p. 169.

35. Ibid.

36. The programme announces the first ensemble number as 'Alexander's Ragtime Band', while the new edition of the libretto Joan Littlewood published in 2000 'to restore the life of the play to my memory of the first production at Stratford East in 1963' identifies the opening number as 'Johnny Jones', alternatively called 'Row, Row Row, Way up the River'. This may be partly revealing of the fallibility of memory, but also highlights the fluidity of the text in Littlewood's productions, which were constantly adapted.

37. Littlewood had begun her career at Radio Manchester, where she learned to juxtapose facts in order to make a point without needing to comment, and it was this skill that she used to create the hard-hitting political commentary in *Oh What a Lovely War!*.

38. Littlewood, *Oh What a Lovely War!*, 2000, p. 75

39. Ibid., p. 76.

40. Holdsworth, *Joan Littlewood*, p. 91.

41. Littlewood, *Oh What a Lovely War!*, 2000, p. 51. The style of black humour in the production derived from *The Wipers Times*, a newspaper produced by soldiers in the trenches, a section of which is reproduced in the 1963 programme.

42. Littlewood, *Oh What a Lovely War!*, 2000, pp. 81–2.

43. Ibid., pp. 87–8.

44. Richard Eyre and Nicholas Wright, *Changing Stages*, London: Bloomsbury Publishing, 2000, p. 269.

45. Holdsworth, *Joan Littlewood*, p. 113.

46. Carol Ilson, *Harold Prince: A Director's Journey*, New York: Limelight Editions, 2000, pp. 61–2.

47. Leach, *Theatre Workshop*, p. 203.

48. Quoted in Leach, *Theatre Workshop*, p. 211.

49. This overview focuses on London with limited reference to equally dynamic developments elsewhere in the UK. This is unavoidable given the limited space

here and the higher impact of London-based theatre on the commercial musical theatre sector. For more information about ethnic minority theatre companies elsewhere in the country, see Claire Cochrane, *Twentieth Century British Theatre: Industry, Art and Empire*, Cambridge University Press, 2014; Graham Ley and Sarah Dadswell (eds), *Critical Essays on British South Asian Theatre*, Exeter University Press, 2012; and Dimple Godiwala (ed.), *Alternatives Within the Mainstream: British Black and Asian Theatres*, Cambridge Scholars Press, 2006.

50. Ruth A. Tompsett, 'Re-imagining History: An Introduction to the Black Theatre Conference Papers', *Black Theatre in Britain*, Special Issue of *Performing Arts International*, Vol. 1, Part 2 (1996), p. 3.

51. Dimple Godiwala, 'Alternatives Within the Mainstream: British Black and Asian Theatres. An Introduction', in D. Godiwala (ed.), *Alternatives Within the Mainstream: British Black and Asian Theatres*, Newcastle: Cambridge Scholars Press, 2006, p. 7.

52. Colin Chambers, *Black and Asian Theatre in Britain: A History*, London: Routledge, 2011, p. 151. For example, Cy Grant had appeared on the BBC TV's *Tonight* programme as a calypso news singer in the late 1950s, and in a musical TV documentary on civil rights called *Freedom Road: Songs of Negro Protest* (1961).

53. For more on the development of the Black Theatre Forum, see Alda Terracciano, 'Mainstreaming African, Asian and Caribbean Theatre: The Experiments of the Black Theatre Forum', in Godiwala, *Alternatives*, pp. 22–60.

54. Chambers, *Black and Asian Theatre*, p. 142.

55. Ibid.

56. Ilona Sekacz is an influential theatre, film and television composer, with credits including Royal Shakespeare Company, Royal National Theatre, www. imagineerproductions.co.uk/content/6965/godiva_awakes/godiva_2012/ artists_and_partners/artist_profiles/ilona_sekacz. Accessed 2 March 2015.

57. Beaton was one of the instigators of Dark and Light (with Frank Cousins), was an actor in the opening production by Talawa, an actor at the Royal Court and National Theatre, and performed in *The Black Mikado* (1975) before becoming an established television performer.

58. Chambers, *Black and Asian Theatre*, p. 144.

59. www.blackplaysarchive.org.uk/explore/companies/temba-theatre-company. Accessed 13 February 2015.

60. Chambers, *Black and Asian Theatre*, p. 148.

61. Terracciano, 'Mainstreaming', in Godiwala, *Alternatives*, p. 39.

62. Paulette Randall quoted in Terracciano, 'Mainstreaming', p. 40.

63. Felix Cross quoted in Terracciano, 'Mainstreaming', p. 41.

64. Ibid.

Notes

65. Paulette Randall quoted in Terracciano, 'Mainstreaming', p. 41.

66. Brewster had already worked in the mainstream and was part of the development of a more fluid and open interaction between mainstream and minority ethnic companies, as well as in the promotion of women and the development of co-productions with theatres around the country (Chambers, *Black and Asian Theatre*, p. 191).

67. The archives of Talawa are available in the V&A theatre and performance collection.

68. www.nitro.co.uk/about/. Accessed 13 February 2015.

69. Philip Hedley, 'Black Theatre Development at Theatre Royal Stratford East', *Performing Arts International* (1996), Vol. 1, No. 2, p. 26.

70. Ibid.

71. Revived in 2007 and transferred to the Barbican Theatre and then the Playhouse in 2008.

72. http://rifcoarts.com/shows/britains-got-bhangra. Accessed 13 March 2015.

73. Michael Billington, 'Britain's got Bhangra', *The Guardian*, 29 April 2010, www.theguardian.com/stage/2010/apr/29/britains-got-bhangra-review. Accessed 13 March 2015.

74. Ibid.

75. http://rifcoarts.com/shows/bollywood-yet-another-love-story. Accessed 13 March 2015.

76. Lyn Gardner, 'Bollywood: Yet another love story', *The Guardian*, 28 March 2003, www.theguardian.com/stage/2003/mar/28/theatre.artsfeatures. Accessed 13 March 2015.

77. Chambers, *Black and Asian Theatre*, p. 159.

78. Naseem Khan, *The Arts Britain Ignores: The Arts of Ethnic Minorities in Britain*, London: Commission for Racial Equality, 1976, referred to in Graham Ley and Sarah Dadswell (eds), *British South Asian Theatres: A Documented History*, Exeter: University of Exeter Press, 2011.

79. For more about this company, see Ley and Dadswell, *British South Asian Theatres*, pp. 13–57.

80. Ibid., p. 29.

81. Chambers, *Black and Asian Theatre*, p. 160.

82. Ley, *British South Asian Theatre*, p. 32.

83. Ibid., 46.

84. Ibid., 44.

85. She later expanded her practice to incorporate many other forms of contemporary dance and performance. For more information, see www.shobanajeyasingh.co.uk/company//obana-jeyasingh. Accessed 29 January 2015.

86. Ley and Dadswell, *British South Asian Theatre*, p. 47.

87. Ibid., pp. 50–1.

88. Kapur 2008 quoted in ibid., p. 51.

89. Chambers, *Black and Asian Theatre*, p. 161.

90. Ibid., p. 162.

91. Jatinder Verma, 'Indian Folk Theatre in Britain', *Asian Theatre Newsletter*, Vol. 4 (September 1985), p. 1. Quoted in ibid., p. 53.

92. Ibid., p. 56.

93. Ibid., p. 79.

94. Ibid., p. 84.

95. Ibid., p. 94.

96. Ibid., p. 102.

97. For more on the history of Tamasha, see www.tamasha.org.uk/about/history/. Accessed 3 February 2015.

98. For more information about Nitin Sawhney, who has composed for film, dance and theatre, see www.nitinsawhney.com/. Accessed 3 February 2015.

99. The show won the Barclays Theatre Award for Best New Musical and for Parminder Nagra (who had also starred in *A Tainted Dawn*) it led to a lead role in the film *Bend It Like Beckham*. She later became a regular character in the American television drama *ER*.

100. The programme of the original production that contains this interview is available at www.tamasha.org.uk/uploads/images/publicity/fourteen-songs-programme.pdf. Accessed 3 February 2015.

101. Ibid.

102. Jen Harvie, *Staging the UK*, Manchester: Manchester University Press, 2005, pp. 161–2. In making this case, she references Vijay Mishra, *Bollywood Cinema: Temples of Desire*, London: Routledge, 2002, p. 8; and Jane Feuer, *The Hollywood Musical*, London: Macmillan, 1993, p. x.

103. Harvie, *Staging the UK*, p. 176.

104. Harvie, *Staging the UK*, p. 176.

105. www.tamasha.org.uk/wuthering-heights-2/. Accessed 13 January 2016.

106. Claire Allfree, 'Bollywood Takes on Bronte', *Metro*, 21 April 2009, http://metro.co.uk/2009/04/21/bollywood-takes-on-bronte-40400/. Accessed 4 February 2015.

107. Chambers, *Black and Asian Theatre*, p. 167.

108. Chambers, *Black and Asian Theatre*, p. 173.

109. Ibid., p. 196.

110. Suman Bhuchar, 'The Marketing of Commercial and Subsidised Theatre to British Asian Audiences', in G. Ley and S. Dadswell (eds), *Critical Essays on British South Asian Theatre*, Exeter: Exeter University Press, 2012, p. 145.

Notes

111. From an interview with Lucy Skilbeck at Theatre Royal, Stratford East conducted by the author on 18 October 2013.

112. Née Feroza, but changed her name to Meera in the mid-1980s. Her writing had been developed through her work with Tara Arts, the Hounslow Arts Cooperative (HAC), the Asian Cooperative Theatre (ACT) and the Asian Women's Writing Collective (AWWC). (Ley and Dadswell, *British South Asian Theatres*, pp. 63, 89).

113. *Goodness Gracious Me* was on Radio 4 from 1996–98, then transferred to BBC2 from 1998–2001. This comedy sketch show, created by Syal with Sanjeev Bhaskar and Anil Gupta, had arguably given British second-generation Asians a contemporary and less stereotyped voice within British mainstream culture.

114. *Billy* (Barry, Clement and LaFrenais, 1974), and with Andrew Lloyd Webber, *Tell me on a Sunday* (1979 recording, 1982), *Aspects of Love* (1989), *Sunset Boulevard* (1993) and *Stephen Ward* (2013).

115. Interview, 18 October 2013.

116. Bhuchar, 'Marketing', p. 145.

117. Interview, 18 October 2013.

118. Bhuchar, 'Marketing', p. 133. The difficulty Bhuchar notes is that Asian communities do not constitute a single, homogeneous group. The marketing of *Bombay Dreams* was unique in commercial theatre in marrying the established techniques of the marketing company Dewynters with the community outreach practices used in subsidized theatre conducted by Hardish Virk and Bhuchar.

119. Ibid., p. 145.

120. Susan Bennett, 'Theatre/Tourism', *Theatre Journal*, Vol. 57 (2005), pp. 407–28.

121. Brantley, 'Coloring By the Numbers', E1:1, quoted in Bennett, 'Theatre/Tourism'.

122. Robert Gore Langston, 'First Night', *Daily Express*, 20 June 2002; Georgina Brown, 'Hooray for this Bite of Spicy Bollywood', *Mail on Sunday*, 23 June 2002; Michael Billington, 'Deliriously Dotty Bollywood', *The Guardian*, 20 June 2002. All quoted in Bhuchar, 'Marketing', p. 146.

123. In David Whitton, 'Bombay Dreams: Commodity Production', in R. Chaturvedi and B. Singleton (eds), *Ethnicity and Identity in Global Performance*, Jaipur: Rawat Publications, 2005, pp. 288–96, the author argues that *Bombay Dreams* is a 'deracinated cultural hybrid designed to occupy a position in a global market where multi-culturalism constitutes a brand' (p. 290). It is commodified, since a consequence of the 'mainstreaming of what might be considered "authentic" Asian culture is the spawning of hybrid cultural commodities designed to target the crossover market that has opened up' (p. 289). But he concludes that it is different from previous Western infatuations with India in that it contains a 'knowingly post-modern cultural masala', a 'satisfying affirmation . . . of feel-good cultural hybridity' in an 'unproblematized version of the multi-cultural global village' (p. 295).

124. Jerri Daboo's critique of *Bombay Dreams* in, 'One Under the Sun: Globalization, Culture and Utopia in Bombay Dreams', *Contemporary Theatre Review*, Vol. 15, No. 3, (2005), pp. 330–37, allows that there are 'pockets of resistance to the dominant ideology of the utopia of entertainment in *Bombay Dreams* mainly provided in moments of irony, self-parody, and kitsch' (p. 335).

125. It has only recently been followed by another multicultural mainstream musical, *Bend It Like Beckham*, the musical version of which opened in the West End in 2015. In the meantime the confidence of the subsidized sector and the visibility of British Asians has been transformed.

126. Erika Fischer-Lichte, 'Interculturalism in Contemporary Theatre', in Patrice Pavis (ed.), *The Intercultural Performance Reader*, London and New York: Routledge, 1996, p. 38.

127. This notion of cycles derives from Gramsci and is applied to vocal style in John Potter, *Vocal Authority*, Cambridge: Cambridge University Press 1998, pp. 190–9. It describes the cultural and political process of the accretion and transformation of signification through time. Sociologists explore other aspects of the communication process, in particular focusing on the listening subject.

128. The song won the 1961 Ivor Novello Award for music and lyrics, and a Grammy in 1963.

129. John Snelson, *Andrew Lloyd Webber*, New Haven: Yale University Press, 2004, p. 6.

130. Ibid., p. 60.

131. Ibid., p. 61.

132. Ibid., p. 63.

133. Ibid., p. 59.

134. For more on the development of the rock musical predominantly in the United States, see Elizabeth L. Wollman, *The Theatre Will Rock*, Ann Arbor: University of Michigan Press, 2006.

135. The Who's concept album *Tommy* was also staged as a rock musical in London in 1979.

136. For more detailed analysis, see Snelson, *Lloyd Webber*, pp. 65–9, and Jessica Sternfeld, *The Megamusical*, Bloomington: Indiana University Press, 2006, pp. 27–54.

137. For more on the way vocal timbre and performance contributes to signification, see 'Performativity as Identity' in Dominic Symonds and Millie Taylor (eds), *Gestures of Music Theater: The Performativity of Song and Dance*, Oxford University Press, 2014, pp. 109–11.

138. Universal Pictures UK, Oct 2000. ASIN: B00004YVEG.

139. Snelson, *Lloyd Webber*, p. 69.

140. Snelson, *Lloyd Webber*, p. 160. Unless stated, these dates refer to the West End opening and not to any earlier try-outs, tours or music releases. Copyright dates are as follows: *Jesus Christ Superstar* (1970), *Starlight Express* (1984), *Joseph and the Amazing Technicolor Dreamcoat* (1971), *Evita* (1976) and *Cats* (1981).

141. Ben Macpherson, 'Dynamic Shape: The Dramaturgy of Song and Dance in Lloyd Webber's *Cats*', in Symonds and Taylor (eds), *Gestures of Music Theater*, p. 66.

142. Snelson *Lloyd Webber*, p. 182.

143. Ibid., pp. 8–9.

144. John Bush Jones, 'Utopia Limited', *Educational Theatre Journal*, Vol. 28, No. 1 (1976).

145. http://en.wikipedia.org/wiki/The_Black_Mikado. Accessed 23 March 2015.

146. www.willyrussell.com. Accessed 11 December 2014.

147. There was some additional music including two songs by Willy Russell. After its run in Liverpool it moved to the Lyric Theatre in London, where it won the Evening Standard Award and the London Critic's Award for Best New Musical in 1974. The work can no longer be performed because of problems with licensing the music from Sony. Angela Levin, 'Willy Russell: I want to Talk About Things that Matter', *The Daily Telegraph*, 15 October 2012. www.telegraph.co.uk/culture/theatre/9605796/Willy-Russell-I-want-to-talk-about-things-that-matter.html. Accessed 12 December 2014.

148. Herbert Kretzmer, 'Review', *Daily Express*, 16 August 1974. www.barbaradickson.net/reviews_john_paul_george.html. Accessed 12 December 2014.

149. The story is a combination of *The Tempest* and the science fiction film *The Forbidden Planet*. It won the Olivier Awards in 1989 and 1990.

150. John Doyle also explored actor musicianship in regional theatre, but his productions were often of existing American musicals, though he also directed devised shows. In recent years he has directed actor musician productions of some of Sondheim's musicals in the UK and United States.

151. It opened in the West End in 1995, and won the Laurence Olivier Award for Best New Musical in 1996.

152. Winner of the 2003 Olivier Award for best new musical, directed by Matthew Warchus.

153. Leigh Bowery, Marilyn (the pop singer), Steve Strange and Philip Sallon and was part of the New Romantic club scene of the 1980s.

154. It ran in the West End from 2002 until 2014. At the 2011 Laurence Olivier Awards, the show won the Audience Award for Most Popular Show.

155. Galileo and Scaramouche set out to fulfil the prophecy by finding the hidden instruments and restoring music to the world. They meet the Bohemians Brit

(Britney) and Meat (Meatloaf), who have been trying to make instruments to play music. The Killer Queen and Khashoggi, the chief of police, try to stop the group from making progress, and Brit is killed, while the other Bohemians are brainwashed. Only Galileo and Scaramouche realize that the clue is in the Freddie Mercury statue pointing to Wembley, and they go to Wembley, play music and find the instruments. The show ends with a performance of 'Bohemian Rhapsody'.

156. Born in 1930 to a large poor family of Jewish immigrants, his father was a tailor in London's East End. Bart's surname was originally Begleiter. Bart died in 1999 having made and lost a fortune.

157. Unity Theatre developed from the Worker's Theatre Movement and was a left-wing political organization. Being a club meant that its scripts did not need approval by the Lord Chamberlain. Its members had full-time jobs (in Bart's case as a printer) and worked at the theatre in the evenings doing whatever was required.

158. His first theatre review as a writer was for *Turn It Up* (1953), in which he was described as 'one of Britain's most talented composers, and his fast, rhythmical melodies are after the style of the immortal Sullivan'. Quoted in David Stafford and Caroline Stafford, *Fings Ain't Wot They Used T'Be: The Lionel Bart Story*, London: Omnibus Press, 2011, p. 35.

159. Originally Tommy Hicks.

160. A reference to the old music hall song 'My Old Man'.

161. A satire of greed and lust by Ben Jonson (1605) that is still ranked among the best Jacobean comedies. No script has been found of Bart's adaptation.

162. Colin Chambers, *The Story of Unity Theatre* quoted in Stafford, *Fings*, p. 58.

163. Although it was a huge hit at the time, Stafford remarks that for modern ears the dialogue seems corny, the slang dated, the gender politics offensive and the songs humdrum. Stafford, *Fings*, p. 75.

164. An adaptation of *Rape Upon Rape: Or The Justice Caught In His Own Trap* by Henry Fielding (1730).

165. Bart and Jonson won the Novello Award for Best Score for Film or Theatre in 1960 for *Lock Up Your Daughters*.

166. Samantha Ellis records that it cost £15,000 in her article 'Lionel Bart's *Oliver!* June 1960', *The Guardian*, 18 June 2003. www.guardian.co.uk/stage/2003/jun/18/theatre.samanthaellis/print. Accessed 12 June 2013. Meanwhile Kurt Gänzl records that Donald Albery raised £14,000 to capitalize the venture, including £3,000 of his own money. For more about the development of the first and subsequent productions, see Kurt Gänzl, *The British Musical Theatre: Volume II, 1915–1984*, London: Macmillan, 1986, pp. 770–4 and pp. 777–9.

167. Stanley Green, *Broadway Musicals: Show by Show*, Sixth Edition, Milwaukee: Applause Books, 2008, p. 201

168. Gänzl, *The British Musical Theatre*, p. 771.

169. Ethan Mordden, *Open A New Window: The Broadway Musical in the 1960s*, London: Palgrave Macmillan, 2002, p. 165.

170. Milton Shulman, 'First Night – *Oliver!*', *Evening Standard*, 1 July 1960. n. p. There are clips available on YouTube that give a sense of what Sean Kenny's set looked like. Sally Dexter as Nancy and ensemble performing 'It's a Fine Life' in a Royal Variety Show performance of Sam Mendes' 1994 production, which used Sean Kenny's set design: www.youtube.com/watch?v=4zewCcXKSZ8. Accessed 2 August 2015. The trailer for the 2009 revival of *Oliver!* at the Theatre Royal Drury Lane, which was based on Sam Mendes' 1994 production and Kenny's sets, is available at: www.youtube.com/watch?v=CxhPm8YpvZQ. Accessed 2 August 2015.

171. *Independent London News*, 16 July 1960.

172. *The Observer*, 31 July 1960.

173. There is a clear line of development from the work of Sean Kenny to, for example, the designs for *Les Misérables* by John Napier.

174. There seem to have been rumours that Bart's secretary, Joan Maitland, who was later awarded a co-writing credit for the book of *Blitz!*, had in fact also contributed to the book of *Oliver!* – but no writing collaborators have ever been credited. Bart is also reported as having said that he never read the novel but knew the story from the David Lean film. (Stafford, *Fings*, p. 89).

175. For this show he was awarded a Novello Award for Outstanding Contribution to the Score of a Stage Play, Film, TV or Radio Programme in 1960, and a Tony in 1963. Nancy's ballad from *Oliver!* 'As Long As He Needs Me' also won a Novello Award for The Best Selling and Most Performed Song of 1960.

176. For a detailed analysis of this, see Sharon Aaronofsky Weltman, '"Can a Fellow be a Villain All His Life?": *Oliver!*, Fagin, and Performing Jewishness', *Nineteenth-Century Contexts*, Vol. 33, No. 4 (Sep 2011) pp. 371–88.

177. *Tatler*, 27 July 1960.

178. Quoted in Mark Steyn, *Broadway Babies Say Goodnight*, Faber and Faber, 2000, p. 173.

179. Ibid.

180. This analysis of Bart's use of musical genres in *Oliver!* is adapted from the chapter by Millie Taylor, 'Lionel Bart: British Vernacular Theatre', in Robert Gordon and Olaf Jubin (eds), *The Oxford Handbook of the British Musical*, New York: Oxford University Press, 2016.

181. Bart, Lionel *Oliver!* Vocal Score (n.d.) p. 59.

182. Ibid., p. 60.

183. Ibid., p. 85.

184. Ibid., p. 87.

185. The original cast recording of this song, sung by Georgia Brown is available at www.youtube.com/watch?v=n2RylUgMrvM. Accessed 4 August 2015.

186. Although the trade is illegal, it reveals the workings of a capitalist economy and the opportunities available to the dispossessed within it (in a similar style to the narratives of John Gay's *The Beggar's Opera* and Bertolt Brecht and Kurt Weill's *The Threepenny Opera*).

187. Weltman, 'Can a Fellow be a Villain', p. 377. Klezmer is an Eastern European style of dance music that is partly improvised and may derive from the Ashkenazy Jews.

188. Bart, *Oliver!* Vocal Score, pp. 114, 116, 118, 119.

189. 16 July 1960.

190. This practice began in Sydney in 1970, originated by Brian Thomson, with whom Jim Sharman was then working. Raymond Knapp, *The American Musical and the Performance of Personal Identity,* Princeton: Princeton University Press, 2006, p. 241.

191. http://rockyhorror.co.uk/tickets-tour-dates. Accessed 18 June 2015.

192. Cast recordings have been made with casts from London, Los Angeles, Australia, Brazil, Mexico, Norway, New Zealand, Germany, Iceland, Finland, Denmark, South Africa, Korea, Peru, The Philippines, Vancouver, Panama, Poland and Japan – and in some of these countries there are several cast recordings from different productions and casts.

193. W. Stephen Gilbert, 'Rocky Horror Show', *Plays and Players* (n.d.). Contained in the reviews file at the Theatre and Performance Collection of the Victoria and Albert Museum.

194. *Melody Maker* review after the move to the Chelsea Classic cinema, 20 October 1973.

195. In fact Michael Coveney comments on the difficulty of recreating the 'environmental quality he achieved so spectacularly in the Theatre Upstairs' once the show moved to the Classic. *Financial Times*, 16 August 1973.

196. Knapp, *The American Musical*, p. 240.

197. Ibid., p. 241.

198. www.rockyhorror.com/history/timeline.php. Accessed 18 June 2015.

199. S. Piro (n.d.), *Creatures of the Night*, www.rockyhorror.com/history. Accessed 25 February 2006.

200. The agency of the performers, creative team and producers in this transferral is difficult to quantify, but as I document in '"Don't' Dream It, be It": Exploring Signification, Empathy and Mimesis in Relation to *The Rocky Horror Show*', *Studies in Musical Theatre*, Vol. 1, No. 1 (2007), pp. 57–71, when the show was taken to Budapest immediately after it emerged from behind the Iron Curtain in 1991, the audience was taught the responses since this was perceived to be an essential part of the show's aesthetic (p. 67).

201. An LP, or Long Playing record, was the size of record on which whole albums were released. It preceded the CD.

Notes

202. www.rockyhorror.com/history/timeline.php. Accessed 18 June 2015.

203. Austin John Marshall, 'The Rocky Horror of it All', *NME*, 27 October 1973, p. 41.

204. John Walker, 'Something to Offend Everyone', *Observer Magazine*, 27 July 1975.

205. Note in this photograph that although microphone technology was available, microphones were not yet wireless, so shows had to be choreographed around microphone cables.

206. Walker, 'Something to Offend Everyone', *Observer* 1975.

207. Keir Keightley, 'Reconsidering rock', in S. Frith et al. (eds), *The Cambridge Companion to Pop and Rock*, Cambridge: Cambridge University Press, 2001, pp. 109–42, pp. 131–9.

208. This analysis is adapted from an earlier, more extended argument in Millie Taylor, *Musical Theatre, Realism and Entertainment*, Basingstoke: Ashgate, 2012, pp. 29–30.

209. A 1913 song by Chris Smith and Jim Burris that was later used in the films *For Me and My Gal* (1942), *On the Riviera* (1951) and later in the mock-horror *Haunted Honeymoon* (1986). https://en.wikipedia.org/wiki/Ballin%27_the_Jack. Accessed 19 June 2015.

3 Narrative and story-telling in the British musical since 1970

1. Jessica Sternfeld, *The Megamusical*, Bloomington/Indianapolis: Indiana University Press, 2006, p. 2.

2. Ibid., p. 2.

3. Ibid., p. 4.

4. Ibid.

5. Cited in Michael Coveney, *Cats on a Chandelier. The Andrew Lloyd Webber Story*, London: Hutchinson, 1999, p. 111 (italics in the original).

6. Tim Rice, *Oh, What a Circus. The Autobiography 1944–1978*, London: Hodder and Stoughton, 1999, p. 191.

7. Ibid., p. 24.

8. Rice and Lloyd Webber found themselves later in exactly the same situation with *Evita*, where for instance the non-sequitur in the musical's most famous song, 'Don't Cry For Me, Argentina' ('Don't cry for me, Argentina, / The truth is I never left you'), a result of last-minute changes in the recording studio, didn't prevent the track from becoming one of the most successful singles of the 1970s.

9. Rice, *Oh What a Circus!*, p. 193.

10. See *Jesus Christ Superstar* (2000), Universal DVD 902 011 2.

11. Harold Prince, 'Foreword I', in Foster Hirsch, *Harold Prince and the American Musical Theatre*, Cambridge/New York: Applause Theatre Books, 1989, p. xiii.

12. Rice, *Oh, What a Circus*, p. 171.

13. Kurt Gänzl, 'Andrew Lloyd Webber', in Carl Dahlhaus (ed.), *Pipers Enzyklopädie des Musiktheaters. Oper, Operette, Musical, Ballett. Volume 3*, Munich/Zurich: Piper, 1989, p. 520.

14. John Snelson, *Andrew Lloyd Webber*, New Haven/London: Yale University Press, 2004, p. 24.

15. Coveney, *Cats on a Chandelier*, p. 105.

16. Snelson, *Andrew Lloyd Webber*, p. 22.

17. Rice, *Oh, What a Circus*, p. 187,

18. Ulrich Prinz, '*Jesus Christ Superstar* – eine Passion in Rock. Ansätze zu einer Analyse und Interpretation', in *Musik und Bildung*, Vol. 4 (1972), p. 194.

19. *Jesus Christ Superstar. A Rock Opera*. Lyrics Booklet, Original Cast Recording 1970. Double Disc Set, MCA Records MCD 00501. All further references will be included in the text.

20. He gushes: 'You've made it!'

21. http://biblehub.com/john/19-41.htm. Accessed 25 July 2015.

22. Snelson, *Andrew Lloyd Webber*, p. 64.

23. Ibid., p. 24.

24. I have written about the consistent theme of the rock/pop star phenomenon in Tim Rice's work at length elsewhere: Olaf Jubin, 'Tim Rice: The Pop-Star Scenario', in Robert Gordon and Olaf Jubin (eds), *The Oxford Handbook of the British Musical*, New York: Oxford University Press (forthcoming 2016).

25. Jack Kroll, 'Theater', *Newsweek*, 25 October 1971.

26. Prinz, '*Jesus Christ Superstar*', pp. 196–8.

27. Stephen Holden, 'Lloyd Webber: Hits but no Hit Songs', in *The New York Times*, 3 July 1983.

28. Hansgeorg Mühe, *Die Musik von Andrew Lloyd Webber*, Hamburg: Verlag Dr. Kovac, 1993, p. 32.

29. Sternfeld, *The Megamusical*, p. 29.

30. Michael Walsh, 'Lloyd Webber: Now, but Forever?', in *The New York Times*, 9 April 2000.

31. Joseph Swain, *The Broadway Musical. A Critical and Musical Survey*, New York: Oxford University Press, 1990, p. 297.

32. Martin Gottfried, *More Broadway Musicals since 1980*, New York: Harry N. Abrams, 1981, p. 70.

33. Coveney, *Cats on a Chandelier*, p. 55.

34. Walsh, 'Lloyd Webber: Now, but Forever?', p. 9.

Notes

35. *Jesus Christ Superstar* amortized its production costs on 12 August 1972 (Walsh, *Andrew Lloyd Webber*, p. 74).

36. 'I felt it wasn't worthy of the furore, enthusiasm and ire that it has aroused' (Richard Watts: 'A Passion in a Rock Beat', *New York Post*, 13 October 1971).

37. Clive Barnes: 'Theater: Christ's Passion Transported to the Stage in the Guise of Serious Pop', *New York Times*, 13 October 1971.

38. *Jesus Christ Superstar* (1973), Universal DVD 823 053 8; *Jesus Christ Superstar* (2000), Universal DVD 902 011 2; *Jesus Christ Superstar* (2012), Universal DVD 8291943-11.

39. Michael B. Druxman, *The Musical. From Broadway to Hollywood*, Cranberry/London: Barnes, 1980, pp. 157–8.

40. Both Michael Walsh (*Andrew Lloyd Webber. His Life and Works*, London/New York: Penguin Books, 1989, pp. 81–2) and Keith Richmond (*Die Musicals von Andrew Lloyd Webber*, Berlin: Henschel Verlag, 1996, p. 31) insist that the Universal Pictures release did not find an audience.

41. Jonathan Mantle states that the worldwide box office receipts were $30 million, which would have made *Jesus Christ Superstar* a substantial hit. (Joseph Mantle, *Fanfare. The Unauthorized Biography of Andrew Lloyd Webber*, London: Michael Joseph Ltd., 1989, p. 141.) This ties in with a report in *Variety* which declares the film to have earned $10.8 million in North American cinemas throughout 1973 (Anon., 'Big Rental Films of 1973', *Variety*, 9 January 1974).

42. As discussed by the Post Punk Cinema Club (http://p-pcc.blogspot.co.uk/2008/07/jesus-christ-superstar-1973.html, accessed 21 June 2015). It is also regarded as the only film musical to come out of the 1970s to rival *The Rocky Horror Picture Show* (1975) in terms of its cult following (www.metrocinema.org/film_view/3006/, accessed 21 June 2015).

43. Irving Wardle, 'Little Here for Card-Carrying Christians', *The Times*, 10 August 1972.

44. Andrew Lloyd Webber, 'The Music of *Evita*', in Andrew Lloyd Webber and Tim Rice, *Evita: The Legend of Eva Peron 1919–1952,* London: Elm Tree Books, 1978, unpaginated.

45. David Chandler, 'Andrew Lloyd Webber: Haunted by the Phantom', in Gordon and Jubin, *The Oxford Handbook of the British Musical.*

46. Scott McMillin, *The Musical as Drama,* Princeton/Oxford: Princeton University Press, 2006, p. 11.

47. Walsh, *Andrew Lloyd Webber*, p. 122.

48. Michael Coveney, '*Starlight Express*', *Financial Times*, 28 March 1984.

49. 'What attempts there are at telling a story and plumbing emotional depths, or even shallows, are pathetic'(Edwin Wilson: '*Starlight Express*', *The Wall Street Journal*, 16 March 1987).

50. Michael Radcliffe: '*Starlight Express*', *The Observer*, 1 April 1984.

51. Margaret Vermette, *The Musical World of Boublil and Schönberg*, New York: Applause Theatre & Cinema Books, 2006, p. 104.

52. Cited in Bruce Weber, 'When the Commercial Theatre Moves in on Nonprofits', *The New York Times*, 10 October 1999.

53. Mackintosh cited in Vermette, *The Musical World*, p. 178.

54. Cited in ibid., p. 98.

55. Ibid., p. xi.

56. Gerald McKnight, *Andrew Lloyd Webber*, New York: St. Martin's Press, 1984, p. 153.

57. Sheridan Morley, 'Twice Knightly', in *Punch*, 30 April 1975.

58. Vermette, *The Musical World*, p. xi.

59. Ibid., p. 42.

60. Snelson, *Andrew Lloyd Webber*, p. 36.

61. His co-author was Richard Stilgoe.

62. Sternfeld, *The Megamusical*, p. 241.

63. Nicholas Hytner cited in Vermette, *The Musical World*, p. 152.

64. Kenneth Hurren, '*Aspects of Love*', *Mail on Sunday*, 23 April 1989.

65. The New York production lost $11 million (Gottfried, *More Broadway Musicals*, p. 74).

66. John Sutherland, 'Introduction', in Wilkie Collins, *The Woman in White*, Oxford: Oxford University Press, 1998, p. vii.

67. The characters' names already signal their main personality trait: the Count is sinister ('fosco' is Italian for 'dark' and 'gloomy'), Laura is fair, and Walter has his heart in the right place. Marian, on the other hand, has that most undesirable of female attributes, a moustache (Collins, *The Woman in White*, p. 32), which immediately disqualifies her as a potential love interest.

68. This term was used on the musical's poster, cast recording and publicity material.

69. Walter's propensity for drink is hinted at early on, and Laura's sleepwalking is mentioned several times throughout the first act so that later, when Glyde and Foscoe attribute her 'death' to that condition, it seems both logical and plausible.

70. In London it ran for 500 performances, while the New York production shuttered after a mere 109 performances.

71. The musical ran for only six and a half months, but was taped and is available on DVD: *From Here to Eternity. The Musical*, Cinestage DVD, OVDVD2.

72. Quoted in Rosie Bannister, 'Overheard at the Theatre: More Funny Audience Comments', www.whatsonstage.com/london-theatre/news/more-funny-audience-comments-theatre_37636.html. Accessed 19 June 2015.

73. Edward Behr, *Les Misérables. History in the Making*, London: Pavilion Books Ltd., 1996, p. 36.

Notes

74. Ibid., p. 39.

75. William A. Henry III, 'An Epic of the Downtrodden', *Time Magazine*, 23 March 1987.

76. Behr, *Les Misérables*, p. 21.

77. The production at the Palais des Sports sold 500,000 tickets (ibid., p. 51).

78. Ibid., p. 74. For a detailed summary of the musical's plot see its Wikipedia entry, https://en.wikipedia.org/wiki/Les_Misérables_(musical). Accessed 5 July 2015.

79. In 1992, an English version of the show – one of the few to feature an original storyline – with lyrics by Tim Rice was released on CD under the title *Tycoon* (Sony Music Entertainment, Epic 471923 2).

80. www.thisistheatre.com/londonshows/notredamedeparis.html. Accessed 4 September 2015.

81. Matt Wolf, 'Review *Romeo and Juliet, the Musical*', *Variety*, 7 November 2002.

82. Lyn Gardner, 'Review *Romeo and Juliet – the Musical*', *The Guardian*, 6 November 2002.

83. Behr, *Les Misérables*, p. 47.

84. It's ironic that the British composer didn't respond in kind when years later he saw *Les Misérables*: according to Cameron Mackintosh, Lloyd Webber 'clearly didn't like it' (cited in ibid., p. 142).

85. Ibid., p. 50.

86. Sternfeld, *The Megamusical*, p. 218.

87. As Trevor Nunn underlines, 'most of [the show's] effects employ a bare stage with minimal scenery' (cited in Vermette, *The Musical World*, p. 126).

88. Frank Rich, 'Stage: *Misérables*, Musical Version Opens on Broadway', *The New York Times*, 13 March 1987.

89. Behr, *Les Misérables*, p. 103.

90. Edward Behr, 'A Splendid *Les Misérables*', in *Newsweek*, 4 November 1985.

91. Rich, 'Stage: *Misérables*', p. 362.

92. The Penguin Classics edition, translated and slightly abridged by Norman Denny, has 1,201 pages.

93. Cited in Vermette, *The Musical World*, p. 86.

94. Ibid.

95. Cited in Henry III, 'An Epic of the Downtrodden'.

96. Sternfeld, *The Megamusical*, p. 190.

97. Cited in Vermette, *The Musical World*, p. 69.

98. Kathryn M. Grossman and Bradley Stephens, '*Les Misérables*: From Epic Novel to Epic Musical', in Gordon and Jubin, *The Oxford Handbook of the British Musical*.

99. Schönberg cited in Vermette, *The Musical World*, p. 49.

100. Ibid.

101. Henry III, 'An Epic of the Downtrodden'.

102. Vermette, *The Musical World*, p. 51.

103. Cited in Behr, *Les Misérables*, p. 74.

104. John Caird, cited in ibid., p. 71.

105. Sternfeld, *The Megamusical*, p. 190.

106. Vermette, *The Musical World*, p. x.

107. Ibid., p. 66.

108. Behr, *Les Misérables*, p. 82.

109. Vermette, *The Musical World*, p. 131.

110. Behr, *Les Misérables*, p. 79.

111. 'Libretto' in ibid., p. 168. Other examples include the comment, 'The old man's a goner for sure' (p. 170), Madame Thénardier's use of the word 'inebriate' (p. 174), and Eponine's complaint that she doesn't 'have a face to say hello to' (p. 182). Page numbers for all further references to the lyrics will be given in the text itself.

112. Clive Barnes, 'Smashing. *Les Misérables*, Here at Last, Is the Stuff of Theatrical Legend', *New York Post*, 13 March 1987.

113. Behr, *Les Misérables*, p. 75.

114. Ibid., p. 126.

115. Caird cited Vermette, *The Musical World*, p. 133. For an in-depth comparison between the novel and the musical, see Grossman and Stephens, '*Les Misérables*'.

116. Rich, 'Stage: *Misérables*', p. 362.

117. Grossman and Stephens, '*Les Misérables*'.

118. Ibid.

119. Ibid.

120. Ibid.

121. Ibid.

122. Behr, *Les Miserables*, p. 74 and p. 96.

123. Cited in Vermette, *The Musical World*, p. 133.

124. *Les Misérables*. Original Broadway Cast 1987. Two Disc Set, Geffen Records 9 24151–2.

125. John Caird calls him 'a religious obsessive, [. . .] a fundamentalist' (cited in Vermette, *The Musical World*, p. 122).

126. Ibid., p. 78.

127. Nunn cited in Behr, *Les Misérables*, p. 78.

128. Cited in Vermette, *The Musical World*, p. 132.

129. John Caird cited in ibid., p. 132.

130. In Act One, Scene 5, Javert already informed Valjean: 'Men like you can never change' (p. 172).

131. Nunn cited in Vermette, *The Musical World*, p. 122.

132. Grossman and Stephens, 'Les Misérables'.

133. Behr, *Les Misérables*, p. 38.

134. Ibid., pp. 11–12.

135. Ibid., p. 43. All of these interpolations were cut for the musical version.

136. Norman Denny, 'Introduction', in Victor Hugo, *Les Misérables*. Translated by Norman Denny, London: Penguin Classics, 1982, p. 7.

137. Sternfeld, *The Megamusical*, p. 203.

138. Behr, *Les Misérables*, p. 134.

139. Caird cited in Vermette, *The Musical World*, p. 134.

140. Behr, *Les Misérables*, p. 156.

141. Grossman and Stephens, 'Les Misérables'.

142. Mackintosh cited in Vermette, *The Musical World*, p. 181.

143. Behr, *Les Misérables*, p. 140.

144. These facts and figures have been taken from the musical's website www.lesmis.com/uk/history/facts-and-figures/. Accessed 28 July 2015.

145. Jack Kroll, 'Revolution on Broadway,' *Newsweek*, 23 March 1987.

146. Cited in Andrew Billen, 'Not Just a Pretty Face', *The Observer*, 7 July 1995.

147. Coveney, *Cats on a Chandelier*, p. 127.

148. Walsh, *Andrew Lloyd Webber*, p. 176.

149. Coveney, *Cats on a Chandelier*, pp. 178–9.

150. According to Hart, around 80 per cent of the lyrics in the final version are his; Stilgoe contributed the remaining 20 per cent (ibid., p. 130).

151. Later printed versions of the libretto give the year as 1911 (Snelson, *Andrew Lloyd Webber*, p. 81).

152. *The Phantom of the Opera. Libretto*, in *The Phantom of the Opera*. Original Cast Recording 1987, Polydor LP 831 273–11987, unpaginated. Further references are included in the text.

153. An 'I Am' song, often the second number of the evening, is a solo for the main character that allows the audience to get more closely acquainted with the protagonist by highlighting her/his beliefs, dreams and hopes.

154. Why would Christine be 'waking, silent and resigned' after losing her former love, especially as she still obviously has his affection? ('When you find / That once / Again, you long / To take your heart back / And be free').

155. 'Look at your face / In the mirror – / I am there / Inside!'

156. 'Behind the Mask: The Story of *The Phantom of the Opera*', in *Das Phantom der Oper*. Special Edition, DVD, Concord 1527. The documentary is also available in several instalments on YouTube.

157. Snelson, *Andrew Lloyd Webber*, p. 121.

158. Sternfeld, *The Megamusical*, p. 242.

159. Snelson, *Andrew Lloyd Webber*, p. 87.

160. Ibid., p. 13.

161. Walsh, *Andrew Lloyd Webber*, p. 203.

162. Ibid.

163. The septet 'Primadonna' is reminiscent of Puccini, while 'Point of No Return' has echoes of Verdi (Mühe, *Die Musik von Andrew Lloyd Webber*, pp. 112–13).

164. Consequently, the show was denigrated as 'grand opera for non-operagoers' by some critics (Sigrid Löffler: 'Das importierte Wunder', in *Profil* 1 (1989), p. 61).

165. 'The trouble is that the moment you give people a lot of melody in one evening it's awfully difficult for them to take in. [...] They *will* not take a vast amount of melody invention in an evening' (cited in McKnight, *Andrew Lloyd Webber*, p. 246; italics in the original).

166. Sternfeld, *The Megamusical*, p. 230.

167. Coveney, *Cats on a Chandelier*, p. 131.

168. Carol Ilson, *Harold Prince. From Pajama Game to Phantom of the Opera*, Ann Arbor/London: Limelight Editions, 1989, p. 349.

169. Ibid., p. 133.

170. Cited in Ilson, *Harold Prince*, p. 345.

171. Sheridan Morley, '*The Phantom of the Opera*', *Punch*, 22 October 1986.

172. Michael Billington, '*The Phantom of the Opera*', *The Guardian*, 11 October 1986.

173. Cited in Hirsch, *Harold Prince*, pp. 168–9.

174. He is ranked as the eighth-worst director ever on www.pajiba.com/guides/the-ten-worst-directors-in-hollywood.php. Accessed 7 August 2015.

175. David Chandler rightfully asserts that it 'was not nearly so successful as an expensive screen version of the world's then most popular musical could, and should, have been' (Chandler: 'Andrew Lloyd Webber').

176. When I saw the film at a London cinema on 9 January 2005, a woman in the row behind me cried out: 'That's not that bad!'

Notes

177. Jack Kroll, 'The *Phantom* Hits Broadway', *Newsweek*, 8 February 1988.

178. Sternfeld, *The Megamusical*, p. 271.

179. Worldwide, the musical has been seen by more than 140 million people and has earned more than $6 billion (www.thephantomoftheopera.com/the-show/facts-figures. Accessed 12 August 2015).

180. Coveney, *Cats on a Chandelier*, p. 137.

181. Michael Walsh, *Andrew Lloyd Webber. His Life and Works*, London/New York: Penguin Books, 1989, p. 14.

182. William A. Henry III, 'They Just "Keep Rolling Along"', *Time*, 2 September 1991.

183. Gottfried, *More Broadway Musicals*, p. 53.

184. Steven Suskin, *More Opening Nights on Broadway*, New York: Schirmer Trade Books 1997, p. 492.

185. Rice, *Oh, What a Circus*, p. 68.

186. Tim Rice, 'Introduction', in Benny Andersson, Björn Ulvaeus and Tim Rice, *Chess. The Musical. (London Stage Version)*, London: Samuel French Ltd., 1994, unpaginated.

187. Jane Edwardes, '*The Beautiful Game*', *Time Out*, 4 October 2000.

188. Kate Bassett, '*The Beautiful Game*', *Independent on Sunday*, 1 October 2000.

189. Susanne Baum, '*The Beautiful Game*', *Jewish Chronicle*, 29 September 2000.

190. Kate Chopstick, '*The Beautiful Game*', *The Scotsman*, 28 September 2000.

191. This version has been released on DVD: *Love Never Dies* (2011), Universal DVD 8287548.

192. George Rodosthenous, '*Mamma Mia!* and the Aesthetics of the 21st Century Jukebox Musical', in Gordon and Jubin, *The Oxford Handbook of the British Musical*.

193. www.tonightsthenightontour.co.uk//ow. Accessed 21 August 2015.

194. Baz Bamigboye and Sarah Bull, 'Spice Girls Left "Gutted and Devastated" as It's Announced Musical *Viva Forever* Will Close in Eight Weeks', *The Daily Mail*, 2 May 2013.

195. Tim Walker, '*Viva Forever!*, Piccadilly Theatre, Review', *The Sunday Times*, 19 December 2012.

196. David Benedict, 'Review *Viva Forever*', *Variety*, 13 December 2012.

197. Cited in Anon., 'The Final Phase. The Making of "The Visitors"', *ABBA. The Visitors. Deluxe Edition 2012*, Polar Music 00602527925295, p. 3.

198. In 1983 it was announced that the band would take a break, so that its members could pursue other projects, but it never reformed and thus simply disbanded quietly.

199. Anon., 'The Final Phase', p. 3.

200. Ibid., p. 13.

201. www.officialcharts.com/chart-news/abba-overtake-the-beatles-to-score-uk-s-second-biggest-selling-album__3041/. Accessed 27 August 2015.

202. Karl French, *ABBA Unplugged*, London: Portrait 2004, p. x.

203. Cited in Ann Donahue, 'Kathy Nelson: The Billboard Q & A', *Billboard*, 16 August 2008.

204. Craymer was in no doubt that Andersson and Ulvaeus would 'never agree to that' (cited in Benny Andersson, Björn Ulvaeus and Judy Craymer, *Mamma Mia! How Can I Resist You? The Inside Story of Mamma Mia!,* London: Weidenfeld and Nicholson, 2006, p. 138).

205. Libby Sutcliffe, 'Abba's Eurovision Win in Brighton Remembered 40 Years on', www.bbc.co.uk/news/uk-england-sussex-26901044. Accessed 27 August 2015.

206. Adam Sherwin, 'It's ABBA on the Phone Making a Lot More Money, Money, Money', *The Times*, 19 April 2006.

207. Richard Corliss, 'That Old Feeling: ABBA, without Apologies', *Time*, 23 October 2001.

208. Cited in James Inverne, 'The Show Must Go On. . . and On', *Time,* 27 May 2002.

209. Carline Bainbridge; '"Knowing Me, Knowing You": Reading *Mamma Mia!* as Feminine Object', in Louise FitzGerald and Melanie Williams, *Mamma Mia! The Movie. Exploring a Cultural Phenomenon*, New York: I. B. Tauris & Co, 2013, p. 80.

210. Michael DeAngelis, 'ABBA', in David A. Gerstner (ed.), *The Routledge Encyclopedia of Queer Culture*, New York: Routledge 2006, p. 3. Since the lexicon is organized alphabetically, ABBA is actually the very first entry.

211. Cited in Andersson, Ulvaeus and Craymer, *Mamma Mia!*, p. 165.

212. Sue Harper, 'Afterword: When All Is Said and Done', in FitzGerald and Williams, *Mamma Mia!*, p. 225.

213. Catherine Johnson cited in Andersson, Ulvaeus and Craymer, *Mamma Mia!*, p. 210.

214. Strains of 'Summer Night City' are heard during the overture and during scene changes.

215. I. Q. Hunter, 'My, My, How Did I Resist You?', in FitzGerald and Williams, *Mamma Mia!*, p. 146.

216. Millie Taylor, *Musical Theatre. Realism and Entertainment*, Surrey: Ashgate Publishing Ltd., 2012, p. 161.

217. Louise FitzGerald, 'What Does Your Mother Know? *Mamma Mia!*'s Meditation of Lone Motherhood', in FitzGerald and Williams, *Mamma Mia!*, p. 205.

218. Ulvaeus cited in Andersson, Ulvaeus and Craymer, *Mamma Mia!*, p. 112.

219. Cited in ibid., p. 200.

220. Ibid., p. 207.

Notes

221. Ibid., p. 208.

222. Ibid., p. 209.

223. Georges-Claude Guilbert: 'Dancing Queens Indeed: When Gay Subtext is Gayer than Gay Text', in FitzGerald and Williams, *Mamma Mia!*, p. 187.

224. Malcolm Womack, '"Thank You for the Music": Catherine Johnson's Feminist Revoicings in *Mamma Mia!*', *Studies in Musical Theatre*, Vol. 3, No. 2 (2009), p. 202.

225. Guilbert, 'Dancing Queens Indeed', p. 187.

226. Melanie Williams, '*Mamma Mia!*'s Female Authorship', in FitzGerald and Williams, *Mamma Mia!*, p. 54.

227. Jamie J. Weinman, 'My Mother Slept Around. Ha Ha Ha Ha Ha!', *Maclean's*, 28 July 2008.

228. It is also disconcertingly similar to the poster of *Muriel's Wedding*.

229. Hunter, 'My, My, How Did I Resist You?', p. 146.

230. Sarah Godfrey, 'The Hero of My Dreams: Framing Fatherhood in *Mamma Mia!*', in FitzGerald and Williams, *Mamma Mia!*, p. 201.

231. FitzGerald, 'What Does Your Mother Know?', p. 210.

232. Ibid., p. 208.

233. Louise FitzGerald and Melanie Williams, 'Facing Our Waterloo: Evaluating *Mamma Mia! The Movie*', in FitzGerald and Williams, *Mamma Mia!*, p. 8.

234. Andersson, Ulvaeus and Craymer, *Mamma Mia!*, p. 9.

235. Cited in 'The Making of *Mamma Mia!*', *Mamma Mia! The Movie*, DVD 2008, Universal 825 560 8.

236. Rodosthenous, 'Mamma Mia!'.

237. Steve Moles, 'ABBA, ABBA, Hey!', *Entertainment Design*, Vol. 33 (August/September 1999), p. 9.

238. Cited in Andersson, Ulvaeus and Craymer, *Mamma Mia!*, p. 194.

239. Lloyd cited in ibid., p. 166.

240. Treherne cited in ibid., p. 226.

241. Cited in Ian Nathan, 'Yo Mamma!', *Empire*, January 2009, p. 158.

242. Screenwriter Diablo Cody opined: '[The movie's] most disturbing scene features Pierce Brosnan singing "S.O.S."' (Diablo Cody, 'Batman? ABBA? Why Choose?', *Entertainment Weekly*, 15 August 2008).

243. As Ceri Hovland puts it: 'It is easier to ignore the potential embarrassment of singing along to ABBA badly when you are in such good company' (Ceri Hovland, 'Embracing the Embarrassment: *Mamma Mia!* and the Pleasures of Socially Unrestrained Performance', in FitzGerald and Williams, *Mamma Mia!* p. 123).

244. Kate Egan and Kerstin Leder Mackley, 'The Same Old Song? Exploring Conceptions of the "Feelgood" Film in the Talk of *Mamma Mia!*'s Older Viewers', in FitzGerald and Williams, *Mamma Mia!*, p. 135.

245. FitzGerald and Williams, 'Facing Our Waterloo', p. 1.

246. Ulvaeus cited in Anon., 'The Final Phase', p. 16.

247. Ulvaeus cited in Andersson, Ulvaeus and Craymer, *Mamma Mia!*, p. 130.

248. Ulvaeus cited in ibid., p. 64.

249. Sarah Bridge, 'Super Troupers . . . 16 Years on and Hit Musical *Mamma Mia* Still Rakes in Money for Producers Littlestar', *Mail on Sunday*, 3 January 2015.

250. This figure is given on the show's international website www.mamma-mia.com.

251. Andersson, Ulvaeus and Craymer, *Mamma Mia!*, p. 6.

252. Rodosthenous, '*Mamma Mia*'.

253. For a detailed discussion of how it differs from the movie, see the Wikipedia entry of the musical (https://en.wikipedia.org/wiki/Mary_Poppins_(musical), accessed 21 August 2015).

254. Cited in Sabine Durrant, '*Sunset Boulevard*', *Independent on Sunday*, 18 July 1993.

255. Mark Steyn, '*Sunset Boulevard*', *Mail on Sunday*, 18 July 1993.

256. Robert Hewison summed up his negative impression of the adaptation with: 'Wilder's hard-boiled has become Lloyd Webber's soft-boiled' (Robert Hewison, '*Sunset Boulevard*', *The Sunday Times*, 18 July 1993).

257. Coveney, *Cats on a Chandelier*, p. 179.

258. John Gross, '*Sunset Boulevard*', *The Sunday Telegraph*, 24 April 1994.

259. Michael Billington, '*Sunset Boulevard*', *The Guardian*, 21 April 1994.

260. Robert Hewison, '*Sunset Boulevard*', *The Sunday Times*, 24 April 1994.

261. David Benedict, '*Whistle Down the Wind*', *The Independent*, 3 July 1998.

262. Charles Spencer, '*Whistle Down the Wind*', *The Daily Telegraph*, 2 July 1998.

263. Coveney, *Cats on a Chandelier*, p. 266.

264. Jane Edwardes, '*Whistle Down the Wind*', *Time Out*, 8 July 1998.

265. Matt Wolf, '*Whistle Down the Wind*', *Variety*, July 13–19, 1998.

266. Stephen Citron, *Sondheim and Lloyd-Webber. The New Musical*, New York: Oxford University Press, 2001, p. 401.

SELECTIVE BIBLIOGRAPHY

The following bibliography is designed to serve as a first step towards further research, so the books and essays listed below have been included because they offer helpful background information on British composers and lyricists, detailed readings of their works or exhaustive overviews of the artistic movements in the period after the Second World War. Literature focusing on specific musicals has been limited to those secondary publications that supplement the twelve case studies.

Aaronofsky Weltman, Sharon, '"Can a Fellow be a Villain All His Life?": *Oliver!*, Fagin, and Performing Jewishness', *Nineteenth-Century Contexts*, Vol. 33 (Sep 2011), No. 4, pp. 371–88.

Andersson, Benny, Ulvaeus, Björn and Craymer, Judy, *Mamma Mia! How Can I Resist You? The Inside Story of Mamma Mia!* (London: Weidenfeld and Nicholson, 2006).

Bart, Lionel, *Oliver!* Vocal Score (London: Lakeview Music Publishing, not dated).

Behr, Edward, *Les Misérables. History in the Making* (London: Pavilion Books Ltd., 1996).

Bennett, Susan, 'Theatre/Tourism', *Theatre Journal*, Vol. 57 (2005), pp. 407–28.

Bhuchar, Suman, 'The Marketing of Commercial and Subsidised Theatre to British Asian Audiences', in Ley, Grahan and Dadswell, Sarah (eds), *Critical Essays on British South Asian Theatre* (Exeter: Exeter University Press, 2012), pp. 133–53.

Chambers, Colin, *Black and Asian Theatre in Britain: A History* (London: Routledge, 2011).

Chilton, Charles, 'Authors' Notes' in *Oh What a Lovely War*. Programme, London, 1963.

Cochrane, Claire, *Twentieth Century British Theatre: Industry, Art and Empire* (Cambridge: Cambridge University Press, 2014).

Coveney, Michael, *Cats on a Chandelier. The Andrew Lloyd Webber Story* (London: Hutchinson, 1999).

Daboo, Jerri, 'One under the Sun: Globalization, Culture and Utopia in *Bombay Dreams*', *Contemporary Theatre Review* Vol. 15 (2005), No. 3, pp. 330–7.

Eyre, Richard and Wright, Nicholas, *Changing Stages* (London: Bloomsbury Publishing, 2000).

FitzGerald, Louise and Williams, Melanie (eds), *Mamma Mia! The Movie. Exploring a Cultural Phenomenon* (New York: I. B. Tauris & Co, 2013).

Gänzl, Kurt, *The British Musical Theatre: Volume II, 1915–1984* (London: Macmillan, 1986).

Godiwala, Dimple (ed.), *Alternatives within the Mainstream: British Black and Asian Theatres* (Cambridge: Cambridge Scholars Press, 2006).

Selective Bibliography

Gordon, Robert and Jubin, Olaf (eds), *The Oxford Handbook of the British Musical* (New York: Oxford University Press, forthcoming 2016).

Gottfried, Martin, *More Broadway Musicals since 1980* (New York: Harry N. Abrams, 1981).

Graber, Naomi, 'Memories That Remain: *Mamma Mia!* and the Disruptive Potential of Nostalgia', *Studies in Musical Theatre*, Vol. 9 (2015), No. 2, pp. 187–98.

Green, Stanley, *Broadway Musicals: Show by Show.* (Milwaukee: Applause Books, 2008).

Harvie, Jen, *Staging the UK* (Manchester: Manchester University Press, 2005).

Hirsch, Foster, *Harold Prince and the American Musical Theatre* (Cambridge/New York: Applause Theatre Books, 1989).

Holdsworth, Nadine, *Joan Littlewood* (London and New York: Routledge, 2006).

Ilson, Carol, *Harold Prince: A Director's Journey* (New York: Limelight Editions, 2000).

Keightley, Keir, 'Reconsidering Rock', in Frith, Simon et al. (eds), *The Cambridge Companion to Pop and Rock* (Cambridge: Cambridge University Press, 2001), pp. 109–42.

Khan, Naseem, *The Arts Britain Ignores: The Arts of Ethnic Minorities in Britain* (London: Commission for Racial Equality, 1976).

Knapp, Raymond, *The American Musical and the Performance of Personal Identity* (Princeton: Princeton University Press, 2006).

Leach, Robert, *Theatre Workshop* (University of Exeter Press, 2006).

Ley, Graham and Dadswell, Sarah (eds), *British South Asian Theatres: A Documented History* (Exeter: University of Exeter Press, 2011).

Ley, Graham and Dadswell, Sarah (eds), *Critical Essays on British South Asian Theatre* (Exeter: Exeter University Press, 2012).

Littlewood, Joan, 'Introduction' in *Oh What a Lovely War.* Script (London: Methuen Drama, 2000).

Lloyd Webber, Andrew and Rice, Tim, *Evita: The Legend of Eva Peron 1919–1952* (London: Elm Tree Books, 1978).

McGrath, John, *The Cheviot, The Stag and the Black, Black Oil* (London: Methuen, reprint 1981).

McMillin, Scott, *The Musical as Drama* (Princeton/Oxford: Princeton University Press, 2006).

Mordden, Ethan, *Open a New Window: The Broadway Musical in the 1960s* (London: Palgrave Macmillan, 2002).

Napolitano, Marc, *Oliver! A Dickensian Musical* (New York: Oxford University Press, 2014).

Nichols, Peter, *Poppy* (London: Methuen, 1982).

Rice, Tim, *Oh, What a Circus. The Autobiography 1944–1978* (London: Hodder and Stoughton, 1999).

Snelson, John, *Andrew Lloyd Webber* (New Haven: Yale University Press, 2004).

Stafford, David and Stafford, Caroline, *Fings Ain't Wot They Used T'Be: The Lionel Bart Story* (London: Omnibus Press, 2011).

Sternfeld, Jessica, *The Megamusical* (Bloomington: Indiana University Press, 2006).

Steyn, Mark, *Broadway Babies Say Goodnight. Musicals Then and Now* (London: Faber and Faber, 2000).

Swain, Joseph P., *The Broadway Musical. A Critical and Musical Survey* (New York: Oxford University Press, 1990).

Symonds, Dominic and Taylor, Millie (eds), *Gestures of Music Theater: The Performativity of Song and Dance* (New York: Oxford University Press, 2014).

Taylor, Millie, '"Don't' Dream It, Be It": Exploring Signification, Empathy and Mimesis in Relation to *The Rocky Horror Show*', *Studies in Musical Theatre*, Vol. 1 (2007), No. 1, pp. 57–71.

Taylor, Millie, 'Continuity and Transformation in Twentieth-Century Pantomime', in Davis, Jim (ed.), *Victorian Pantomime* (Basingstoke: Palgrave, 2010).

Taylor, Millie, *Musical Theatre, Realism and Entertainment* (Basingstoke: Ashgate, 2012).

Vermette, Margaret, *The Musical World of Boublil and Schönberg* (New York: Applause Theatre and Cinema Books, 2006).

Walsh, Michael, *Andrew Lloyd Webber. His Life and Works* (London/New York: Penguin Books, 1989).

Whitton, David, '*Bombay Dreams*: Commodity Production', in Chaturvedi, Ravi and Singleton, Brian (eds), *Ethnicity and Identity in Global Performance* (Jaipur: Rawat Publications, 2005), pp. 288–96.

Wollman, Elizabeth L., *The Theatre Will Rock* (Ann Arbor: University of Michigan Press, 2006).

Womack, Malcolm, '"Thank You for the Music": Catherine Johnson's Feminist Revoicings in *Mamma Mia!*', *Studies in Musical Theatre*, Vol. 3 (2009), No. 2, pp. 201–11.

Wright, Adrian, *A Tanner's Worth of Tunes. Rediscovering the Post-War British Musical* (Woodbridge: The Boydell Press, 2010).

DISCOGRAPHY

Ace of Clubs. A Musical Play (1950). Original London Cast with Bonus Tracks, Bayview Classics, CD001.

(Noël Coward's) *After the Ball* (2005). The Irish Theatre Repertory Theatre Production, Kritzerland KR 20015-1.

Ann Veronica (1969). London Cast Recording, Stage Door Records, STAGE 9042.

Aspects of Love (1989). Original Cast Recording, 2 CD Set, Really Useful Recording, 9874436.

(Andrew Lloyd Webber and Ben Elton's) *The Beautiful Game* (2000). Original Cast Recording, Telstar Records, TCD3160.

Bend It Like Beckham. The Musical (2015), Original Cast Album, Sony Classical, 88875136992.

Billy Elliot. The Musical (2005). Original Cast Recording, Polydor, 987 521-6.

Betty Blue Eyes (2011). Original Cast Recording, First Night Records, CASTCD111.

Bless the Bride. A Musical Show (1947). Original London Cast, Sepia 1124.

Blitz! Lionel Bart's Musical (1962). Original London Cast Album, EMI Records Limited, 00946-311822 2 6.

Blondel (1983). Original Cast Album, MCA Records, MCD 11486.

Blood Brothers (1995). The International Recording, First Nights Records, 88561-1539-2.

(A. R. Rahman's) *Bombay Dreams* (2002). Sony Classic Musical, 508435 2.

The Boy Friend. A New Musical Comedy of the 1920s (1954). Original London Cast, Sepia 1042.

By Jeeves. Original Cast Recording (1996), Really Useful Recording/Polydor, 533 187 – 2.

The Card (1994). 1994 London Cast Recording, First Night Records, OCR CD6045.

Cats (1981), Really Useful Recording, 817810-2.

Charlie and the Chocolate Factory (2013). The Original London Cast Recording, Sony Classics, 88883780332.

Charlie Girl (1986), Original London Cast, First Night Records, OCR CD9.

Chess (1984). The Original Recording. Remastered Deluxe Edition, Polar Music, 00602547018335.

Chitty Chitty Bang Bang (2002). Original London Cast Recording, Chitty UK Ltd., MR BB001.

The Crooked Mile (1959). The Classic 1959 London Cast Recording, Must Close Saturday Records, MCSR 3002.

Evita (1976). 20th Anniversary Edition, MCA Records, DMCX 503.

Expresso Bongo. A Musical Play (1958). Original Cast Recording, AEI-CD 020.

(Lionel Bart's) *Fings Ain't Wot They Used T'Be* (1959). Original London Cast, Bayview Records, RNBW011.

Discography

Five Guys Named Moe (1994). Original London Cast Recording, First Night Records, OCR CD6050.

From Here to Eternity. The Musical (2013). Live Cast Recording (2014), Absolute Records, OVCD11.

Gay's the Word (1951). Original London Cast, Bayview Classics, CS001.

(Anthony Newley sings) *The Good Old Bad Old Days* (1972), Stage Door, Stage 9038.

Grab Me a Gondola (1956). Original London Cast, Sepia Records, Sepia 1101.

Half a Sixpence. A New Musical (1963). An Original Cast Recording, Deram, 820 589-2.

The Hired Man in Concert (1992). 2-CD Box Set, That's Entertainment Records (TER), CDTER2 1189.

Honk. A Musical Comedy (1998). Original Scarborough Cast Recording, Dress Circle Records, Dress CD 004.

Jerry Springer – the Opera. Live (2003). Original Cast Recording, Sony Music, 514 792 2.

Jesus Christ Superstar. A Rock Opera (1970). Double Disc Set, MCA Records, MCD 00501.

Johnny the Priest (1960). Original London Cast, Must Close Saturday Records, MCSR 3051.

Joseph and the Amazing Technicolor Dreamcoat (1974). MCA Records, MCLD 19023.

Just So (2006). World Premiere Cast Recording, First Night Records, Cast CD 95.

Les Misérables (1985). The Original London Cast Recording, First Night Records, Encore CD1.

The Likes of Us (2005). Live from the Sydmonton Festival, Really Useful Records, 978 4834.

Lock Up Your Daughters (1959). Original Recording, Hallmark Music, 710532.

London Road (2011). Original Cast Recording, National Theatre, RNT001.

The Lord of the Rings (2007). Original London Production, Cadiz Music, LOTR1001.

(Andrew Lloyd Webber's) *Love Never Dies* (2010). Deluxe Edition, Really Useful Records/Polydor, 2724801.

Maggie Mae (1964). Original Cast Recording, Bayview Records, RNBW020.

Make Me an Offer. A Musical (1959). Original London Cast, Sepia, Sepia1155.

Mamma Mia! (1999). Original London Cast. 5th Anniversary Edition, Polydor, 986 630-7.

Mary Poppins (2004). Original London Cast Recording, First Night Records, CAST CD93.

Martin Guerre (1995). London Cast Recording, First Night Records, CAST CD59.

(Roald Dahl's) *Matilda. The Musical* (2011). Original Cast Recording, Royal Shakespeare Company, RSCE 002.

The Match Girls (1966). The Original Cast Recording, AEI, AEI-CD 019.

Metropolis (1989). Original London Cast, 2 CD Set, JAY Productions Ltd., CDJAY2 1248 (1).

Miss Saigon (1989). Original London Cast Recording, Geffen Records, GED 24271-1.

Oh What a Lovely War! (1963). Original London Cast, Must Close Saturday Records, MCSR 3007.

Oliver! (1960). An Original Cast Recording, Deram, 820 590-2.

Pacific 1860 (1946) & South Pacific, Box Office Recordings, ENBO-CD #8/93.

The Phantom of the Opera (1986). 2 CD Set, Original Cast Recording, Really Useful Records, 543 929-2.

Pickwick (1965). The Musicals Collection, TER, MUS C N13.

The Roar of the Greasepaint – the Smell of the Crowd (1965). Original Broadway Cast Recording, RCA Victor, 60351-2-RG.

The Rocky Horror Show (1973). Original London Cast, First Night Records, OCR CD6040.

Salad Days (1991). Highlights from the Revival London Cast Recording, Showtime, SHOW CD009.

Scrooge (1970). The Musicals Collection, TER, MUS C N26.

Shockheaded Peter (1999). CD + DVD, NVC Arts/Warner Music, 3984 26522 2.

Soho Cinders (2011). Live Concert Recording, SIMG Productions, SimGR-CD09.

Starlight Express (1984). Original Cast Recording. 2 CD Box Set, Polydor, 00663702.

Stephen Ward (2013). Original Cast Recording, Decca, 3760237.

Stop the World – I Want to Get Off (1963). Original Recording, Hallmark Music, 710782.

(Andrew Lloyd Webber's) *Sunset Boulevard* (1994). American Premiere Recording, Polydor, 523508-2.

(Boy George's) *Taboo* (2002). Original London Cast, First Night Records, CAST CD86.

Trelawny (1972). Original 1972 London Cast Recording, Must Close Saturday Records, MCSR 3008.

Twang!! (1965). Original London Cast, TER, DDJAY7004.

Twenty Minutes South (1955). An Original Cast Recording, Must Close Saturday Records, MCSR3032.

Valmouth (1958). The Musicals Collection, TER, MUS C N37.

(Jeff Wayne's Musical Version of) *The War of the Worlds* (1978). Remastered and Repackaged, Columbia/Sony Music, OPCD96000.

The Water Gypsies (1955). Original London Cast, Sepia, Sepia 1060.

Wedding in Paris (1954) & Can-Can. Original London Cast, Sepia, Sepia 1041.

We Will Rock You (2002). Original London Cast, Live at the Dominion, EMI Records, 7243 5 80003 2 0.

(Andrew Lloyd Webber and Jim Steinman's) *Whistle Down the Wind* (1997). Original Cast Recording, Really Useful Records, 547 261-2.

The Witches of Eastwick (2000). Original London Cast Recording, First Night Records, CAST CD79.

The Woman in White (2004). Original Cast Recording, Really Useful Record/EMI Classics, 7243 5 57983 2.

Zip Goes a Million (2001). Original 2001 London Cast Recording, Bayview Records, RNBW014.

FILMOGRAPHY

Acorn Antiques! The Musical (2006), DVD, Channel 4, C4DVD10033.

Billy Elliot. The Musical. Live (2014), DVD, Universal, 830 064 6.

By Jeeves (2001), DVD, Universal, 0785542.

Cats (1998), DVD, Universal, 9025509.

Chess in Concert (2009), DVD, Reprise Records, 517636-3.

Chitty Chitty Bang Bang (1968), Special Edition, DVD, MGM, 16153CDVD.

Evita (1996), DVD, Paramount, GE 104545.

Expresso Bongo (1959), DVD, Prism Leisure, 3037090553R.

From Here to Eternity (2014), DVD, Cinestage, OVDVD2.

Half a Sixpence (1967), DVD, Paramount, 06721

The Heat Is On. The Making of Miss Saigon (1989), DVD, Freemantle Media, FHE02241.

The Heat Is Back. The Remaking of Miss Saigon (2015), DVD, Universal, 8304735.

Jeff Wayne's Musical Version of The War of the Worlds (2013). Special Edition, DVD, Universal, 8245673.

Jerry Springer – the Opera (2005), DVD, Pathé, P-OGB P917701000.

Jesus Christ Superstar (1973), DVD, Universal, 823 053 8.

Jesus Christ Superstar (2000), DVD, Universal, 902 011 2.

Jesus Christ Superstar. Live Arena Tour (2012), DVD, Universal, 8291943-11.

Joseph and the Amazing Technicolor Dreamcoat (2000), DVD, Universal, DSD 0537032.

King's Rhapsody (1955), DVD, Network, 7954977.

Les Misérables. 10th Anniversary Concert at the Royal Albert Hall (1995), 2-Disc Collector's Edition, 2 Entertain Vidio, VCD0435.

Les Misérables. The World's Longest Running Musical. In Concert. The 25th Anniversary (2010), DVD, Universal, 8280665.

Les Misérables (2012), DVD, Universal, 002519215048.

London Road (2015), DVD, Spirit Entertainment Limited, 534703.

(Andrew Lloyd Webber's) *Love Never Dies* (2011), DVD, Universal, 8287548.

Mamma Mia! The Movie, DVD, Universal, 825 560 8.

Oh What a Lovely War!, Paramount, PHE 9258.

Oliver! (1968), Collector's Edition, DVD, Columbia Home Entertainment10048.

Our House. A Musical Love Story (2004), DVD, Universal, 8227140.

The Phantom of the Opera (2004), DVD, Warner Home Video, 0085393895129.

(Andrew Lloyd Webber's) *The Phantom of the Opera at the Royal Albert Hall* (2011), DVD, Universal, 8286011.

The Rocky Horror Picture Show (1975), DVD, 20th Century Fox, 0142408.

Filmography

Salaam Bombay Dreams. The Behind-the-Scenes Story of the Spectacular Musical Sensation (2004), DVD, Universal, 8226063.

Shockheaded Peter and Other Songs. Live in Concert in New York (1999), DVD, Warner Vision International, 3984-26522-9.

Taboo. The Hit Musical (2003). Original London Production, DVD, Cornerstone Media, VCS 48927.

That Day We Sang (2014), DVD, Universal, 8303993.

Tommy. The Movie (1975), 2-Disc Collector's Edition, DVD, Prism Leisure, ODX20290.

INDEX

Index

Index

Index

Index

Index

Index

Index

Printed in Poland
by Amazon Fulfillment
Poland Sp. z o.o., Wrocław

49885243R00163